WILD-LOOKING BUT FINE

WILD-LOOKING BUT FINE

Abbey Theatre Actresses of the 1930s

CIARA O'DOWD

UNIVERSITY COLLEGE DUBLIN PRESS
PREAS CHOLÁISTE OLLSCOILE BHAILE ÁTHA CLIATH
2024

First published 2024
by University College Dublin Press
UCD Humanities Institute, Room H103,
Belfield,
Dublin 4

www.ucdpress.ie

ISBN 978-17-3-90863-29

CIP data available from the British Library

Typeset in Dublin by Gough Typesetting Limited
Text design by Lyn Davies
Printed in England on acid-free paper by
CPI Antony Rowe, Chippenham, Wiltshire.

For Christine Frances O'Connor Shields

Contents

Acknowledgements

One of the greatest joys of my life has been the many people that I encountered during the research for this book, all of them taking 'my ladies' to their hearts and supporting me in this journey. Some, such as the kindly porter in Hotel Edison, remain anonymous; others I am now proud to call friends.

Firstly, to Adrian Frazier, for teaching me what non-fiction writing can be. Lionel Pilkington, Patrick Lonergan, Charlotte McIvor, David Clare, Stacey Wolf, Jill Dolan and Aoife Monks were crucial to my completing my PhD. Barry Houlihan and all at Special Collections in the James Hardiman library; Mairead Delaney at the Abbey Theatre; the archivists at the National Library, at the New York Public Library, Columbia University and at Yale University's Beinecke Library; you are all heroes.

In California, I am grateful to Maureen Shay, J. J. Harrington, Maire Clerkin and Laura Haupt. Carrie Marsh of Claremont University was the most gracious host. Katharine Weber answered an email others would have dismissed as crazy and brought such wisdom. Helen Sheehy continues to be an inspiration as a biographer and feminist writer. Finola Finlay (and family) shared a precious Milk Tray box of letters and photos as well as her humour and friendship. Mary McCullough and Helen de Geus graciously shared details of the Mulhern family. Niall and Síle Mooney continue to honour Ria's memory and I am delighted that Janet has given the family another Ria. Susan Slott spoke of her family with such sensitivity. Sheila Robinson provided a vital piece of the puzzle. Patrick Laffan and Val Mulkerns were the most wonderful of interviewees, and I am so grateful to have recorded their thoughts now they are no longer with us. Maev Kennedy carries on her mother's diligent work and kindness.

For listening patiently: Laura Brock; Jocelyn Clarke; Jen Coppinger; Iseult Dunne; Sarah Durcan; Olwen Dawe; Bea Kelleher; Ciara L. Murphy; David Parnell; Gerald Dawe as well as all the readers of my blog, *Chasing Aideen*. I was honoured Róisín McBrinn and Jane Brennan so quickly agreed to contribute. My colleagues at SGI and the Culture Company never blanched at my interests and the staff in Chatterbox and Johnstown make my working possible by caring for my son. My peer reviewers, Noelle Moran, Órla Carr, and UCD Press for taking this, and me! on.

Christine Shields shared her mother with me so graciously and embodies Aideen's beauty and sense of adventure. I think so often of our time in California.

Thanks to my parents, Deirdre and Pat, my brothers, Killian and Oran, my sisters-in-law Marina and Hana, my nieces and nephews and to the Conway family.

Over a decade ago, Thomas Conway invited me to walk the prom in Galway to discuss my research. It has been a long way back, and now Saul walks between us, but you have held my hand the whole way.

Thank you all.

Ciara O'Dowd
Dublin, May 2024

Foreword

These our actors as I foretold you were all spirits, and are melted into air, into thin air...

The famous lines from *The Tempest* came to mind as I read this book. It made me wonder why so few biographies have been written about women in Irish theatre. Why don't we know more about their lives and achievements? Why, for example, is Ria Mooney not more widely remembered as the renaissance woman she was? Why had I never before heard of Aideen O'Connor (but am well acquainted with the name and reputation of her husband Arthur Shields). This book, focusing in particular on these two women, provides some important answers in the context of the times through which they lived.

Although I was familiar with her name and have always admired the wonderful portrait of her as the Widow Quin that hangs in the Abbey Theatre, I had only previously read about Ria Mooney in Phyllis Ryan's autobiography, *The Company I Kept*. There is a beautiful insight into her mentoring style in the story of Phyllis's first audition for the Abbey at the age of 12. She insisted that Phyllis called her Ria and not Miss Mooney. (My mother, Daphne Carroll, who was a student at the Abbey School back in those days, told me that you would never dare speak to a senior actor in the company, let alone call them by their first name!) After 'lovely patient Ria' had rigorously put her through her paces in a gentle and practical way, she told Phyllis, 'You broke every rule but you have real talent.' In this book, Ciara O'Dowd gives us the background to Ria's sympathetic and nurturing approach. She was mentored in New York by Eva La Gallienne at the Civic Repertory Theatre and Le Gallienne's philosophy of supporting, mentoring and assisting respectfully made a lasting impression on Ria. The breadth of her career is extraordinary. It includes studying painting and drawing for two years at the Metropolitan School of Art in Dublin, to her time at the Civic Repertory Theatre in New York, to acting and writing for the Gate Theatre, (MacLiammóir seems to have had real respect for her) and of course her devotion to the Abbey. I was amazed to learn that although she was never officially given the title of 'Artistic Director' of the Abbey, she effectively was, as Director of Plays in English, and she produced an astonishing amount of work during her tenure.

Aideen's career on the other hand was short and more difficult but had its moments. She was a beautiful and talented young actor and she and her pal Frolie Mulhern should have had bright futures ahead of them at the Abbey and further afield. Ciara O'Dowd relates their heartbreaking stories with real compassion and insight.

I was fascinated to read about these very different women. They were courageous, well read and passionately interested in the development of their craft. But what this book demonstrates is that there was a price to pay. I was struck by how both actors had to navigate the perils of playing women of 'loose morals' at a time of religious conservatism in Ireland. They were so convincing, Ria as Rosie Redmond in *The Plough and the Stars* and Aideen as Jesse Taite in *The Silver Tassie*, that it led to them being personally disapproved of. The notion that talent, hard work, research and close observation might have had something to do with it or that acting is an act of empathy, transformation and not 'being', was not really considered. The creator was tainted by the creation. We've come a long way!

The stresses and strains of juggling domestic life with a career is something that a lot of women can relate to, and this book emphasises how these women sought to be recognised for their life's work rather than their life choices. I was very moved by it and it made me think of my own mother. For over 20 years she had to abandon a career in theatre which was her first love, to work in the Radio Rep, where she had financial security. It was a medium she grew to love but putting food on the table and caring for her family was her priority. Happily, she did eventually get to return to the stage.

Ciara O'Dowd is to be congratulated on this excellent, timely and rigorously researched book highlighting the lives and contributions of Ria and Aideen and the resilient women they represent throughout the history of Irish theatre.

Jane Brennan
March 2024

Introduction

On a blustery February day, I check in to the Hotel Edison on West 47th Street, just off Times Square, in New York. I am on my own, lugging a suitcase that I've brought on the subway from Harlem, where I was staying while using the archives in Columbia University. I'm given a room on the sixth floor, and as darkness falls I watch from the window as taxis pull up at the Richard Rodgers Theatre to dispense people going to see Scarlet Johansson perform in *Cat On A Hot Tin Roof.*

Temperatures dipped to below freezing this morning, and now there are flurries of snow in the sky. I unpack necessities: not clothes and toiletries but books and notebooks. I line up pens on the armoire and I spread out the photocopied sheets I have brought with me. These sheets of faded writing paper bear the logo of the Hotel Edison at the top, along with a small sketch of the 22-storey building and the contact details, including the telegram number. The pages are filled with tightly-packed cursive writing, sometimes drifting into a scrawl. The dates at the top often don't include a year, but somebody has helpfully pencilled in '1937'. I open the drawer in the armoire to find a navy-blue folder of hotel writing paper. I take some of the newly-designed paper and photograph both sets side by side. The before and after. What she wrote and what I will write. I hope. I sit cross-legged on the bed and hope.

The letters sent from the Hotel Edison were written by an Irish actress named Aideen O'Connor. I found them in an archive of her husband's papers, in a university library on the west coast of Ireland, and I have read and re-read these photocopies endlessly. Aideen visited the hotel in November 1937, while touring with the Abbey Theatre Company in the US for approximately six months. The company stayed here for weeks, including spending Christmas day in its restaurant and bar. She wrote home about the theatre, about the city, about relationships and plans, and she dispensed advice about life to her sisters in Dublin.

At 24 years of age, Aideen was the youngest in the touring company, but she had a firm ally in another actress just turned 30, Frolie Mulhern. On previous tours, they shared a bedroom. On this tour, they each were granted the grown-up privilege of a room of their own. As they gossiped and laughed, running to and from each other's rooms to share clothes and makeup and discuss the evening's social entertainment, another woman in the company wasn't having such a good time.

In a room down the hallway, a small, raven-haired woman named Ria Mooney was in bed, laid low by an illness no doctor could diagnose. Aideen and Frolie would drop in occasionally, to see if she needed anything. Or they left her alone. Ria had performed briefly on the company's arrival in the city, but now couldn't be coaxed from her bed. At 34, Ria was a more experienced member of the company, although not the most senior in age. She knew New York better than any of the actors she was travelling with, having lived and worked in Greenwich village for a number of years at the end of the 1920s, as the member of a company based on 13th Street.

I am 34 on this trip to New York, the same age as Ria. I am a failed actress, a failed academic and a writer not by virtue of publication, but by nature and habit. In my room on the sixth floor, I stay quiet and still, hoping against hope to hear the traces of these women, the whispers of the walls. There is nothing but the incessant knocking of the plumbing (probably not replaced since Aideen's visit) and the honking of horns that is New York's serenade.

I believe that Ria's illness over this period, leaving her listless and prone in bed right over the festive season, was as much psychological as physical. I think her return to the fabulous city where she'd forged her professional career threw her into a depression. I don't have medical records, but my understanding of her nature, the evidence of her own and others accounts of her time in New York, as well as her personal life in Dublin around that time, all lead me to that reading of that moment in her life. I am fallible, as are my instincts, but that reading is supported by a hard-earned understanding, a discipline of listening, reading, thinking and waiting. It is, I hope, touched with compassion (but not too much) for these women.

I can't find out which rooms housed these women. The Abbey company manager, F. R. Higgins, or Fred to his friends, was on the 12th floor but he was relieved to be separated from the actors, none of whom mourned his loss. I do know the hotel had a roof garden, which was used by the company during the day and at night to relax and survey the city. So when I've gotten bored listening for nothing, I find a hotel porter and persuade him to let me take the lift to the 21st floor, to the now-abandoned fitness centre, and then to climb the back staircase to the 22nd floor, where I can't go outside but I can look out the full-length windows to the same section of sky enjoyed by these travelling women in 1937. I take it all in, the skyline, the cloudless sky pierced by the skyscrapers. And I stay there while the buildings burnish golden, until the sun sets over the city and the theatre lights far below blaze. I wonder what these three women dreamt about in their comfortable beds high above Times Square, after seeing this view. I wonder what I will dream about here.

This book centres on the lives of two Irish actresses that worked with Ireland's Abbey Theatre in the 1930s. They had different backgrounds, ambitions and creative visions and would pursue very different paths. They were united by one thing: a devotion to theatre and to Ireland's National Theatre in particular. They came of age in an Ireland desperate to control and restrict women: their sexuality; their professional careers; their independent lives. Their chosen profession as an actress in the 1930s defined and unmade them. They were friends, competitors, colleagues and allies.

To elucidate my title: 'Wild-Looking but fine' is the character description given by John Millington Synge to the central character of Pegeen Mike in his 1907 play, *The Playboy of the Western World*. Pegeen Mike is an iconic figure in Irish theatre. Norway has Ibsen's Hedda Gabler; England has Shakespeare's Rosalind and America has Tennessee Williams' Blanche; Ireland's equivalent is Pegeen Mike. Synge's description is literal, conjuring a good-looking woman who is windswept and messy. But I like its capacity to be read as something more: as a woman with ambition and rebellious potential, who also has the resilience to cope with whatever life brings her way. Only one of the women presented here was asked to play Pegeen; Ria Mooney's performance was controversial and divided critics. This one casting decision says much about the two different women, which I will explore.

The visit to New York in 1937 was not the climax of their careers, nor was it perceived by these women as a pivotal moment in their lives, at the time. Both had visited New York before; they would do so again. It was simply a moment, a job, another stop on a lengthy tour. Ria was unwell; Aideen bought her first electric hairdryer. And yet, for each of them, things would take a turn after that stay in the Hotel Edison, and paths would separate. Individual fates, or decisions, or ambitions, would intervene and the women would not tour together again. I cannot know what they spoke of, dreamt of, planned in these hotel rooms. But this book is my letter home from my visit to their world, and my tribute to those adventurous souls.

The biographies presented here recount the life stories of women elided in the recorded history of Irish theatre. There are limited accounts of the achievements of these women and, with the exception of Ria Mooney, no prior written accounts of their lives. Therefore, I draw on extensive archival research and shape the hitherto unknown material into narrative. These are life stories that intersect and interweave, that separate and come together. These biographical accounts can be read as case studies of female lives in Irish theatre during the first half of the century, but they are also individual life stories. They are the stories of women who dedicated their lives to the stage. It is this dedication to Irish theatre I wish to draw out, rather than any notion of success, or of lasting influence. They strove relentlessly against all odds; their determination is inspirational. This book is not an attempt to honour them as some kind of romantic idols, but to understand them as women, doing their best with their lives, their ambitions, and the fortunes they faced. The challenges of forging an artistic career in the 1930s as an Irish woman were monumental; some of those challenges remain today. I sense these women had much wisdom to share about life as an Irish woman, and as a professional actress. They knew as much about failure as they did about success; they lived through and beyond it.

I realised during my stay in Hotel Edison that to really appreciate that moment of their careers, the time they spent here, it is necessary to funnel back, into each of their backgrounds, before projecting forward, to what came next. It's vital to meet each of the ladies on their own terms. So, I have told the two life stories separately, with an interlude to illustrate how their careers overlapped during their fateful tour with the Abbey Theatre Company in 1937 to spring 1938. Both had lives that were complex and were sometimes difficult to trace. As I did my best to tease out their stories into clear narratives, I grappled with their artistic theories; their economic situations; their personal circumstances. I have done my best to simplify and clarify these matters without concealing the complexity. I have listened carefully and quietly for hours, so that you might hear the whispers more fully.

The stories, pulsing with life, full of detail about the women, their craft, their theatre, have been written with a focus on synchronic time. There is a chronology observed, but to tell a life story chronologically is always somehow to invoke cause and effect, to trace meaning from the ending, and to let the final reckoning with life outweigh everything that came before. I choose to work, rather, with a form of syncopated time, where I select the notes to amplify, to let the arc of the story take a different form. This synchronic time allows us to step in or out at any time, to delve into the stay at the Hotel Edison, for example, and treat it as a moment with the same gravity as a death or a marriage. This seeks to reflect life as it is lived, rather than as we read and tell it.

Life is not linear; we choose ways of living and reading it. Readers who feel in need of context, both social/historical and to understand the performance context, may find it useful to refer to the appendices. Others may wish to begin with the life stories and revert if needed to the appendices at a later point. But please do so knowing that you are shaping these lives for yourselves, just as I have shaped them for myself and for you. How we absorb these life stories into our understanding of history, the theatre, the world, should be a conscious and meaningful decision.

Chapter 1

Aideen O'Connor (1913–50)

Ambition and devotion

A photograph of Una Mary O'Connor was taken in the green room of the Abbey Theatre before she went on to the main stage for the first time in 1933.[1] In the picture, she barely raises her eyes to the camera as she sinks into the corner of a flowery couch. Her hair is pinned back to reveal an elfin face and on the wall behind her head is a photograph of the Abbey Players on a recent American tour. In her lap, her right hand grips the fingers of her left; both hands hover above the swathes of gingham that make up the too-large costume. To my eyes, there's a determination in her face as well as an anxiety. She has the air not of someone who doesn't want to be there, but of someone who is terrified because she so badly wants to be there.

O'Connor had grey eyes, a button nose and hair of 'a copper colour … a mass of tiny ringlets'.[2] She was five foot two and a half inches tall and of slight build (106 pounds).[3] She was a Catholic girl, living at home with her father and working as a secretary in the office of Polikoffs' clothing factory during the day. On Wednesday 6 September 1933 she turned 20 and the following Monday she made her first professional appearance in Brinsley MacNamara's play, *Margaret Gillan*.

Una Mary was aware of the better-known actress Una O'Connor, born in Belfast and a member of the Abbey company from 1912. The latter left for Hollywood in the 1920s, but her name remained known in Dublin. To differentiate herself, Una Mary chose the name Aideen. The name comes from *Étaíne*, from *Tochmarc Étaíne* in the mythological cycle of Irish legends and the word roughly translates as 'fire'. It has connotations of jealousy and passion. For a few years, she would be Una at home in Ranelagh and Aideen in the theatre. Then she moved between the identities, as some (including her future husband) always used Una, while for others she would sign off personal letters as Aideen. It was to become a life-long performance, sometimes drawing on the one identity, sometimes the other, to serve the particular 'scene' in her life. For my part, I use Aideen whenever I can—the woman she aspired to be.

MacNamara's play, *Margaret Gillan*, in which she made her debut, centres on the relationship between a mother and a daughter: a recently widowed woman is dismayed when the only man she ever loved asks for her daughter's hand in marriage. O'Connor was replacing the actress Kitty Curling, whom she had seen perform as Esther Gillan one month earlier. The script was familiar to her from classes and performances in the Abbey School of Acting. It is a play full of repressed passions, showing a woman struggling with aging, with financial and practical realities, along with the death of her own dreams and a burning jealousy of her daughter's youth and beauty. Abbey stalwart May Craig played the title role. Tentatively entering Margaret's sitting room late in the first act, Aideen O'Connor raised her head and asked, 'Did you want me, mother?'[4] In the telling of any life story, a mother is a good place to begin.

Hollybank Avenue, Ranelagh

I traced the letters on the screen of the Irish Census of 1911 (publicly available on the Internet) with my finger. I compared the Fs with the Cs, one in 'O'Connor' and the other in 'Roman Catholic', denoting the religion of the household. The genealogist from the National Library gives the name on the Enumerator's Form as 'Flora Crowley O'Connor'. I leaned towards 'Clara Crowley O'Connor'.[5] It wasn't possible to be definite. But in this tracing, this guessing, I was inventing someone in 'Clara', or obliterating somebody by the name of 'Flora'. Such conundrums and decisions are an intrinsic part of archival research. Later, I would use both names to search church records, civil registers and discover the challenges of apostrophes. I would trace the name many times, and discover it was Clara—It was the website that had obliterated her by failing to decipher the cursive script.

Mrs Clara Crowley O'Connor was 22 years old when the Census Collector called to the door of 53 Hollybank Avenue on the south side of Dublin city. He canvassed the entire 'Avenue', which is a grandiose title for the neat cul de sac of terraced, red-bricked houses in this long-established suburb. Number 53 was considered a large house (three bedrooms and an outside privy) for a couple with a single domestic servant. Another Catholic family lived on one side of the O'Connors', on the other side were Methodists.[6] The lady of the house had been married for less than a year to Vincent De Paul O'Connor, who worked at the Mercantile Office in Dublin Port. It was April 1911; it was spring. If Mrs O'Connor was already expecting her first daughter, Eileen, this pregnancy wasn't recorded. The Census heralded the start of something: the O'Connor family proper.

At 9.40am on 26 August 1913 the trams stopped running, leaving idle the 50 miles of track that linked the centre of Dublin with the suburbs of Clontarf, Rathmines, Blackrock and Kingstown (now Dún Laoghaire).[7] The abrupt absence of bells announcing the trams' arrival left the streets quiet. Four days later, rioting broke out in Ringsend (a working-class area close to the port) and the disturbances spread rapidly to other working-class districts. An industrial dispute over workers' rights to unionise began to unravel and some of the city's employers threatened a lockout.

On the first Saturday of September, the *Irish Catholic* newspaper described events on the streets of the capital as 'Dublin's Peril', saying that 'most self-respecting and educated men and women' were 'heartily ashamed' of the rioting and disputes spilling out from various industries.[8] Many believed an unbridled class war was on the verge of breaking out. At the same time, according to historian Padraig Yeates, Irish nationalists (such as Vincent De Paul O'Connor) opposed the Lockout and the influx of goods from overseas it would encourage.[9] The weather was mild for autumn and the city re-assumed a relaxed, weekend air as the threat of violence remained at a remove. Journalists noted that the police were not obtrusively visible and there was generally good humour and the 'the usual harmony'.[10]

That same Saturday, 6 September, Una Mary O'Connor was born. The following day, the O'Connors celebrated their third wedding anniversary. Any parents would fear for a child born into a city threatening to descend into lawlessness. From his desk in Dublin Port, Vincent De Paul O'Connor could see the men on the docks gathering to unload the ships arriving with food supplies and (as the crisis developed) boats leaving for Liverpool where children were promised Catholic homes with food and schooling. Later, official documents would claim that Mr O'Connor was the Superintendent of the Mercantile Marine Office.[11] It is an unlikely title, given that he was an Irish Catholic working in the civil service at a time when promotions or leadership roles were denied to many of his faith. He was a lower-middle-class man striving to raise a young family in a city under siege from industrial disputes, from poverty and from endemic diseases.

Aideen was born in the midst of the 1913 Lockout. By the end of that year, infant mortality would have risen by almost 50per cent.[12] Clara would have another daughter within two years, but she didn't survive to see her children grow into young women. It's tempting to say that Aideen was born with the defiant energy of the Lockout in the air; the malevolent despair that found its way into every nook of the city in the winter of 1913 shaped her personality. It's tempting to say this, but it's a theory I can't prove or support with evidence. As much as I'd like the idea of this shaping force to linger in the reader's mind, it was simply a moment in the life of the city and this woman.

The threatened Lockout did happen but the city moved on. In February 1925, Vincent De Paul O'Connor made the difficult trip to officially record his wife's death.[13] She had pneumonia, which brought on a heart attack. Other death records on the same page of the register detail the duration of illness, as requested. The absence of this detail for Clara suggests it was a sudden death. Clara O'Connor was 36 years old and Aideen was 12, about to begin secondary education at the Dominican Convent in Donnybrook. The widower, Vincent De Paul O'Connor, was left to bring up his daughters as respectable middle-class women alone.

Her father was an Irish speaker but where Aideen attended school she learnt to speak French, to play tennis and to compose elegant business letters. In the early 1930s, William Fay of the Abbey Theatre was taking afternoons away from Marlborough Street to coach young convent girls around Dublin in elocution and Shakespeare.[14] If he included Muckross College on his weekly rounds, O'Connor came under his watchful eye. She liked attention, this middle child who considered herself the plain sister.[15] She found out about the evening classes in the Abbey, even as the Muckross nuns educated her for a job in an office with prospects and a steady wage. Polikoffs' Factory was an achievement for O'Connor: a job in the office above the factory floor where men and women stitched and sewed all day. But she already had her eye on a different life and was taking the tram into the city a few evenings a week to be tutored by Lennox Robinson and M. J. Dolan in classes at the Abbey Theatre.

M. J. Dolan kept one of his adjudicators' sheets: a typed sheet of names on which they made handwritten notes as they auditioned scores of hopeful performers for the Abbey School of Acting on the Peacock stage. O'Connor's notes are not recorded but others were considered with the following observations:

> Miss Rose O'Shea
> I don't think so: weak and uninteresting.
>
> Eleanor O'Connell
> Anxious & nervous. Not bad voice in reading.
> Recitation: Gesture bad and not so good in reading: – enunciation.
>
> Nora O'Neale
> Made sense of what she was reading. Robust: good strong voice.
> Clear enunciation (often) Dramatic sense.
> Recit[ation]: flexibility and word painting good. Face expression.[16]

There is much emphasis on voice and recitation, on the strength of voice and enunciation. Little else is revealed about the qualities they required from students.

In April 1933, O'Connor received her certificate in acting from Lennox Robinson at a small graduation ceremony.[17] One morning in the house on Hollybank Avenue, Vincent De Paul O'Connor noticed a postcard addressed to his middle daughter in the post. He was presented in writing with a formal indication of her hard work in the evening classes. He could simply turn it over to see the typed request for 'Una' to call to the theatre as soon as possible to see Mr Arthur Shields. He wrote 'Go n-eirí an t-áidh leat. Daidí', (sic) in pencil across the card, wishing her luck in Irish.[18] Soon after that meeting, O'Connor began to prepare for her first professional appearance.

Aideen's siblings, Eileen and Maeve O'Connor, were 'not Abbey-goers'.[19] There was one friend and mentor who celebrated O'Connor's every performance, although she could rarely travel to Dublin. Sister Mary Monica Hanrahan (whose real name was Martha) was born in Cork city and at 18 years old joined the Sisters of Mercy convent in Cobh. She was a friend, or possibly relative, of Mrs O'Connor, who stayed in touch with the children of her dead friend. Living close to O'Connor's extended family in the centre of Cobh and teaching at the local primary school, Hanrahan took pride in Aideen's work and growing fame.

I later learn, from the Congregational Archivist for the Sisters of Mercy that Sister Hanrahan was a 'handsome' woman, 'cultured, gracious and ladylike.' She spoke with a 'fine accent' and taught speech and drama to all her students. As well as the standard elocution and verse-speaking lessons, Mary Monica encouraged her students to produce their own plays, tableaux and sketches.[20] She met a four-year-old Aideen in Cobh and, however she felt about O'Connor's future decisions, letters sent many years later to her family indicate that Sister Mary Monica loved Aideen like a mother.[21]

After a six-night run of *Margaret Gillan*, O'Connor returned to work at Polikoffs' factory and attended rehearsals in the theatre in the evenings. Two weeks later, she had a small part in *The Plough and the Stars* as Mollser, a 15-year-old teenager who looks little more than ten because consumption has 'shrivelled her up. She is pitifully worn, walks feebly, and frequently coughs'.[22] She subsequently played Delia, the young sweetheart of doctor-to-be Denis, in Robinson's hit comedy, *The Whiteheaded Boy*. With little stage time, O'Connor had the opportunity to watch the rest of the cast, to read plays closely and to learn the technique and habits not taught in an acting class.

At the end of her first year with the Abbey company, O'Connor was cast as Helena in Lennox Robinson's comedy about a theatre company visiting a small Irish village, *Drama At Inish*. At its uproarious first night the year before, Robinson had made a speech explaining the play:

> I wanted to confound the critics. It's really an absurd play based on an impossible situation. The critics would have described it as such, so you see I am saying it before them.[23]

There's a note of self-pity and desperation beneath the eloquence. Robinson's alcoholism had reached dire conditions. Playwright Teresa Deevy, then a protégé of Robinson, said at this time that she 'felt like crying when [she] saw him' because he was 'very bad'.[24] Robinson was growing thinner, more morose, and becoming increasingly unreliable. Many of the cast knew this play well and could cope with his erratic attendance at rehearsals. Arthur Shields was designated assistant director to help the new actors learn the meta-theatrical jokes.

Unlike the ingénue parts she had played to date, Helena in *Drama at Inish* was a soubrette, a neat servant unused to the ways of theatrical people. In the first act, she voices the shock of an Irish girl at the sleeping arrangements for the couple leading the theatrical troupe. Lizzie explains that she's keeping a double room for Mr de la Mare and Miss Constantia; the salacious idea alarms her servant:

Helena: (*shocked*) Mr—and Miss Constantia! Glory, miss!

Lizzie: It's quite all right, Helena. Actresses they are – I mean, she's an actress and so is he—I mean, he's an actor and so is—well, anyhow, they're man and wife these years and years. O'Hara or some name like that I believe they are really.

Helena: I see, Miss.[25]

The servant obediently swallows her shock at the ways of theatrical life. She took it all in, saying little but learning the secrets of the clandestine arrangements, much as O'Connor was doing backstage.

Despite her apparent naïvety, Helena in *Drama At Inish* has a troubling secret: she gave birth out of wedlock and her baby subsequently died. Stills from the production show a frenzied Helena with her arms around the neck of a startled man. Her face isn't visible; the context for the physical situation is not clear to those unfamiliar with the plot. The male character is the honest, handsome 'Boots' in the hotel, Michael; he was played by the assistant director, Arthur Shields. Helena's problems are neatly resolved when she disappears off to the church to marry fellow servant Michael. Respectability was restored as O'Connor tucked her arm into that of the tall, reedy figure with the sensitive face and gentle manner. O'Connor was already fond of the kind and fatherly figure of Shields; he offered her advice and shared his experience. Together, they bowed and left the stage. For O'Connor, the negotiation of her social and theatrical life with her job in Polikoffs' and as the daughter of a Catholic widower would be harder to resolve than Helena's wedding resolves the plot of *Drama at Inish*. But already, Aideen's strong and determined personality was shaping the life that she wanted for herself.

Frolie Mulhern: Scrapbooks and stories

Many of the Abbey Theatre actresses of the 1930s kept scrapbooks as they toured, piecing together newspaper cuttings, gluing photos and programmes into place.[26] They worked on their scrapbooks in hotel bedrooms between shows, or clenching them on their knees in rocking train carriages. Coming home, they brought heaps of paper folded into the back of the books to be sorted and smoothed. It was a task as well as a memento, a shaping as well as a sharing of their memories and stories. The books served, professionally and personally, as evidential proof of their hard work and success. On the inside cover of one such scrapbook now in the National Library of Ireland, the name 'Frolie Rutledge-Mulhern' is inscribed in a loping, youthful hand.[27]

Frolie Mulhern was a girl from an upper-class family with a gift for comedy and mimicry that brought her huge popularity in Ireland and America. She forged a close friendship with Aideen O'Connor at the Abbey and on tour. The training, performing and personal lives of these friends consistently intertwined and overlapped.

The first page of Mulhern's scrapbook, which she curated so carefully, contains her black and white headshot.[28] The newspaper photo captures the star of this scrapbook: a dark-haired, sallow woman with a round face and molten brown eyes that revealed much even when she was silent. She is in her 20s, but there's an innocence and openness in her expression, as if the photographer's attention has startled her. Other newspaper photographs contained therein date the scrapbook to the autumn of 1934, when Frolie was a 27-year-old actress with the Abbey company.

Ailesbury Road Sunday suppers

Frances Mulhern was born in Enniskillen, Co. Fermanagh in 1907.[29] The baby of the Mulhern family quickly became known as Frolie to her five older sisters and one older brother; the name stuck. When the Abbey took her on tour to the US for the first time in 1934, Frolie and Aideen were dubbed the 'babies of the company'.[30] Aideen was 21; Mulhern 27 years old. There was a naïvety to both women, who still lived in the family home. Both had only one surviving parent in Dublin.

Frolie lived in 'Belvedere', a luxurious home on the upmarket Ailesbury Road, under the watchful eye of her mother, Bridget. The census shows that Bridget Mulhern had been widowed before her youngest daughter turned four. She buried her husband, James, in Enniskillen, and transplanted to Dublin to manage his business affairs and ensure a proper education for her seven children. A formidable businesswoman and publican as well as a strong maternal presence, she carried on the management of her husband's substantial bottling company.

Frolie's elder sisters went to boarding school, but Frolie—the youngest and weakest—wasn't suited to the discipline of boarding-school life. It is rumoured that she tried a number of different convent schools, including a Sacred Heart convent close to the city centre, but wasn't a prize pupil of the nuns.[31] Mulhern didn't need to earn a living, but it was expected that she become a respectable Catholic lady, mix in the right social circles and marry well. While many of her sisters went on to university, she joined the Abbey School of Acting in 1929. If she were to devote her life to acting, it would be in a respectable cultural institution.

With her confidence and natural gift for mimicry, it didn't take Frolie long to graduate from William Fay's evening lessons in the Abbey school to a full-time position in the company. In April 1930, she appeared in the premiere of George Shiels' comedy, *The New Gossoon*. Directed by Arthur Shields, she played Mag Kehoe. This servant girl is described as 'A coarse girl, with dirty bobbed hair, about thirty-five years old.'[32] The comedy opens with Mag entering the stage and 'flinging aside her old sun-bonnet' to say:

> Curses on them and their hay! I wish there wasn't a hay-field in broad Ireland. (*She wipes her face and neck with a cloth.*) I'll be as red as a crab, and peeled like an onion...[33]

She goes on, complaining about her lot:

> They've kept me working in the hayfield to within an ace of six o'clock, and now I've a day's work to do before bedtime. Cows to milk and calves to feed and pigs to feed, and potatoes to wash and boil for to-morrow morning. The man that freed the blacks in America should be President of Ireland...[34]

The New Gossoon was a huge hit for the Abbey company, accumulating 188 performances between 1930 and 1951, as well as being a staple part of the repertoire on American tours.

Throughout her career, Mulhern would continue to play the customary servant girl, or 'homely colleen' role. A review of *Nineteen Twenty* by F. X. O'Leary in 1933 declared that, 'the honours must go to Frolie Mulhern for a very amusing rendering of Liz Ann, the servant girl'.[35]

She also played Baby in Lennox Robinson's play, *The Whiteheaded Boy*, the character being described as 'a great lump of a girl' in the script.[36] Here, then, was the upper-class girl drawing on her own impressions of the home help her mother employed to amuse audiences.

Bridget Mulhern ran a busy household, with six of her own children as well as three members of the extended family that came to live under her care. Her charges ranged in age from 40-years-old to young teenagers and her own elderly sister also lived there, helping to keep order. The age range meant Frolie had young nephews at home awed by her glamorous lifestyle, often sitting in the passenger seat of her motorcar as she raced around Dublin and eagerly awaiting the gifts she brought home from abroad.[37]

Sunday night suppers at Belvedere were a regular feature of Abbey Theatre social life. Young charges would be sent to bed after the tea and cakes, but the company would gather in the drawing room, around the piano, where each guest would be invited to share a poem, a song or a dramatic speech. Frolie always garnered special attention from her family, due to her illness: at birth, the doctors had said one of the chambers in her heart wasn't pumping blood efficiently. With no cure available, Mrs Mulhern did her best to keep Frolie safe and healthy; she balanced this care with allowing Frolie to enjoy her independence and indulge her theatrical passion.[38]

An American debut

The same month that O'Connor and Mulhern appeared in *Drama at Inish*, whispers began backstage about the members of the company to be included in an upcoming tour of America. O'Connor wanted the adventure but was pragmatic enough to consider the impact of leaving Ireland. She negotiated conditions with the Abbey management, or was assisted in doing so, and her weekly wage was increased to £3 10s when she resolved to give up her job to go on the tour. Frolie remained on the sum of £2 a week.[39] She could rely on her family for assistance when she needed funds. Veteran actor William O'Gorman agreed to Mr O'Connor's request that he be an unofficial 'chaperone' to Aideen on her travels; he would regularly send notes to the widower to confirm that his daughter was 'as happy as when she was at home and unchanged'.[40] Aideen had set in motion her dreams of life as a full-time actress.

It was publicly announced that the Abbey was transporting 'fourteen players, three stagehands with the necessary scenery, costumes and property' to the US and Canada.[41] A press release from Fred W. Jordan given on 17 August 1934 stated that this would be 'one of the largest theatrical tours on record'.[42] As assistant producer of the Abbey company, Arthur Shields was in charge of the company, while the American producer Mr Elbert Wickes was granted 'personal charge' throughout the tour.[43] After arriving in Boston in October 1934, the company would spend November in Canadian and eastern cities including Montreal, Toronto, Ohio and Detroit before appearing on Broadway. The return journey took them to San Francisco, Seattle, Minneapolis and St Paul before finishing in Boston in early June 1935.

Aideen joined Frolie and the other actors in Westland Row train station in Dublin, where they took the train to Belfast and then a boat to Liverpool. The liner, the Scythia, sailed from Liverpool port, with 177 passengers on board. Many of the company already knew this journey: its luxury, its boredom and the occasional bouts of seasickness. For O'Connor, it was new: the glamour of dressing for dinner each evening, the dancing, the drinking and the sunbathing on deck. At dinner, the actors spotted the British toffee magnate, Sir Harold Mackintosh, and his wife.[44] Gales held back docking for an entire day but they eventually managed to dock in East Boston as darkness fell on an autumn evening.[45]

The White List of 1934/35

The *Cincinnati Post* mentioned on 15 December 1934 that while there was a 'crusade against salacious stage plays launched by the Catholic Church in New York', the Abbey Players were one of only four theatre companies to be put on a 'white list' by the Church.[46] This 'white list' confirmed they provided respectable entertainment and the endorsement bolstered both the prestige of the company and audience numbers. Recalling the Abbey tour two years earlier when 'through the fog of that ominous period the actors from Dublin played on', *The Sunday Tribune* in Chicago in December 1934 declared the Abbey company to be 'heroes of [the] bank panic period' and urged theatre-goers not to miss a chance to see a performance.[47]

Max Stein of the *Cincinnati Post* declared the Abbey productions of 1934 to be 'Romantic, Weird', but the performances were a resounding popular success.[48] Cocktail parties and dinners were held in honour of the Irish players and the women regularly appeared in social columns.[49] When the *Chicago Herald* announced a supper dance would be held after a performance at the Harris Theatre with 'Aideen O'Connor to be toast of the evening', Frolie might have been irritated by the attention heaped on O'Connor, as the blonde ingénue.[50] Or, more likely, given her spirited personality and sense of humour, she was amused by the headline.

As for any touring theatre group, resilience was a feature of the actors, and O'Connor was getting a true experience of the itinerant life and its demands. There were long, uncomfortable train journeys and sometimes disappointing houses as well as enthusiastic reviews. In some cities, notably the Cass Theatre in Detroit, the audiences were 'regrettably small'.[51] Their visit to the Harris Theatre in Chicago was more successful, with the run extended from two weeks to three. Playing minor roles such as the young girl, Honor Blake, in Synge's *The Playboy of the Western World*, Aideen began to hone her craft. While finessing her performances on-stage, she was also learning how to present herself off stage.

Against the mature talent and sophistication of many of the Abbey players, Aideen was said to sparkle like a 'child of nature' straight from the mist of Yeats' Celtic Ireland.[52] Or rather, the American press, who described her this way, imposed on her the role of Celtic colleen. Noting its publicity value, O'Connor embraced the notion. A photographer convinced her to sit for an art exhibition, and he took photographs of her in character without even 'a bit of lipstick'.[53] She complained to her sisters of weariness from the demand 'to be "nice" and "sweet" to everyone I meet'.[54] Yet she obligingly told stories of fairies in the bogs of Connemara and:

> she talked reverently of William Butler Yeats ... and described him as a SO handsome gentleman with snow white hair, one lock of hair which is always dripping over his forehead ... [55]

The *Chicago Herald* deemed both ladies to be 'pert and capable'.[56] If Aideen and Frolie vied for press attention, their different physical attributes and acting styles meant they did not compete for roles. In a strange twist, their usual roles were subverted in 1934, when O'Connor was cast as the servant girl Helena in *Drama at Inish* by Lennox Robinson. The play, re-titled *Is Life Worth Living?* for American audiences, pokes fun at provincial towns 'blue-mouldy for a bit of innocent scandal', at theatre companies, and at acting itself.[57] Of course, this shift in character types was not so much a 'twist', as a kind of restoration of the social order that theatre so gleefully throws over. Mulhern played Christine Lambert, 'a capable-looking, handsome' accountant, who is spurning the advances of a young man to concentrate on the books of a local factory.[58] The plot teaches Christine that there is more to life than work and as the curtain fell, Christine/Frolie was in a joyful dance with her new husband.

In January 1935, the *Detroit Times* featured a head-and-shoulders shot of O'Connor with the caption: 'Hollywood already has its collective eye on this new and bright-eyed colleen from the Abbey Players'.[59] Judy O'Grady, social columnist of the *Detroit News*, caught her sweet and innocent persona eloquently in the same month. After having tea with the Company, O'Grady wrote on 24 January:

> Her blue eyes sparkled as she talked of the American impressions ... she wore a sparkling afternoon frock that exactly matched those dancing eyes, too, She talked of tea in Ireland which is composed of homemade cake and heavily buttered scones (pronounced scons) ... she talked of how Irish girls walked so much more than we Americans, but admitted that there wasn't a city in Ireland where one couldn't be right out in the country after walking for ten minutes ... [60]

Early in the new year, the *Detroit Press* deemed O'Connor, along with Frolie Mulhern, to be 'mere novices' alongside the rest of the established company.[61] While some of the papers still recalled Kate Curling, the Abbey actress who had left the company (and Ireland) to marry an American businessman, O'Connor was making an impression.

Since their arrival in New York in November, O'Connor and Mulhern had been playing frolicking teenagers in Robinson's comedy, *The Far-Off Hills*, to the delight of audiences. The play had been in the repertoire of the Abbey company since it premiered in October 1928, with Shelah Richards and Kitty Curling playing the sisters. Mulhern, cast by Robinson while she was still studying at the Abbey School, took on Richards' role of Pet later that year. Frolie initially appeared with an actress called Susan Hunt, who left the company after two years. Aideen took over the role of Ducky in 1934 and it remained one of her favourite plays for the next five years. The success of their on-stage partnership in *The Far-Off Hills* owed something to the close, if tempestuous, friendship of Mulhern and O'Connor. Many of the newspapers commented on their talents, with C. J. Bulliett declaring a lengthy scene between them in *The Far-Off Hills* to be 'one of the major delights of the whole repertory'.[62]

By the time they arrived in San Francisco in the spring, American touches had been added to the set of the girls' bedroom that opened the second act. In the 'simple, pretty room' where the two beds are 'side by side, their ends towards the audience' there is the refraction of the hotel bedrooms O'Connor and Mulhern shared while on tour.[63] On the walls of the set, posters of American heartthrob Ramon Navarro now hung alongside the holy pictures. The girls were made up in shadow, rouge and lipstick, which they preferred to bring from Ireland.[64] Ducky, played by O'Connor, was the 17-year-old elder sister who is reading in bed while 16-year-old Pet (Mulhern) brushes her hair by candlelight. Amid girly gossip, they are secretly trying to plot their father's second marriage.

'All this silly wait-till-you're-asked business', Ducky grumbles in *The Far-Off Hills* about women awaiting an engagement, while Pet bemoans the shape of her nose.[65] Pet blows out the candle, kicks off her slippers and makes for bed. Ducky is quick to ask, 'Have you said your prayers?' Pet tartly responds, 'Mind your own business.'[66] As the sisters settle down to sleep, whispering to each other in the darkness and recalling the events of the day, there is an outbreak of giggles and they cannot conceal their laughter. The stage directions read: 'They both laugh until the beds shake.'[67] A similar sense of youthful exuberance marked Mulhern and O'Connor's friendship on their first American tour.

While her chaperone O'Gorman may have seen her as unchanged, the performances and the press attention began to alter O'Connor's perception of all that she could achieve in her career.[68] She wrote home to 'My Dear Daddy', and joked, 'It will be funny to go home and settle down as the least good-looking of the family.'[69] The letters to her father are polite and innocent; she is the child of nature and the girl of the Celtic twilight that was a darling to the US journalists. To her sisters, she revealed the private changes in this naïve Catholic girl.

By the spring of 1935, the company were enjoying the glorious sunshine of the West Coast. O'Connor believed that she had grown taller and gained seven pounds, although she retained 'a pale face' with 'hollows in the cheeks' from all the hard work.[70] When she wasn't performing, shopping and socialising took much of her energy. Despite the innocence of her press interviews, she was meeting and dating American men. After a dalliance with a 'concert and radio' tenor called Alban Knox in Chicago, she met a divorced man called Bob. This mysterious man, with an unknown surname, was the first serious relationship of her life. Bob planned to visit Dublin for the horse show after Aideen's return to Dublin. She was relieved that her sisters didn't abhor the idea, saying 'I'm glad you both don't have a fit at the idea of a divorced man, it cheers me up.'[71]

O'Connor was also being exposed to modern ideas about femininity. As she commiserated with elder sister Eileen, who was suffering from menstrual pains, she scorned traditional Irish ideas and advised her:

> I've given up that silly old-fashioned idea and bath[e] the same as usual, it's much more hygienic and all the [docto]r's here tell you to. [Y]ou feel much better too after a bath with plenty of bath salts and a rub over with Eau de Cologne, just you try it.[72]

Some of the actors arranged to see a production by Eva Le Gallienne during their stay in Chicago. O'Connor was 'crazy about her' and corresponded with the actress/director briefly, entertaining the idea that if she were sacked by the Abbey Theatre she would approach Miss Le Gallienne for a job.[73] Le Gallienne's work proffered the role model of an independent professional career for a woman in the theatre. O'Connor's suggestion that she could easily be 'sacked' suggests she knew that her position with the Abbey was precarious, or at least was dependent on her observing certain standards. This was to prove prescient in the years to come.

For all her sophistication, O'Connor remained devoted to her sisters, leaving herself 'financially embarrassed' by spending her earnings on gifts for them and clothes for herself in Los Angeles. She sent letters packed with the minutiae of Hollywood gossip—which actor had said what to her, how shy Maureen O'Hara was, the colour of the 'bathing suit' she bought.[74] In March 1935, she wrote home from San Francisco:

> This city is glorious. I am typing this at an open window of my bedroom. Frolie has just left the room like a young hurricane to have her hair done, and when she comes back we are going to do a bit of shopping, a movie and dinner somewhere before the show.[75]

The hurricane-like Frolie was easily roused to a temper by the petulant Aideen, but arguments blew over as quickly as they ignited. They had a close, tempestuous relationship, sharing confidences and covering one another's parts when illness struck, joking and giggling, rowing and making up again. During their stay in Los Angeles, the two women went shopping with film star Maureen O'Sullivan, 'in Bullocks Wiltshire, the rendezvous of all the stars'. Despite O'Sullivan's shyness, they all 'became great friends'.[76] Photographs often show Mulhern with a cigarette in one hand and a drink in the other: both Frolie and Aideen worked hard and played harder.

The 'babies' were becoming accustomed to the life of a professional actress, albeit with the family support from the rest of the company. As well as the friendly chaperoning of O'Gorman, Arthur Shields and his wife Bazie (known as Mac) acted *in loco parentis* to the young charges. Mac fussed over them when they were sick; she dosed O'Connor with painkillers for period cramps and gave advice.[77]

At her open window in the Sir Francis Drake Hotel, O'Connor made a decision about the trajectory of her life. Ranelagh and Polikoffs' factory belonged to a dull and distant world. Yet, she had also turned down opportunities in the Hollywood film industry. Despite her interest in Le Gallienne's troupe, what she really wanted was for the Abbey company to keep her on permanently. She declared, 'I shall stick to the stage for good or evil now'.[78] If Una Mary, self-conscious novice and ingénue, had left on tour that September, it was Aideen O'Connor, ambitious professional actress, that disembarked from the train in Westland Row in June 1935.

Options, ideas and Jessie

Aideen spent the months after her return from the US writing to her new friends in Chicago and getting used to life as a full-time actress. The theatre closed for the usual summer break and for additional renovations, but Arthur Shields was busy casting 18 actors for a new play and finding places to rehearse while the theatre was inaccessible. There is no record that her American beau Bob did arrive in Dublin for the horse show in August. An ocean lay between them and he may have cited business reasons, or O'Connor lost interest and told him not to come; but this is speculation. In any case, the early weeks of August were packed with work and she had little time to mourn his absence.

The main events of Horse Show Week were held during the day in the Royal Dublin Society, a large green space on Dublin's southside. Abbey management arranged social outings around it each year; they brought the actors and board members to watch the equestrian events.[79] If the days were full of porter and laughter, the evenings of Horse Show Week brought everyone promptly back to the theatre. The event attracted wealthy, sophisticated visitors to Dublin, and the RDS was close enough to raise attendance at the theatre substantially. The repertoire was always carefully chosen for the influx, and in 1935 the board of directors decided to use the event to coincide with the premiere of *The Silver Tassie* by Seán O'Casey.

Early on Monday 12 August 1935, 'HOUSE FULL' notices were displayed on the exterior of the theatre. The first-night invited audience would include the American, French and German ministers with their wives, the Consul for Sweden and the Netherlands, the Earl and Countess of Longford, Senator and Mrs Blythe, as well as a host of literary and theatrical celebrities. The playwright himself did not attend.[80]

Seven years after the Abbey Theatre had rejected his script for *The Silver Tassie*, O'Casey had managed a tentative reconciliation with W. B. Yeats. Finding himself ill in London, Yeats invited O'Casey for dinner, and they managed to overcome their differences on *The Silver Tassie*. They continued to correspond by letter, and Yeats asked O'Casey for permission to stage his 1934 play, *Within The Gates*. At O'Casey's urging, Yeats got permission to present both plays; Yeats' interest was in *Within The Gates*, and this play was put into rehearsal immediately. However, Brinsley

MacNamara, now a director, and a devout Roman Catholic, took exception to *Within The Gates* and stopped rehearsals. He was no more in favour of *The Silver Tassie*, but he failed to prevent its opening the new season.[81] The Protestant Arthur Shields was asked to direct. He had the advantage of being able to discuss the play with his brother, Barry Fitzgerald, who had played a lead role in the London premiere.

This controversy over the play electrified the atmosphere for those arriving at the theatre that night and made for a high degree of anxiety back stage. O'Connor had had her first taste of success and fame in the US, but such scandal was a new experience. Michael Scott's newly-designed theatre lobby and modernised auditorium, as described in the newspaper columns, added to the sense of anticipation. The black and gold hallway, where portraits of the theatre's stars had hung in semi-darkness, had been replaced. Now there was a bright, spacious lobby where celebrities could more comfortably mingle. In the auditorium, there were new cushioned seats and the orchestra, under the direction of Dr Larchet, was warming up to play. Permission had been granted by the directorate, after years of a ban, and many of the audience now enjoyed the novelty of smoking throughout the performance.[82]

Aideen had acted for Arthur Shields on numerous occasions, but her casting as Jessie Taite in this production suggests Shields was beginning to look at her in a different light. The part, though minor, represented a significant change from the young ingénue roles she had played on the American tour. Jessie is the young woman in love with Harry Heegan, a successful footballer and handsome hero, at the opening of the play. Later, when Harry returns maimed from World War I, he finds Jessie in the arms of another man. One of the newspapers described the character as 'a mindless little minx'.[83] O'Casey introduces the character in the script of *The Silver Tassie*:

> Jessie is twenty-two or so, responsive to all the animal impulses of life. Ever dancing around, in and between the world, the flesh and the devil. She would be happy climbing with a boy among the heather on Howth Hill, and could play ball with young men on the swards of the Phoenix Park. She gives her favour to the prominent and popular.[84]

In original notes for this play, Jessie Taite was 'Sara', and was a year younger, at 21.[85] The final line of the published description is more tame and circumspect than O'Casey's initial vision of the character. In his notebooks, O'Casey recorded how 'Sara' loved playing with the boys, and when one caught her in his arms:

> she recognizes in the struggle the pleasures of this young man's desire for her. [A]nd she thrills when she sees their lightning glances at the frills and [things] she shows in the ardour of the expression.[86]

This is a confident woman: her sexuality and desire are displayed and used. Later in *The Silver Tassie*, at the local dance, two observers describe her allure:

> Simon: And Jessie's looking as if she was tired of her maidenhood, too.
> Mrs Foran: The thin threads holdin' her dress up sidlin' down over her shoulders, an' her catchin' them up again at the tail end of the second before it was too late.[87]

On her very first entrance to the stage, a bystander comments, 'look at the shameful way she's showing her legs'.[88] With her appearance as Jessie, O'Connor stepped out onto the stage as a sexualised Irish woman: a portent of danger to her respectable Catholic community.

While prostitute Rosie Redmond partly triggered the upset about the morals of *The Plough and the Stars*, objections to Jessie Taite and her morals were almost lost in the greater furore about other aspects of *The Silver Tassie*. The character of Jessie is intricately drawn; she is both more complex and nuanced than Rosie. Both support themselves with their sexuality, but Jessie does so in covert ways. She adores Harry for his athletic prowess, his medals and his popularity. She has good work in the war ammunitions factory and has been squirreling away every penny in her savings book to secure her independence. She remains unperturbed by her potential mother-in-law's feelings about her. When her childhood sweetheart comes back from the trenches paralysed, Jessie throws him over for better prospects and for his best friend.

In O'Casey's indictment of violence and war, the men are irreparably damaged; the women fare better. They use both their intelligence and femininity to forge a different life for themselves. Jessie isn't afraid to display her sexuality and to enjoy it. She earns her financial independence and seizes happiness for herself, despite how society tries to shame her for it. In one of the final scenes of the play, Jessie Taite stands her ground before the 17 characters at a party. They scorn her for her behaviour and perceived immorality; she demands the right to make her own decisions. In playing this part, O'Connor experienced the sensations of public humiliation. It was an insight into how life could be for a Catholic woman in the Irish Free State who dared to cross certain societal boundaries.

By curtain fall that Monday, the cast knew the production was an abject failure. The reviewer from the *Irish Independent* expressed distress that some of the country's best performers had been forced to take parts in such an 'epileptic fit of cleverness'.[89] The play was pronounced a 'vigorous medley of lust and hatred and vulgarity' by the Church, a description which, according to O'Casey, terrified theatre-goers who had procured tickets for the sold-out run but then wouldn't attend.[90] Many never saw it; it closed after six performances and was hastily replaced by Shaw's play, *John Bull's Other Island*. 'M. B.' reported that 'Arthur Shields's production was without fault', but it was to be the last play he directed at the Abbey Theatre.[91]

Following *The Silver Tassie* debacle, it was back to business for the Abbey company. They toured to the Cork Opera House in October 1935 with *Autumn Fire* by T. C. Murray (a play set in Cork) and the reliable comedy, *Drama at Inish*. O'Connor now took on secretarial duties in the theatre when she wasn't rehearsing: she acted as an administrative assistant to newly-appointed manager Hugh Hunt.[92] This was financial necessity for O'Connor as well as serving the theatre; she no longer had a day job. Hunt appreciated her work; later events suggest other directors objected to having an actress privy to business affairs.

At the beginning of August 1936, Hunt gave O'Connor permission to go to London briefly for an audition, but the other directors subsequently decided O'Connor's excursion was insubordination. On 14 August, the board 'considered the position of Miss A. O'Connor in relation to the office work and decided that her services be dispensed with.'[93] However, their chosen replacement (Miss Ann Clery) refused to take the post 'owing to the circumstances under which Miss O'Connor had lost the position.' Frank O'Connor then demanded a statement from Miss O'Connor, 'as to her behaviour'. O'Connor acquiesced, and her letter was read at a board meeting on 1 September 1936. In it, she stated that she went to London briefly with Hunt's permission and under the impression that she was not required the following week. Ostensibly, the board accepted this explanation and restored Miss O'Connor to her position, but by 11 September she had been replaced as secretary by Eric Robinson, a brother of Lennox.[94]

Higgins said at one meeting that Miss O'Connor was not 'sufficiently efficient' but Ann Clery's minuted response suggests that for the board, O'Connor's real felony was daring to consider a career for herself outside of the Abbey.[95] At this point, O'Connor was fighting for greater recognition in the company and the London audition was an opportunity to show her potential. According to Laurie Shields, it was in 1936 that Arthur Shields and O'Connor began their affair.[96] Thus, it may also have been that the directors were aware of her personal life and, to compound this, her appearance as Jessie Taite was impacting her reputation. Where Eileen Crowe insisted on 'being the mouthpiece', on presenting rather than embodying women viewed as unsavoury and immoral, O'Connor was being seen to embody them, on and off the stage. Her removal from the administrative position was to be her first experience of dealing with the Abbey directorate effectively punishing her for how she behaved off the stage.

By August 1936, Holloway was recording that 'bombshells still continue to be exploding'.[97] The changes backstage at the Abbey Theatre were continuing at pace. The administration staff were in 'a mild panic' at the re-structuring that was taking place, as a result of a long-standing conflict on the board between Frank O'Connor and F. R. Higgins.[98] O'Connor and Higgins were vying to succeed Yeats, and on Higgins' appointment as managing director, Frank O'Connor was effectively pushed out of the theatre.[99]

The company left behind the chaos for an engagement at the Grand Opera House in Belfast. There, they showed their affection for O'Casey by re-staging *Juno and the Paycock* and *The Plough and the Stars*, along with *Drama at Inish*. Aideen O'Connor, however, was reconsidering her circumstances. She had been re-cast in *The Plough and the Stars* as 15-year-old consumptive Mollser: possibly a cautionary demotion by the directorate. Against this background, newspapers in Belfast broke the news that Aideen O'Connor was to grace the London stage.[100] With no public comment by Abbey Theatre management, she left for London shortly after returning from Belfast. When the newspapers publicised O'Connor's departure for London, the move was not a surprise to her family and colleagues; they had been aware of the prospect for some time. The playwright Michael Egan had come to Dublin specifically looking for an Irish accent and had seen her perform. After her London audition, Aideen agreed with her family that she would play the part and then return to Dublin for Christmas.[101]

On the London stage and home again

On the stage of the Embassy theatre in Hampstead, London in November 1936, during a production of a new play entitled *The Dominant Sex*, a character gave a heartfelt rendition of the *Londonderry Air* in Irish. Afterwards, journalists speculated about the scene. One was adamant that the tune was sung by an invisible substitute in the wings, not by the actress that played the part. Others praised O'Connor's vocal talent.[102] Reading through theatre reviews, one sees only refractions of the real performer, much like watching actors through opera glasses. This image of the journalists craning their necks, trying to get a proper sighting of this woman in the wings, is the only image available of O'Connor at this time, a shadowy figure with a crystal-clear voice, a woman still exploring and revealing her talents, preparing to step out onto the world stage.

There are press cuttings, but no letters or diaries detailing her emotions as she left for London and set up temporary home there. It's possible that O'Connor only wanted to broaden her horizons while earning some money. There is no evidence she saw it as a permanent move, although her prospects at the Abbey were being diminished. If one can rely on the dates provided by Laurie Shields, O'Connor was now in a relationship with Arthur Shields .[103] But Aideen left for London alone, to focus on her craft and on her future.

The Dominant Sex, which opened on 23 November 1936, is set in a studio in Chelsea. The play centres on a bohemian artist, Maurice Holmes, who is trying to choose a wife from a trio of female types. As Sheila, O'Connor played the convent-educated daughter of Mr Holmes's butler. Once again, she is the wide-eyed and demure colleen. The play reviews are mixed, but they all note Aideen's stage presence. One of the London papers said:

> Miss Aideen O'Connor, the young Abbey actress, whose first part in London this is, made everybody feel her charm and admire her grace and the deftness of her art. She has moreover obviously much talent that is still latent. Her personality is winning and her power will grow with her technique, which is already remarkable for such a young actress.[104]

There were rumours of a West End transfer but, as promised, O'Connor came home to spend Christmas with her family. She had kept up to date with friends in Dublin. Reviews of *Wind from the West*, in which both Mulhern and Shields appeared, made their way to her lodgings and she glued them into her scrapbook, alongside her own reviews. London offered opportunities, but she was drawn back to the comfort and stability of the Abbey Theatre. She had also been cast in Paul Vincent Carroll's play, *Shadow and Substance*, due to open in January 1937.

Audiences and actors alike were clamouring to see the new script by the tubby, bespectacled Dundalk writer. Advance notices of the play declared its controversial nature. Critics said of Carroll: 'Not since O'Casey has there been an author who gave such vital characters to the Abbey stage and who moved them with such effect.'[105] Despite predictions of scandal, *Shadow and Substance* was a huge and popular hit. It was deemed by some to be 'The most remarkable play produced at the Abbey for many years.'[106]

Shadow and Substance is set in the home of an elderly canon in Co. Louth. Canon Skerritt finds himself out of harmony with two young curates and an agnostic schoolmaster over the declarations of a young girl who insists she has been visited by the Virgin Mary. He questions his own judgment when confronted with the mystic servant, who was played by a 16-year-old girl from the Abbey School: Phyllis Ryan. Shields took the pivotal role of Canon Thomas Skerritt, and Aideen played his niece and namesake, Thomasina Concannon. Production photographs show the tall French windows of the set and imposing Sacred Heart ideograph over the heads of O'Connor and Shields. She has her head cocked in a smile; his black robes swish around his feet and his face is startled as if disarmed by her outspoken attitude.[107]

O'Connor and Shields developed a close friendship with Carroll over the course of rehearsals. For Carroll, the urbane, intellectual Skerritt was a calculated attempt to bring Dean Jonathan Swift back to life and to 'throw him into the modern mental turmoil in Ireland'.[108] While much of the press focuses on the mesmeric performance of the young Phyllis Ryan, it was also held to be Shields's strongest performance on the Abbey stage. Most of the comments on O'Connor's performance focus on the character's behaviour. Her depictions of young Irish ladies were again being watched for its expression of Irish femininity, rather than for her acting abilities.

Thomasina Concannon is described in Carroll's text as 'a "bunty" girl of about twenty-two' with 'full animal spirits, a round fat face, all dimples and given to giggling laughter'.[109] She tries the patience of her uncle with her antics, including reading a novel entitled *Love's Purple Passion*, and then leaving it under his pillow. For Lennox Robinson, Thomasina was the epitome of a type of Irish female increasingly seen around Dublin. This female type was a problem for Robinson. He explained:

> the perfect type for all time of the desperate and, to me, quite unfaceable problem of the country-girl who has become what we in the Gaelic League call 'Anglicised', what the West Briton would equally unfairly call 'Americanised', what her own neighbours would, I fancy, call simply foolish and what in actual fact is unendurably cheapened, tedious, and embarrassing…[110]

To imbue such a role with a sense of sincerity, without becoming a simpering fool that disgusts the audience, required a delicate balance.

The cast tramped through the January sleet and flurries of snow each evening to perform in *Shadow and Substance*. Frolie Mulhern doesn't appear on the cast list for the premiere production of the play, but newcomer Phyllis Ryan remembers Mulhern as a 'quirky young comedienne' who whispered and conspired with O'Connor in the dressing room.[111] Even when she wasn't strictly required at the Abbey, there was Frolie, supporting her friend. Ryan disliked the arrangement, feeling uncomfortable with the women's conspiratorial whispering. She was convinced that, 'They felt they were being pushed out by the new arrival and their attitude naturally lacked warmth.'[112]

Aideen had little time or patience for niceties; Ryan was correct in her assumption that their roles were threatened by the arrival of a younger ingénue. But Aideen worked hard under Hunt's guidance and played the role of Thomasina with a vibrancy that delighted audiences. One of the newspapers provides a precious description of her physical style:

> Aideen O'Connor's rendering of the canon's niece, the only person not afraid of him, was outstanding not merely for her priceless giggle, but for the use of [her] body to suggest a gawky 'flapper' whose mind, clothes, coiffure, and voice were all of a piece with her passion for bullseyes – her best performance for a long time.[113]

O'Connor now had the skill and confidence to move effortlessly from demure servant in *Drama At Inish* to flirtatious flapper. The chain of adjectives describing her performances since the American tour of 1934/35 track the emergence of a particular style. The newspapers (previously quoted) describe her as 'pert'; they talk of her 'grace' and of her 'deft' technique. She was precise in her physicality, each gesture considered and deliberate. Despite her small frame, she could command a stage. Her range was growing, as were her confidence and ambition. She was thriving under the discipline imposed by Hunt and the gentle attention of Arthur Shields. But despite (or because of) her expanding range, the parts available to her in the Abbey company were diminishing. However, there remained some roles in the Irish classics that could challenge her.

A more self-assured Aideen found herself on the boat to England in February 1937; this time, Mulhern and Shields were travelling with her as the Abbey company set out for the Cambridge Arts Festival. Hunt had cast her as Mary Boyle in *Juno and the Paycock*, where she'd play the daughter of Juno (being played by Eileen Crowe). She was ready for the challenge, and the reviewer for *The Cambridge Gownsman* was impressed by her interpretation, calling it 'fresh and sensitive'. He said, 'The character becomes more complex in the course of the play, and Miss

O'Connor showed a full understanding of every aspect of it.'[114] On stage, she continued to be respectful: 'She did not let it obtrude melodramatically on the other phases of the action.'[115]

If she was courteous to her elders on stage, off stage the 'pretty juvenile actress' was playing a more dangerous game.[116] On the Cambridge trip, it was impossible to hide her romantic relationship with Shields. Given the Catholic morals of the other actors along with their friendship with Bazie Magee, it was only a matter of time before the affair was public knowledge.

Genevieve (Bazie) Magee, whom Shields had married in Chelsea in 1920, was 'quick-witted, reasoned like a man, [was] sharp-tongued and quick tempered.' She was 'more mentally aware than other women of her day, or perhaps it was just a case of being more outspoken than most.'[117] Magee was a reasonably talented actress, despite having no training, and was a practical, maternal figure during the 1934/35 tour. But Magee had a 'capacious imagination'.[118] Playwright Denis Johnston recalls how, when Magee has visitors, she simply 'talks and talks and talks' until her own mind 'begins to stagger at the conclusions reached.' Johnston recognised when her 'dangerous' behaviour began to lose her friends. He described her as having 'a Pirandellesque mind completely divorced from any relation to reality'.[119]

By the 1930s, this propensity to lose touch with reality was taking over Magee's life. She was performing less and less; a susceptibility to manic moods was exacerbated by her drinking habit. The couple had moved to the seaside village of Sandymount, to a house with a garden where their son, Adam, played and Shields kept a vegetable patch. Yet Shields was finding living with Magee 'impossible'.[120] Aideen O'Connor, for her youth and beauty, resembled Magee in her quick temper and outspoken nature. She was independent and increasingly ambitious, yet nothing prepared her for the fallout from this romantic attachment.

The Abbey green room, with its packed bookshelves and stove, its worn furniture and friendly ghosts, had become a home away from home for O'Connor. She had taken refuge there one evening in late February 1937 when the door swung open to reveal an irate Bazie Magee. Magee had once featured as an affectionate figure for O'Connor. But everything had changed; Magee slapped Aideen across the face. It later transpired that a 'concerned' company member had sent a letter to Magee with all the details of her husband's affair.[121] O'Connor was shamed in front of her colleagues; Shields' reputation was unaffected.

Worse was yet to come: Aideen fled home to discover that an identical letter had been sent to her father. Vincent De Paul O'Connor pitilessly told her to leave the house and she spent two weeks with extended family in Cork before daring to return to Ranelagh. W. B. Yeats refused to tell his wife, George, how he discovered all of the details, although his daughter, Anne Yeats, and many of the other actors witnessed the events that 'reduced Miss O'Connor to such tears'.[122]

O'Connor remained resolute in her devotion to Shields, but she would never forgive the interfering Company member or forget the humiliation of Magee's attack. With Frolie Mulhern and Abbey scenic designers, Anne Yeats and Tania Mosiewitch, O'Connor found a small circle of friends to support her, but the sense of ignominy lingered.

Tania Moseiwitch, a designer who had arrived at the Abbey with director Hugh Hunt the week after *The Silver Tassie* debacle, occupied the paint room. This was at the far end of the corridor backstage at the Abbey, 'past the greenroom, past the wardrobe room, past the dressing-rooms.'[123] If respite was needed from the green room, O'Connor and Mulhern could come here, to a room 'no bigger than a drawing room', and gaze out the sole window onto the laneway behind. It was private, if only because of the pungent smell of size in the air and the crowded untidiness of flats and tools and paint-splattered paraphernalia.[124] Happy to have company while she worked, Moseiwitch kept there, 'an aluminium kettle, a blue jug, a yellow teapot, a small pot of raspberry jam, and a cup and saucer that don't match on an orange tray.'[125] It was a place where O'Connor could seek support and laughter out of earshot of the green room and the offices, but she was learning to be careful whom she trusted with details of her personal life.

As a close friend, Anne Yeats visited Aideen in her family home. There, Yeats could barely hide her horror at the state of the house, which she described to her mother as having a 'filthy kitchen, general dilapidation and breakage everywhere.'[126] George Yeats lamented that 'there seems to be no female of any sort in charge,' as if this was the root of all of O'Connor's issues. '[127]

There is an O'Connor family anecdote that before the actress left Hollybank Avenue for good, Bazie Magee arrived to bang on the door of number 53 and shout insults. O'Connor cowered upstairs, while her quick-witted sister Maeve talked down an inebriated Bazie, coaxing her away with the enticement of a drink in Ranelagh.[128] The following month, Vincent De Paul O'Connor's rage hadn't subsided, and O'Connor packed her bags. She went temporarily to Howth, where Hunt offered refuge in his cottage. Moseiwitch was also staying there but their stay was cut short when the landlady noticed that two unchaperoned women were staying in the house and complained to the Vicar.[129]

Arthur Shields kept thin pocket diaries for most of his life, noting appointments, rehearsal times, production dates. A note on 6 April 1937 reads, 'Marriage 16 years'. On the following page, dated 12 April, is the note, 'Una home'.[130] He was one of the few people to always address her as Una, while others used the name she'd chosen for the stage. The next few months passed in tantrums and despair, in rows and tears.

Aideen O'Connor's promotion into female roles demonstrating a more overt and liberated sexuality coalesced dangerously with developments in her personal life. She no longer wanted to be playing naïve teenage girls, but her reputation off-stage had been tarnished and, in Dublin society, this affected the adult parts she was offered as well as her other duties in the theatre. Officially at least, the affair with Shields ended. This was the only course of action that would allow them both to travel to the US with the Abbey company again in September 1937.

Chapter 2

Ria Mooney (1903–73)

Players and the Painted Stage

Ria Mooney is the only actress that I write about to have published her own memoir. She worked with editor and writer Val Mulkerns in the late 1960s to produce *Players and the Painted Stage*. This was eventually published in journal format in two volumes of *George Spelvin's Theatre Books* in 1978, five years after Mooney's death. Such evidence provides a valuable source of biographical information, but only with a carefully considered strategy for reading and interpreting the memoir. Such evidence should be tempered by an understanding of Mooney's personality, and her art, as well as the context in which the autobiography was prepared.

By the twentieth century, autobiographies of actresses were more often becoming 'a narrative assertion of a professional self which mirrored the increased confidence, social and theatrical acceptability and education of the writers.'[1] Actresses wrote and shared their life stories to assert an identity as professional artists, to share their philosophy and craft as well as acting heritage. Thus, Mooney's failure to find a publisher for her memoirs when she completed the work in the late 1960s was a blow to her artistic integrity and self-belief. At the same time, the writing in the autobiography shows a reticence to proclaim her accomplishments and to assert the ingenuity of her work. She wanted to share her lessons with a younger generation, yet she drew back from asserting her expertise. This pattern of determination halted by reticence to publicise her talent is reflected in much of her practical work as well as in her writing. For a female performer, writing a memoir 'activates the actress's public image.'[2] In Ria Mooney's case, she chose to activate the image of a girl sheltered from moral evils such as prostitution and suicide, guided by religious faith, and succeeding through good fortune rather than her talent and hard work.

In *Players and the Painted Stage*, Mooney's prose suggests a reversion to the type of self-effacing Irish girl idealised by the Free State. The title is both a tribute to W. B. Yeats and a signal of her understanding that she was a minor part of a greater Irish literary tradition. The voice and tone represent a naïve, even superstitious girl. Early on Mooney says, 'This vocation seemed to be thrust on me.'[3] While she lays claim to being gifted with 'second sight', her own agency in life decisions is elided.[4] Later, Mooney suggests, 'Perhaps it was the strength of my desire for change that brought it to me.'[5] Repeatedly, the gentle, sweet tone belies her life experience, her struggles, her patience and work. It also conceals the exposure to life in London and New York, and to political machinations in theatres in Dublin and elsewhere, which made her an astute, worldly woman.

Catherine Maria (Ria) Mooney was born on the last day of April in 1903 and she later used this date to adopt the persona of 'changeling'. It was only on reaching her 30s that Mooney learnt of May Eve changelings: creatures swapped by the fairy folk for children born on April 30. This was a tale that she adopted, a familiar narrative to explain how she looked so much like her siblings but would lead a life entirely different from theirs. A 'changeling' suggests a mystical creature that, without being openly subversive, touches on the 'strangeness' of the American director that would become her mentor: Eva Le Gallienne.

Theatre scholar Robert Schanke has written a biography of Le Gallienne, and he said the following of her two autobiographies:

> Certainly they were well-intentioned, but both are literary shrines to a woman that Eva always wanted to be, not to the woman she was. [...] She did an admirable job of camouflaging herself behind portraits that rob her achievements of their sinew and texture.[6]

The same comments could be made of Mooney's autobiography. Here, I want to exercise such sinews and demonstrate the texture of her achievements.

Mooney's depictions of events are fascinating in how the details work to obscure the people and material reality of events. Instead, she draws heavily on colour and light, creating painterly impressions of important scenes in her life. Mooney swallowed any fury she may have felt at powerful figures; she was always discreet and dignified in her account of the history of the Irish National Theatre. Often, the structure of the slim volume works synchronically, focusing in on apparently inconsequential minutiae and moments of her life until they expand to reveal their impact on the overall narrative. Such intimate descriptions frequently allow her to conceal or evade other critical contexts, including her own emotions at major points.

The biography by James P. McGlone, *Ria Mooney: The Life and Times of the Artistic Director of the Abbey Theatre 1948–63*, drew extensively on Mooney's account of events, supplementing it with newspaper reviews and limited other third-party sources. Its aim was to reassert the importance of Mooney's contribution to Irish theatre, but in doing so it ascribed her a title that she never officially held: Artistic Director. Here, I frequently refer to Mooney's own account of events in her life, but I also work to read between the lines of her 'literary performance' for a deeper understanding of the turning points in her life and the factors that drove and energised her.

Writing on actresses and autobiography, Mary Jean Corbett asserted: 'Whatever sorts of roles it may recount, an autobiography or memoir is less an originary act of self-expression than another formally constrained or determined mode of performance.'[7] *Players and the Painted Stage* does not so much reveal Mooney, as expose the fact that she performed in every way right to the end of her life.

In her appearance as Rosie Redmond in the premiere of O'Casey's *The Plough and the Stars*, as well as in a radically new interpretation of Pegeen Mike for the production of Synge's *The Playboy of the Western World* in 1937, Ria Mooney showed true bravery. She displayed strength of mind that some would call stubbornness or, later on, would view as eccentricity. This courage stemmed from a devotion to the plays, to the characters as written, and to the playwrights that engendered them. It grew through dedication to her acting technique and it led her to make artistic and personal choices and decisions that other Abbey actresses of that time did not, or would not, consider. The sections that follow are not strictly chronological, although they trace the growth and expansion of Mooney's craft and work. They work to show the patterns and motifs in Mooney's life, including unanticipated lurches in her career trajectory. As in any life story, there is rarely an uncomplicated sequence of cause and effect; yet there is a beautiful and brilliant unity of artistic philosophy in Ria Mooney's work.

Member of the Abbey Theatre Company

Pictures of the Abbey Theatre Company on tour in America show Ria Mooney as small and curvy, with large eyes set deep into a moon-shaped face.[8] In those eyes one can still see the raven-haired, eight-year-old girl peering out of a doorway on Baggot Street. This girl watched three gentlemen passing by her father's teashop on Upper Baggot Street and imagined they had stepped out of a fairy tale book. Her father, at work inside, laughed at her question: the men were from the Abbey Theatre.[9]

For the 'changeling' growing up on Baggot Street, the upheaval of the 1916 Easter Rising and the first rumblings of the Civil War were all swept up in the sudden death of her mother. She was 14 years old when her mother passed away. Rather than turn to practical matters like assisting with the family teashop business or raising her younger siblings, she chose to let herself loose upon the world. 'From the day my mother died, I did exactly what pleased me,' Mooney says in her memoirs.[10] If there was no one to tell her when she was doing wrong, there was also no one to tell her when she was doing right. This liberation paved the way for many future adventures.

The 'crimson, gold and cream' of Madam Rock's theatre school performances entranced Mooney at an early age.[11] Her mother had been an amateur actress in her time, and happily watched her daughter dance at the Gaiety Theatre and the Theatre Royal. Madame Rock's dance training taught Mooney poise and rhythm, before she had a basic introduction to acting with the amateur Rathmines & Rathgar Musical Dramatic Society. At the Abbey, she was exposed for the first time to the still, elegant quality of acting fostered by Frank and William Fay. The resplendent theatricality at Madame Rock's meant that the Abbey Theatre was something of a disappointment when Mooney made her first professional appearance there. It was threadbare and dowdy; the theatre's serious intentions did not yet extend to décor and costume. At the age of 21, she appeared in a leopard-skin coat in George Shiels' comedy, *The Retrievers.* All of the actors were charged with providing their own costumes; a penurious Mooney borrowed, along with the coat, a dress and hat.

She relinquished the glamour and vibrancy of her youthful performances for something radically different. Despite her initial disappointment at the lack of colour, Mooney was naturally disciplined, and she devoted herself to achieving the elegance demanded at the National Theatre. While she describes her own accent as 'affected', situated somewhere between her own Dublin brogue and the polite English of her elocution lessons, her elocution impressed director William Fay.[12]

Rosie Redmond

While Ria was working away happily in minor productions for the Dublin Drama League and other 'dramic' (her term for amateur drama) productions in aristocratic drawing rooms, Seán O'Casey was working on a play entitled *The Plough and the Stars.* He completed it in August 1925 and sent it to Lady Gregory who deemed it 'a fine play, terribly tragic.'[13] As was her custom, Gregory read the play aloud to the other directors. While she had no issue with the character of the prostitute Rosie Redmond, O'Casey was wincing. He wrote to Gabriel Fallon: 'It was rather embarrassing to me to hear her reading the saucy song sung by Rosie and Fluther in the second act'.[14] The reading over, he set to thinking about casting and he wondered aloud to his 'buttie' Gabriel Fallon: '[O]ught I to chance young [Shelah] Richards for the part of Nora? Or Ria Mooney? Which of the two would you suggest?'[15] In stage time, Rosie is not a substantial role, but rehearsing and playing the first prostitute on the stage of the National Theatre would require significant strength, firstly, to withstand the Catholic prudery of the rest of the cast and, secondly, to endure the tendentious public reception of the play. Shelah Richards (from a well-off Protestant family) was already known for her outspoken nature, but O'Casey had been watching Mooney's performances intently. Two weeks before he finished *The Plough and the Stars*, the playwright had an altercation with manager M. J. Dolan. O'Casey criticised the production of Shaw's *Man and Superman* on the Abbey's main stage, declaring on 13 August that acting was the 'first essential in drama', and that the performances were 'painfully imperfect'.[16] He went on to tell Dolan that the performers in *Man and Superman* 'were all bad (except Ria Mooney)'.[17] When O'Casey approached her, he told her that she was the only actress fit to play the role. Shelah Richards was cast as Nora Clitheroe.

The building was ahum with the licentious energy of O'Casey's play by January 1926. Upstairs in the offices, Yeats and Robinson were fielding the anxious entreaties of the directorate. Dr George O'Brien, professor of economics at UCD, had been on the board for only two months when he was sent a copy of the play for his approval. He couched his grievances on 5 September 1925 by saying the appearance of a prostitute was 'not in itself objectionable' but that O'Casey's portrayal 'is objectionable' because 'The lady's professional side is unduly emphasised in her actions and conversation'.[18] While O'Brien believed changes could be made, certain elements (in particular the song) 'could not possibly be allowed to stand'.[19] Yeats and Robinson rushed to Rosie's defence:

> [S]he is certainly necessary to the general action and ideas ... It is no use putting her in if she does not express herself vividly and in character, if her 'professional' side is not emphasised.[20]

Dr O'Brien retained his objections and his fear that the character would incite an attack on the theatre proved prescient.

Downstairs in the rehearsal spaces, there was, as Adrian Frazier has described, an embattled 'stand-off between actors and author'.[21] Eileen Crowe gave up her part rather than speak about children being begotten between the Ten Commandments, because of the allusion that there were children who were not. May Craig took the part after Crowe consulted her priest and voiced her decision. F. J. McCormick refused to use the term 'snotty' to his stage wife. In a sleight of hand, the director discovered that McCormick's stage wife, Richards, had no problem with it; she took the line and made it her own.[22] Yeats did insist that O'Casey remove many of the uses of the word 'bitches' but allowed one in the final dramatic scene between Bessie Burgess and Nora Clitheroe to remain. O'Casey wrote to Robinson on 10 January 1926. He pointed out that most of the banned words had appeared in other plays but not all in the same one, and said, 'I draw the line at a Vigilance Committee of Actors'.[23]

While Crowe consulted a priest for advice and compromises, Ria Mooney did not have a 'Father Confessor'.[24] Her mentor was O'Casey himself and he wanted her to play the part. Committed to the role, she took the potentially embarrassing step of frequenting the alley at the back of the theatre to ensure her appearance was authentic. Having studied the streetwalkers, Mooney imitated their 'clown-like make-up' of thick white powder and red circles on their cheeks.[25] But while she could (and would) separate the personal from professional and take on the role, she did nothing that would, to her mind, besmirch her good name or that of her family. 'I need hardly say that it was some of the women who tried to put me off,' Mooney reveals in the autobiography. Unmoved by either 'their self-righteous faces or their arguments', she continued to rehearse the part.[26] It is useful that she states this fact; many social histories focus on the patriarchal suppression of 1930s Catholic Ireland and patriarchal values are often transmitted by women. However, the collusion of women in Ireland's ideology is rarely set out in such startling fashion.

In an interview with this author in July 2012, the editor of Mooney's autobiography, Val Mulkerns, dispelled the famous anecdote around Mooney and Rosie Redmond's profession. Mulkerns was adamant that 23-year-old Mooney was mature and experienced enough to know how a prostitute earned her money. But it *is* true that Ria always insisted that she did not know and says so in her memoirs. Setting the more pragmatic truth (from Mulkerns) against the anecdote yields an insight: Ria probably did understand the nature of prostitution, but off-stage she played the role of a respectable Catholic girl who didn't countenance such things.

Prior to the opening, O'Casey made one significant change to the part of Rosie Redmond. Moved either by his own embarrassment in the wake of Lady Gregory's reading or O'Brien's objections to the bawdy number about a tailor and a sailor, he wrote to Lady Gregory on 11 September to say, 'My little song, I think, has to go'.[27] Thus, Mooney left the stage at the end of the second act without a song. In later years, when she herself came to direct the play, she restored the tune.

Opposition to *The Plough and the Stars* did not break out immediately. A few evenings into the run, actors were subjected to shouts and jeers mid-performance, with lumps of coal and coins being used as missiles during the second act. After an attempt to set the curtain on fire, a decision was made to leave the stage bare for the third act. Mooney watched from the wings as the trouble continued. A boxing match broke out and F. J. McCormick stepped out of his role as Jack Clitheroe to disassociate himself and his wife (Eileen Crowe) from the play. Yeats made an appearance, declaring his fervent support for O'Casey. When the audience verbally attacked him, he admonished them while simultaneously affirming O'Casey's genius with words frequently quoted in the decades since: 'You have disgraced yourselves again ... You have rocked the cradle of genius ... You have sent O'Casey's name around the world.'[28] Many of the actors in the play were shocked to find that the attackers included personal friends. Shelah Richards was yelled at by a woman in the audience every time she opened her mouth; later the actress was disgusted to discover the heckler was someone she had known from childhood.[29] The coalescence of personal and professional lives had become dangerous for the performers, male and female.

There were no further riots in the theatre, but offstage the opposition continued, with letters appearing in the newspapers and some feeble attempts to terrify the main actors, who were instructed not to approach or leave the theatre alone and on foot. Mooney believed they were in danger of being kidnapped, but that the would-be kidnappers did not go through with their plans. The second act was played with auditorium lights up and plain-clothes policemen on hand.

Rosie Redmond is not a crucial element of the plot of O'Casey's play. The prostitute presents an element of Dublin tenement life that others wanted to ignore and she appears only in the pub scenes, disappearing after the second act. The character of Rosie has little to offer beyond her profession or 'type'. She has no storyline, just an outburst when the Covey resents her voicing her opinions at the end of the second act. His announcement that he won't take any 'reprimandin' from a prostitute!' turns her 'wild with humiliation'.[30] She tells him: 'You're no man ... I'm a woman, anyhow, an' if I'm a prostitute aself, I have me feelin's.'[31] Mooney had an emotionally uncomplicated connection to the character that reduced her to tears when Covey reminds her of her position. On the stage of the National Theatre, Mooney asserted the right of all Irish women, including prostitutes, to express emotion and be treated with respect. O'Casey's intention may have been primarily a socialist one, but there's a feminist intent in the line if one is listening for it.

In taking on that role and sustaining her performance during the moral storm that accompanied *The Plough and the Stars*, the actress set her career on a new plane. Ria herself said: 'It was not until that night that I ceased to be an amateur and became a professional actress in the truest sense of the word.'[32] The transformation happened before she hid in the wings, watching the riots; the shift began when she accepted and began to rehearse the role. Unlike many of the females in that company, Mooney had started to separate her personal life and moral concerns from those she adopted on stage. Despite her beliefs, she divested herself of ego and treated the character with respect by going out of her way (and down that alley) to imbue Rosie with an authenticity that may have contributed to the riots. That she refused to publicly admit her understanding of prostitution suggests she hadn't completed the separation of her personal and professional reputations, but the fissure was happening.

After the opening night of *The Plough and the Stars*, O'Casey came to Ria Mooney backstage and told her that she had saved the play. The solemn actress remained devoted to O'Casey, and his work, for the rest of her life. He was a tall, avuncular presence and she responded to his passion for theatre and his generosity towards her. In the summer of 1926, she was missing both Rosie and Seán O'Casey. Once she had saved enough money to pay lodgings in advance and keep enough for a return ticket, she took the boat to London. Ria Mooney never intimated that she followed O'Casey, but he was by then settled in the city.

The Civic Repertory Theatre Company

Early in the spring of 1928, Shelah Richards wrote to her fiancé Denis Johnston from the Belvedere Hotel in New York telling him that Mooney had 'by the by' signed a contract with Eva Le Gallienne to appear in her Civic Repertory Theatre Company.[33] Shelah and Ria were appearing together in a tour of O'Casey plays by an English company. They shared rooms close to the theatre and while Shelah often pined for home, Ria found that her 'pulse responded to the city's rhythm'.[34]

Ria had not stayed in London long. Money ran out quickly, as did her hopes of finding work, and she was close to going home when she was offered the job as understudy to Shelah Richards in New York. Any disappointment about not being on stage was assuaged by the sight of the skyscrapers rising from a mist on the Hudson river like 'a fairy city resting on a cloud'.[35] Yet again in her writing, the romance of the scene conceals any trepidation about the lifestyle change. Soon, she had been cast as Mary Boyle in a production of O'Casey's *Juno and the Paycock*. At the same time, she lost weight and acquired some 'well-cut American clothes', which gave her for the first time in her life 'a presentable figure'.[36] Ria began to present herself as a stylish woman, confident of a place on the New York theatre scene.

They weren't performing during the last week of the tour, and the women set about experiencing what Shelah Richards described as: 'Bored Broadway believing in Better Brighter Plays'.[37] They endured Eugene O'Neill's experimental play, *The Strange Interlude*, which lasted from five pm until eleven thirty pm with a break for dinner and declared it 'marvelous'.[38] Another evening, two polite men called at their rooms to escort them to visit the Civic Repertory Theatre on 14th Street, where *The Three Sisters* was being performed. Richards told Johnston:

'The Three Sisters' was actually good – very good – although I don't imagine it was like the London production; [...] but the acting was extraordinarily good and the best I have seen here, and the most like The Abbey![39]

Shelah was impressed; Ria was captivated. In Dublin and London, she believed in putting herself in the right place and waiting for something to happen. A newly-confident woman took matters into her own hands: she wrote to the director of *The Three Sisters* asking for an audition.

Richards' reporting to Johnston of Mooney's contract with the Civic Repertory Theatre Company was matter-of-fact, but winning a place in the core group of this company was not a straightforward matter. The standards of dedication and discipline held by director Eva Le Gallienne were extremely high. Le Gallienne personally monitored all aspects of productions, as well as taking starring roles. Rose Hobart, Le Gallienne's acquaintance for years before joining the company, was sacked for visiting her husband during a week she wasn't performing without telling the director.[40] Another actress said: 'It was as if we must always be fit, do our best, make the best of everything, because Eva was doing so much.'[41]

Le Gallienne relied on others to scout talent. It was the Civic's literary manager, Helen Lohman, who saw Mooney perform Mary Boyle and granted her an audition after her letter. That season, the permanent core of 20 actors was expanded to 30. The following season, 30 apprentice positions were coveted by over 200 applicants. In those auditions, Le Gallienne tried to 'sense their inner quality ... some trace of sensibility or imagination, humor, or aspiration'.[42] Ria Mooney demonstrated a sensibility Le Gallienne approved of. She completed the tour as understudy to Shelah Richards and returned to Dublin, where she played a teenage girl in Robinson's *The Far-Off Hills* one last time. Then she packed up and said farewell to her family and to her friends in the Abbey. She was returning to New York as an official member of the Civic Repertory Company but, nonetheless, alone.

The Civic Repertory Theatre is no longer visible in downtown New York. It was on the north side of 14th Street (just off Sixth Avenue) and close to two subways. An overground train rumbled past at regular intervals. On the autumn morning of her first day, Mooney walked past a Salvation Army hostel, a second-hand clothes store and the Child's restaurant where she would eat many of her meals for the next few years, to arrive at the neo-classical façade. The building was crumbling, but a few weeks before the new season, Le Gallienne used money she'd won with a *Pictorial Review* award to refurbish the interior.

Ria was introduced to the other actors and the new cast sat around on the stage under a gold proscenium arch reading scripts. The auditorium was freshly painted in green, gold and black and there was a cyclorama of lights and modern footlights. After the first read-through, the actors walked up newly-carpeted aisles and explored the dressing rooms backstage. For all the glamour front of house, the floorboards in the dressing rooms were warped and the radiators wheezed. In the green room, photos of Le Gallienne's estranged father, the Irish/French poet Richard Le Gallienne, hung on the walls.[43] Ria was ready and eager to start rehearsals.

Training and working with Eva Le Gallienne had a life-long impact on Mooney, personally and professionally. It was a period of ferocious hard work, and investment in her skills and talents, which made her such a sensitive actress and astute director. But it was also a challenging time, that led to insecurities about her abilities. It shook her confidence at various points, and those insecurities would re-surface from time to time in the decades after. To understand that period of Mooney's life, it is necessary to understand Le Gallienne: her background, her inspiration, her artistic ideals and the company she led.

Le Gallienne was born in London but raised by her mother, a journalist turned milliner, in Paris. Julie Norregaard separated from her husband, Richard Le Gallienne, after years of emotional abuse. Much of the time, Norregaard was also the main carer to Hesper, Richard's half-Irish daughter from his first marriage. An early feminist, Norregaard raised Eva with the aid of a nurse. Le Gallienne grew up as the sole focus of the energy of these two formidable women and it shaped Le Gallienne's personality. As her biographer Helen Sheehy recognises:

> Her horizons were not circumscribed by traditional expectations and she simply did not recognize any boundaries in her development as a person. [...] Her soul was that of a searching artist; her vitality and her appetite for experience were enormous. And she had the good fortune to grow up in an atmosphere free of stifling bourgeois conventions.[44]

Set on a life on the stage from an early age, Le Gallienne spent many of her summers in Surrey with her half-sister, attending as much theatre as she could. A generous patron paid the fees for Le Gallienne to attend Tree's Academy in Gower Street (the institution that is now the Royal Academy of Dramatic Art). By the age of 16, she was in New York with her mother. Le Gallienne was ambitious and precocious, although behind the precocity there was an educated intelligence and diligent work ethic. Her early influences were decidedly European: Eleonora Duse and Sara Bernhardt were idols she studied and emulated. On first watching Duse perform in London in 1923, she was stunned by her 'superhuman understanding and compassion' along with the 'metaphysical and impersonal creative genius'.[45] In 1966, Le Gallienne would publish a biography of Duse, and in it Le Gallienne demonstrates how the awe of her youth gave way to a careful interrogation of her idol's life and work.

Given her maturity and arrogance, it was not long before taking roles for other production companies failed to fulfil Le Gallienne's ambitions. With a desire for additional training and experience, she planned (with a collaborator) to create a workshop where, in her own words, 'untroubled by outside opinion, we could improve and perfect our instruments'.[46] This would provide a space outside of the long-run system, which she found unbearably suffocating, to work on plays they chose for the pleasure of the rehearsal process. In the event, professional commitments and health problems meant the plans came to naught, but years later Le Gallienne returned to her 'idealistic dreams' and transformed them into practical plans to introduce New York to a proper repertory theatre system.[47]

If Duse and Bernhardt formed the centre of her philosophy on acting, Le Gallienne's craft was indelibly shaped by the work of the Russian theatre director Constantin Stanislavski. The Moscow Arts Theatre first visited New York in 1923, and Le Gallienne frequently saw them perform from her habitual seat in the front row. The Moscow Arts Theatre thrilled the theatre community and Le Gallienne introduced herself to Stanislavski. Her later process shows that she took careful note of his approach, including ensemble work and concentration on the inner reality of characters.

Broadway had become, for Le Gallienne, a male-dominated business focused on stars and marred by long runs, high-ticket prices and typecasting. As she wrote in her second autobiography, *With A Quiet Heart*, 'There was plenty of cake in the showcases of Broadway, but the bread was missing'.[48] She wanted audiences to be exposed to art, regardless of their financial position. The idea that repertory theatre could thrive in New York was an idealistic one; Le Gallienne determined to succeed where others had failed. She was convinced the audience was there for the type of plays she wanted to produce, but such an audience were of modest means and so alternative modes of funding productions were essential. Although she later claimed there was 'no commercial angle' to the original plan, Le Gallienne was charming and alluring in her dealings with potential wealthy benefactors.[49]

There were seven actors in the core company Le Gallienne established, each with a contract guaranteeing 20 weeks of work. Salaries ranged between 60 and 200 dollars. She had also chosen a repertoire of four plays (two by Ibsen, one by Chekhov and one by Benavente) and hired five Russian musicians to provide an orchestra. With a promise from theatre producer Otto Kahn to meet the rent for the first season, Le Gallienne began an intense five-week rehearsal period, involving all four plays.

In the first volume of her autobiography, *At 33*, Le Gallienne describes the rehearsals for their first major hit: the production of Chekhov's *The Three Sisters* that Mooney attended. This particular rehearsal period captures many of Le Gallienne's ideals. The company took over a small inn in Westport, in Essex County, New York. There, the cast sought to identify themselves with the various characters in the play. They called each other by their character names and frequently started work by discussing in character things not actually in the play. Once somebody gave a proper 'cue', the conversation would continue as written in the text. This created a 'tremendous sense of ease and reality' before they began rehearsing on stage where Le Gallienne could give 'actual shape' to the performance.[50] Rarely again would the company have the financial means or the time to immerse themselves in a work in this way, but the essence of this approach was transported back to the crumbling 14th Street theatre, where they would rehearse with a soundtrack of roaring trains and machinery drilling for subways.

For Le Gallienne, acting was not a trade. She refused to support the strikes of the Equity Union, who claimed it was. For her, acting was high art; she considered herself a conscious and endlessly developing artist.[51] This concept of the actor as a creative artist was also a central tenet of the teachings of Stanislavski.

In the sections that follow, it is necessary to distinguish between the original Stanislavski System (as expounded by Carnicke, Benedetti and others) and the tools that formed the basis of the American 'Method' of Lee Strasberg and Stella Adler. The American Method drew on the translation of Stanislavski by Elizabeth Hapgood, and it used many of the principles to commodify actors, create an industry and perpetuate gender stereotypes.[52] The teachings of Stanislavski, conversely, had as their cornerstone the concept of the individual creative artist, who must be respected and supported in their work. The Stanislavski artist used empathy, rather than emotional substitution or 'recall', to explore character and his system balanced psychological work with physical exercise, including yoga.

Le Gallienne was also inspired by the philosophy of Eleonora Duse, and she was committed to Duse's idea that 'in playing, as in any other art, one should abolish the personal and try to place one's instrument at the service of a higher, disembodied force.'[53] Obliterating the ego and submitting to a higher power was not a religious act, except where the religion was acting. This idea was echoed by Ria Mooney many years later when, in June 1962, she wrote a letter to young actor Patrick Laffan. The letter, which set off a successful career and which he kept, says: 'Don't let your brain come between your instinctive acting talent and your audience. Remember the great actor is, or should be, a MEDIUM.'[54] Throughout her career, Le Gallienne's mood was in large part determined by the character that she played at the time. Sheehy's biography reveals an ongoing cycle, from her earliest professional life to her elderly years, in which each new part demands a shift in lifestyle: a new facet to her personality, a new style of movement, often a new partner or living arrangement.[55] At various points throughout her career, Le Gallienne would work herself into a state of nervous exhaustion by complete immersion in a role and intense periods of overwork. If as a director in rehearsals she employed the Stanislavskian ideals of ensemble playing and calm introspection, in her own work she eschewed his notion of dual-consciousness and frequently allowed her immersion in character to dictate her personal life.

Le Gallienne invested the money earned by her success, ensuring the comfort of her mother and providing herself with a solid base, but she remained wary of the 'insidious joys of prosperity'.[56] At the heart of her vocation was a constant struggle: to obliterate her own personality and become each character, at the same time as her adoring (and sometimes scathing) public sought to know the real Le Gallienne, which she wanted to keep private. In her 20s, Eva wrote long, reflective letters to her mother in Europe. While appearing as Julie in a production of Molnár's *Liliom* she wrote:

> It must be wonderful to be able to create away from crowds—out of sight of one's public— it is a source of endless wonder to me, why the medium that has been thrust upon on me should be the most terribly exposed—so glaringly illuminated to all eyes. With my nature it is a curious paradox—& somewhat of a burden.[57]

Le Gallienne simultaneously abhorred and relished this challenge, balancing her internal need for solitude and her professional need for exposure. Sheehy says: 'Eva Le Gallienne refused to be typecast in any part, in the theatre or in her private life'.[58] Despite Le Gallienne's youth, she was already grappling with complex and conflicting desires for privacy and for public recognition. She also loved and wanted to live with women but refused to define herself as a lesbian.[59] She was beginning to realise the difficulty of realising her artistic ambitions in a theatre world dominated by 'show business' and was coming to despise the money-driven values of Broadway.

Le Gallienne was elfin, and she generally kept her brown hair short and dressed in a boyish fashion. Looking at photographs of her (often in costume), it's difficult to penetrate the persona she has created for each one. Her Peter Pan is androgynous and child-like; her Varya in *The Cherry Orchard* is feminine and quiet. There is a *Time Magazine* cover from 25 November 1929 that aims to capture her 'off-stage' appearance. The ink portrait shows her in a royal-blue blouse, her wavy hair cropped and brushed back from the delicate features of her impassive face; her blue eyes are intense with focus. Sheehy suggests that Le Gallienne chose this outfit and persona specifically to depict a 'determined young feminist'.[60] Le Gallienne learnt early to construct and present the woman she wanted to be: a determined, intelligent artist, not restricted by gender or sexuality.

Midway through her biography of Le Gallienne, Sheehy observes:

> it was clear to uptown Broadway folk, especially younger theatre people, that Eva Le Gallienne set herself apart—a pious prig who affected devotion to art and looked down on ordinary actors in commercial plays who just wanted to make money and have fun.[61]

Sheehy goes on to pose the question:

> [Le Gallienne's] industriousness, her very nature, seemed both a challenge and a rebuke. She appeared overly serious and humorless. What was she trying to prove? Why was she working so hard? What was wrong with her?[62]

The exact same questions hovered around Mooney's life in Dublin. Her childhood and haphazard introduction to theatre, while she continued to dance or to imagine becoming a visual artist, could not have been more different to Le Gallienne's sheltered and spoilt upbringing. But they shared a solemnity and quiet ambition. Denis Johnston captured Mooney's curious mix of innocence and maturity when she was included in his pen sketch of the Abbey green room. The playwright described 'the dark, square charm of Ria Mooney and her full mellow voice belying so quaintly the naivety of everything she says.'[63]

McGlone cites Mary Manning (an understudy to Mooney for extended periods), who remembered her close friend as getting on well with various casts; although, 'She wasn't very humorous. She was very earnest and ambitious.'[64] Similarly, Micheál MacLiammóir of the Gate Theatre commented that, after her return from New York:

> ... her head was full of their theories; she would labour at some small technical point for hours together and be ready for endless discussions about the theatre; she was a serious person.[65]

MacLiammóir goes on to say, somewhat tetchily, that Ria lacked 'the national passion for malicious commentary'.[66] Like Le Gallienne among New York actresses, Mooney was set apart from her female contemporaries in the Abbey by her solemn demeanour and intellectual devotion to her craft. Frolie used her talent for mimicry to connect with people; Aideen was a blonde, button-nosed 'teaser'.[67] Ria was never the 'overbearingly ambitious' actor that Le Gallienne was, but she was compelled by Le Gallienne's resolve and her vision.[68] Ria was drawn to her serious style and confident persona. She found a challenge in the lofty nature of Le Gallienne's ambitions that only a period of work with the Civic Repertory Company would satisfy.

Ria Mooney was living in New York when the theatre critic George Jean Nathan penned an acerbic article in the popular magazine *American Mercury*. He said that the Civic Repertory was 'praiseworthy only in intent' but that it was a total 'botch', and its 'incompetent' director should step aside to let 'other and more competent producers' fulfil New York's need for repertory theatre. He called on Le Gallienne to give up her belief that 'she is a reincarnated combination of Rachel, Joan of Arc, and Nat Goodwin, with faint but unmistakable overtones of Jesus'.[69] It is a savage attack with little substance, smacking of homophobia and/or misogyny. Nathan's objection appears to be to Le Gallienne's political, business persona while he concedes her intent was 'praiseworthy'.[70] He didn't, or couldn't, countenance a woman that occupied such a paradoxical position.

The contradiction in Le Gallienne was always that the egomaniacal, wildly ambitious businesswoman who sought funding for her theatre concealed an artist consumed by the need to embody dramatic characters and create spell-binding theatre. As Sheehy notes: '[I]n describing Le Gallienne, writers returned again and again to the word 'strange'. Her beauty was unconventional, her mind extraordinary, her sexuality ambiguous...'[71] Mooney was not deterred by this 'strangeness'. She dismissed the gossip and rumours to work with the legend and with the woman. Mooney's own sexuality is opaque, but, in the women of the Civic Repertory Company and those artistic circles in Greenwich village, she found a circle of emotional and creative as well as financial support, affection and empowerment. She also witnessed first-hand the power of artistic vision and creativity when coupled with discipline and ambition, regardless of the gender or sexuality of its bearer.

Helen Dore Boylston and Civic Repertory technique

Le Gallienne describes her rehearsal process in her autobiography, *At 33*, and in her biography Sheehy repeats the details as reported by the director; but a further account of the process supporting this evidence can be found elsewhere, in the most unexpected of archival sources. Helen Dore Boylston was an English-born nurse who settled in Connecticut, becoming famous for a series of young adult books about a trainee nurse called Sue Barton. Boylston was a neighbour and close friend of Eva Le Gallienne. At some point in the 1930s, she spent a year backstage at the Civic researching for a new fictional heroine.[72] *Carol Goes Backstage* was published in 1941 and tells the story of a young girl who comes to New York as an apprentice to a Repertory Company established by a Miss Marlowe.

Dore Boylston's novel expresses with unaffected clarity Le Gallienne's beliefs about the Repertory system in America and many of the central tenets of her philosophy and teaching. The illustrations in the book for young adults (by Frederick E. Wallace) support the contention that Miss Marlowe is modelled on Eva Le Gallienne. The book's depiction of acting and directing techniques tally with other accounts of the Civic Repertory, such as that given by May Sarton, while the details, meticulous if idealistic in places, link directly to the tenets of Stanislavski (as translated by Carnicke).

Early in Carol's training at the Civic, the apprentices are invited to watch a rehearsal being led by Miss Marlowe. They gather midway down the house 'to await spectacular events'.[73] But to their disappointment, the rehearsals are calm and entirely respectful. The cast arrive in comfortable old clothes and simply move around the bare stage reading from scripts, pausing now and then for 'amiable discussion' with little or no physical gestures. '[74] Although there is the occasional joke at which everyone laughs politely, the performers are for the most part quiet and courteous. The cast Carol sees, 'worked, in fact, as a single unit, willingly and hard, with every appearance of enjoying what they were doing'.[75] Despite the touch of fictional idealism, there remains a suggestion of the serene simplicity that Le Gallienne engendered in her cast and saw as vital to any successful interpretation of a play. This was not simply an extension of her personality but derived from a considered directorial ideal and artistic technique.

In Boylston's imaginative rendering of a rehearsal, Miss Marlowe watches from the centre aisle, just behind the orchestra pit, and moves back at times to watch from a distance. The writer describes her: 'She offered only occasional suggestions. She didn't shout or swear, as directors were supposed to do, and she never, for a single instant, lost her temper.[76]

Instead of the notion that a powerful man will use force to extract the performance, to get it 'out of her', Le Gallienne assisted actors to come to their own understanding of their characters and make decisions accordingly.[77] Stanislavski, similarly, sought to 'offer advice to actors of different temperaments who wished to speak through different aesthetic styles'.[78] Le Gallienne resisted imposing her will on the individual creation and artistry of each actor. She was there to support, mentor and assist respectfully.

The future writer May Sarton was also an apprentice in the company. She recollects her time watching rehearsals, sitting in the blackness of the house 'before the huge empty stage where only a work-light threw shadows on the brick wall at the back'.[79] She watched Le Gallienne go down the aisle and climb onto the stage to talk to individual actors intimately, without ever raising her voice.[80] When the apprentices performed, the other professional actors always offered encouragement and guidance, while Le Gallienne's criticism was 'severe, inclusive and exceedingly helpful'.[81] Sheehy asserts that actors' time was never wasted: the director came to each rehearsal punctually and well prepared. As a sign of respect, during working hours Le

Gallienne called each of her actors by their surnames (Miss Mooney, Miss Hutchinson). There was a professionalism and dignity in Le Gallienne's treatment of her actors that echoed Stanislavski's insistence on respect for theatre as an art form and for actors as practicing artists.[82]

Le Gallienne frequently produced plays in a realistic mode, but throughout her career she refused to be bound by gender, playing parts such as Peter Pan, Romeo and Hamlet as well as traditional female roles. In her direction and teaching, she welcomed all connections between actors and characters: there was no distance between the two that could not be bridged. She listened and encouraged attention to detail, to endless questions about personality and motivations. She mentored actors to create characters through meticulous preparation and intellect, as she herself prepared. With such preparation, anything was possible.

At one point in *Carol Goes Backstage*, the heroine observes a friend in a state of terror. Instinctively, she notes the movements and gestures expressing her friend's mental state. Disgusted by her heartlessness, she speaks to Miss Marlowe, and learns this is the way of all great actresses:

> The real artist is driven to absorb and use anything which pertains to his art, and that this necessity is a thing apart, functioning by itself regardless of the personal sympathies of the artist.[83]

The director is adamant that the vital importance of any off-stage experience is their capacity to be used in the portrayal of characters. Again, it is helpful to differentiate this tool from the American Method with its use of personal recall and emotional substitution. Rather, Le Gallienne held with Stanislavski's belief that empathy, as a controllable sensation, is a more powerful prompt to creativity than personal emotion.[84] Emotions are not used for 'recall' or 'substitution'; observations of emotional states and reflections impact on decisions made in the interpretation of stage roles.

During one apprentice rehearsal, the strident young director Mike drills his friends in the basics of grouping and movement on stage. He insists they appear in a triangle, allowing the stage picture to slide effortlessly into something else, without unnecessary or awkward shifts. He sets out rules for movement:

> If you have to cross the stage, do it while you're speaking. But never do it when someone else is speaking. That's supposed to be very unfair – because it makes the audience notice *you* instead of the one who has the lines at the moment. And you must always go across the stage in a straight line.[85]

While it is the strident male establishing the rules for physical movement, the emotional understanding of the method comes first to the female members of the apprentice company. Over time, male and female performers come to work together, drawing on each other's understanding of technique.

The Fay brothers, at the Abbey Theatre, taught Ria never to move while speaking on the stage. That distinction aside, the refined physical gestures and graceful movements of the Abbey school were in keeping with the Civic Repertory style. Ria quickly mastered the physical techniques. She then began to work at developing the mental focus and psychological interpretation engendered by Le Gallienne.

There was a lavish quality to Civic productions that enthralled Ria, as she found herself drinking warmed Chianti on stage and eating caviar during Russian plays.[86] The technical files for the CRTC include a props list with the following instructions:

> Straw coloured bottle full of wine**
> Burgundy bottle full of wine
> **This wine should be the good Chianti and all other wine Dago red
>
> ragout in pot on plate for SERVANT
> ragout in pot on pewter plate
> [...]
> 2 eggs on napkin in bowl for SERVANT
> apple for SERVANT
> The two ragouts should not be the same colour nor substance.[87]

At the Abbey, Ria had been presented with plates of paper ham and pork chops shaped from wood. Here, theatrical reality and practical reality started to overlap. From early rehearsals, Le Gallienne insisted that actors have appropriate costume elements and props to work on their interpretation of roles. Furniture was antique and costumes made of silk (where appropriate). All of this followed Stanislavski's notion that an actor's belief in the world of the play should be induced with costumes, realistic props and sound effects.[88] The Moscow Arts Theatre used make-up and costumes as early as two months before a play opened. Le Gallienne employed similar means to stimulate and engage actors' imagination and emotions.

The thrill of having luxuries on the stage later grated with Mooney's discipline and work ethic. The hearty foodstuffs, she claimed, distracted the poor and hungry actress from her playing on the Civic stage. Mooney said that she had never been as drunk as when she'd sipped lemonade at the bar in the second act of *The Plough and the Stars*.[89] She believed in the power of imagination and commitment to the fiction, but Ria's own sense of theatrical truth had its limits; Le Gallienne meddled with the divisions and affected her imagination. That said, in all of the productions she later directed, Ria Mooney displayed the directorial techniques of gentle intercession with individuals, calm discussion of minute detail and the nurturing of individual styles and temperaments.

Ria Mooney would always hold to the principle of acting she discovered in the Civic Repertory: 'Technique, without feeling and concentration, is ... dead.'[90] The work of the company was incessant. Rehearsals, while calm, were long and painstaking. After they left the theatre, the actors often had dinner together to discuss progress, problems and ideas. Le Gallienne was relentless in her pursuit of perfection; she expected the same of her actors. Ria became engaged in her own constant struggle for excellence. As a naïve girl, Ria put her heart into parts in threadbare productions. In New York, where money was no object to create scenic illusion, she started to lose the conviction to match her skills to the sumptuous presentation. Her sense of inadequacy was reinforced by the trials of working with the perfectionist, Le Gallienne. The more intense the focus on perfection, the easier it is to fall short and see yourself as failing. Even as her performances were being lauded by New York newspapers, Ria began to question her ability. Le Gallienne's criticisms (delivered to everyone, including herself) affected Ria deeply and were never fully overcome.

In the 1950s and 1960s, Abbey actors would refer to Mooney's inept direction and actor Vincent Dowling recalled her approach as 'uptight, defensive'.[91] However, it may be that Ria Mooney was not only the first 'Director of Plays in English' at the Abbey Theatre, but she was the first director to attempt to work within a particularly feminist model in the patriarchal institution. The implicitly feminist style of work she learnt from Le Gallienne, using tools which Le Gallienne derived from Stanislavski but inflected with her own feminism, put the emphasis on a disciplined, meticulous ensemble process with decisions gently considered and ideas calmly discussed. Feeling and concentration were balanced by well-honed technique. At the Abbey, this method was met with resistance from many of the undisciplined male actors, given as they were to ostentatious personal display.

Some of the problems Ria Mooney faced working within the Abbey at this time may correlate with those experienced by Maria Knebel of the Moscow Arts Theatre, who directed *The Cherry Orchard* at the Abbey in 1968. In an essay exploring the rehearsal process of the that production, Roz Dixon reports that Knebel's experiences were largely positive, but that Knebel was not impressed by the 'unprofessional practices of some of her actors.'[92] Their scornful behaviour and reactions to her discipline, methodical character work and ensemble playing suggest the conditions Mooney was faced with in trying to bring Stanislavski tools to bear on the Abbey company.

Ria first heard of Alla Nazimova joining Le Gallienne's company in the summer of 1928, as she was saying farewell to Dublin. Nazimova had trained with Stanislavski at the Moscow Arts Theatre and was, Mooney states, 'the film star par excellence'.[93] In an effort to look even more like her idol, Mooney altered her appearance: 'I fluffed out my black hair, or parted it down the centre, and twitched my nostrils to make myself look more like her.'[94] The star's presence would later prove a catalyst to changes in Mooney's position in the company and in her relationship with Le Gallienne.

Nazimova first came to New York early in the 1900s, where she presented a season of Ibsen on Broadway and met Le Gallienne, before going to Hollywood to make a number of films. The actress had trained with the Moscow Arts Theatre before moving into films and now yearned to return to theatre. While other prominent names had requested roles with the company, Nazimova was the first to commit to becoming a permanent member. After much negotiation with Le Gallienne over her return to New York, the two stubborn women finally struck a deal which meant that Nazimova had a private dressing room with her own bathroom an apartment across the courtyard from that of Le Gallienne and her partner, Josephine Hutchinson, and a salary of $250 a week. However, she would not be 'starred'.[95] The CRTC always listed actors in the programme in the order of character's appearance or alphabetically. Such negotiations (practical and artistic) would be ongoing.

During that season, Mooney had a small part in the production of *The Would-Be Gentleman*. Her first major role was in a symbolist play by the French playwright Jean Jacques Bernand entitled *L'Invitation Au Voyage*. Le Gallienne had brought the play, in a translation by Ernest Boyd, back from a trip to Paris and it would remain forever her favourite play in the repertoire.[96] Ria won the part of Jacqueline, the 20-year-old sister to the bored Marie-Louise, wife of an industrial magnate. Marie-Louise (played by Le Gallienne) is in love with a man that recently fled to the Argentine Republic without knowing anything of her affection. She sustains herself with the dream of their idealised love.

The play is set in 'the present day in the Vosges district.' When the curtains rose, the audience saw tall, arched French windows, 'all wide open on the forest'. The stage was flooded in the 'pink light of a fine afternoon in September, on the wane'.[97] As Marie-Louise, Le Gallienne played a Chopin nocturne on the grand piano. The prompt books for the production, now in the Beinecke Library at Yale University, are immaculately kept with stage directions underlined, occasionally altered in clear handwriting, and neat instructions set out in red pencil. Jacqueline's call to the stage is marked clearly on an early page.

Ria first appeared on the patio outside the window. Le Gallienne wore a bobbed, brunette wig, and Mooney had her own thick black locks cut to match. Both women were made-up sophisticatedly and wore 'some of the prettiest dresses ever worn in 14th street'.[98] Leaning in the window, Ria Mooney uttered her opening line: 'Are you alone, Marie Louise?'[99]

This play was conceived in the symbolist tradition. Much of the script is slow and suggestive: sighs, pauses and hidden tears. As John Leslie Firth points out in his introduction to a later translation of the play, Bernard's work has 'a quietness, a simplicity, an entire absence of "drama" in the crude sense'.[100] Le Gallienne's growing sensibility was for plays that dismissed the traditional notion of 'realism' but worked towards a more esoteric notion of 'truth' or 'art'. In this, her taste differed from the majority of the audiences that came to 13th Street. Such a sensibility would inform Mooney's later interest in play texts of a more abstract nature, including those of Jack Yeats.

There is an intimacy between the two sisters in Bernard's play that can only have been performed by two confidantes. The second act is set in December, with snow heaped on the fir trees outside. Jacqueline (Ria) tells Marie-Louise (Eva): 'I understand much better than you think, believe me. I've eyes in my head. And I know that the Argentine set you dreaming.'[101] With tears in her eyes, Marie Louise confesses: 'I should be so glad if we could talk together gently, you and I. We're very far apart, perhaps. But I've really no one but you, Jacqueline.'[102]

McGlone asserts that Mooney's work 'went unnoticed in the failure' of the play.[103] In fact, Brooks Atkinson of the *New York Times* writes that the play 'lacks substance and dramatic moment' but goes on to say that 'Miss Le Gallienne and her comrades adorn it with an exquisite performance'. Atkinson wrote, 'Mooney plays the part of the sister with as much graphic precision as charm'. Clearly taken with their 'supple charm', Atkinson declares the piece 'discovers the Civic Repertory troupe in one of its most accomplished aspects.'[104] May Sarton never forgot watching 'that extraordinary play of silences' and called the experience 'pure luxury.'[105] Sarton was in a minority; the audiences deplored it. As was usual, Le Gallienne had been rehearsing three plays at the one time. Thus, as quickly as *L'Invitation Au Voyage* closed, *The Cherry Orchard* opened. Le Gallienne starred as Varya and Nazimova played Madame Ranevsky. Ria Mooney was Dunyasha: the small part of a maid. But such was the manner of repertory theatre, from major role to bit part, and Ria got on with it. The show proved a popular hit and she was being paid $50 a week: a paltry sum against New York cost of living but more than her friends in Dublin were receiving from the Abbey.[106]

The final production of the season was *Katerina*, a play by Andreyev that had been included in the repertoire on Nazimova's demand. For years, she had been trying to get a Broadway production of the piece, which was the perfect vehicle to showcase her own talent, although it was not ideally suited to an ensemble company. The play is a 'light-hearted frolic, with marital infidelity, voyeurism, and attempted murder.'[107] When the cast list was hung backstage, Mooney's name was again not on it.

The Civic Repertory Company was now playing to 94 per cent capacity, but relations between Le Gallienne and Nazimova were strained. While they attempted to maintain professional politeness, Le Gallienne was disgusted that Nazimova was advertising *Lucky Strike* cigarettes to supplement her income. In rehearsals, differences in their dramatic approaches were surfacing. Josephine Hutchinson described the Russian as 'a cat', recalling that she was 'very theatrical' while the company were 'much more modern'.[108] In a further affront to Le Gallienne, who thought *Katerina* melodramatic and ridiculous, Nazimova intervened in casting. The star insisted that, given the physical resemblance, the actress cast as Liza (Katerina's sister) should be replaced with Ria Mooney.

Thus, Le Gallienne (the company's founder) and Nazimova (the star celebrity) both insisted on casting the new Irish visitor as their on-stage sister. These women were known to have same-sex relationships; they had a brief romantic dalliance some years before. Ria was dignified and discreet in many aspects of her life, but particularly in her personal and sexual life. Yet here, Le Gallienne and Nazimova were drawing Ria into their intimate circle on the stage and, given how their on- and off-stage lives intertwined, it's not inconceivable that this was happening off stage too. Either way, she now had a key role in the lives of the company's main players.

Katerina opened in February 1929 and despite the problems, Le Gallienne recorded in her diary that Nazimova gave a 'magnificent performance'.[109] Broadway critics agreed, but when the company toured to Philadelphia and Boston the power struggles between Le Gallienne and Nazimova continued. Mooney was torn between her allegiance to Nazimova and her respect for Le Gallienne; but experience had taught her to avoid conflicts. She didn't gossip or slander and she would resist any part in a feud. In any case, a refusal to get involved would have been taken by the egomaniacal Le Gallienne as a sign of dissension.

Although she was on the programme for the next theatrical season, Nazimova finished the tour in Boston and did not return to 14th Street. Mooney's place in the company changed substantially the next season, when Le Gallienne charged her with directing the new apprentices. For Ria, this guaranteed an income she badly needed. Le Gallienne arranged people around her as she desired, and it may be that after the split with Nazimova she wanted 'Miss Mooney' in a less conspicuous role. It's also possible that she identified in Mooney a gift for mentoring young talent that could be used for mutual benefit.

Directing *Romeo & Juliet*

In Boylston's novel *Carol Goes Backstage*, the fictional apprentices are under the tutelage of a lady with the most Irish of surnames: Miss Byrne. Miss Byrne is already in place and working assiduously with her young charges when Carol joins the company. In factual records, it is established that the real apprentice group auditioned by Le Gallienne and put under Ria Mooney's care as the 1929/30 theatre season opened included such future luminaries as May Sarton, Burgess Meredith, Howard da Silva and John Garfield. Both real and fictional apprentices were permitted to watch the main company at work, whilst also having their own schedule of classes and scenes to prepare.

In Mooney's record, she was directing a rehearsal when she noticed that Le Gallienne had come to observe her methods from the balcony.[110] Steeling herself against the prospect of criticism, she carried on, leading them through *The Playboy of the Western World* in the traditional style of the Abbey Theatre. Le Gallienne was impressed; she invited Mooney to become Assistant Director in the forthcoming production of *Romeo & Juliet*. Mooney distinctly remembers how the chorus were instructed to obey Miss Mooney as if she was the director herself.[111] Programmes for the premiere of *Romeo and Juliet* in the Beinecke Library show that Le Gallienne is credited above and below the title of the play. Underneath her name, before the cast are listed (in order of their appearance), is the line: 'Assistant to Miss Le Gallienne, Ria Mooney'. The credit carefully modulates the title: there is a distinction between assistant directing (working with actors) and being an assistant to the director (bringing coffee). Yet in the Administration Files of the CRTC, where the members of the permanent company are listed, it clearly credits Ria Mooney as 'Assistant to Miss Le Gallienne in directing "Romeo and Juliet"'.[112]

Le Gallienne's overarching principle for *Romeo & Juliet* was to convey a sense of Italy during that period: 'Colourful, violent, and above all SWIFT'.[113] Pauses between scenes were eliminated; there was full concentration on flow with a steady increase in tempo and suspense throughout. The prologue was eliminated and the play opened with the pounding of drums and a street brawl. Many apprentices appeared as dancers and a number of the Company were in silent chorus roles.

Working to Le Gallienne's vision, Mooney turned to visual art for inspiration. Le Gallienne also used this method; for her production of *The Good Hope* she used Dutch paintings for formations for group scenes.[114] It was the work of the Florentine painters, with their unique sense of light and colour, which influenced Mooney's direction of the chorus scenes for the Shakespeare play. Using the costume colours, she started to group crowds to circle and highlight the main players. She let the actors move freely and instinctively, with the imperative that they were on the required spot when the cue came. Her technique grew from years of careful watching, at the Abbey Theatre and in the Civic Repertory, as well as her love of visual art.[115] Intent on capturing the fluid, mercurial sense the director demanded, Mooney began to develop her own directorial technique.

In *Carol Goes Backstage*, while the apprentices studied fencing and voice with other company instructors, 'Miss Byrne' works diligently with them on movement, progressing from physical stance to styles of walking, running and abrupt stops that capture distinct characters.[116] In one acting exercise, she calls each actor to cross the stage and deliver a letter, without any dialogue. As they step out to begin, she calls out their character's work or social position: prince, servant, young girl. The objective (delivering the letter) was identical; the distinctions were in the small physical choices the actor had to make quickly and decisively. Such simple exercises consistently reinforced the delicate craft of creating character from within, in the mode of Stanislavski.

Boylston's heroine and her friends also appear as silent chorus in *Romeo and Juliet*. After Miss Byrne has spent weeks 'drilling them in entrances and exits', they make their first public appearance, gaining confidence even while they're acutely aware that they're under 'very close observation'.[117] The pressure of working for Le Gallienne was intense, but Mooney responded warmly to the energy of her charges. Dismissing traditional boundaries between the company and apprentices, she arranged social evenings in her home to introduce the budding actors to established artists. This nurturing of her charges off-stage, which began in New York, set a pattern for her career. In Wicklow in the 1940s and later, she would often hold social evenings in her Glencree cottage. She continued to draw energy from young talent around her, while supporting and encouraging the development of their technique.

Enmeshed as they became in the life of the company, the work of the apprentices differed from that of the main troupe in one specific point. For the apprentice rehearsals and productions described in *Carol Goes Backstage*, there are no props or scenery. The essence of the lesson, Carol understands, is to 'act without self-consciousness in the midst of purely imaginary furniture'.[118] Mooney engendered in her charges the vivifying dramatic imagination that was central to her work in Dublin.

Outside of rehearsals: art and life

The strict discipline of the Civic Repertory Theatre structured her days and if she wasn't performing, Mooney arranged social evenings for her apprentices. There was little time for her own social life; in fact, she made sure of that. To artist friend Patrick Tuohy, Mooney confided that she had decided to leave Ireland to get away from a man and heartbreak.[119] While there is no evidence to suggest the identity of this man, there are pointers to suggest that her leaving for London was linked to O'Casey's settling there. He was single and had showed genuine affection for Mooney and a regard for her talent. His continued support to her was demonstrated by his lending her money when she failed to secure work, but it may have been that when she was in London, she discovered that O'Casey's interest in her was not romantic. In any case, New York brought distractions and encounters that would salve her broken heart and reanimate her.

For the initial visits to New York with Shelah Richards, the two women shared an apartment on Broadway, as close to the theatre as they could afford. A circle of Irish theatre acquaintants, including Maire O'Neill and Sara Allgood, invited them to parties where they made friends with a bohemian group that included sculptor Jacob Epstein and writer/photographer Carl Van Vechten. To reciprocate, they held soirées of their own. The housemates had different temperaments and tastes, but both were smitten with 'the best-looking man' and the 'one with the most charm': professional singer Paul Robeson.[120] At their party, Robeson sang African-American spirituals and talked of his daughter. Richards joked they lived 'on chocolates, gin and oranges, trying to get with New York society.'[121]

As the lovesick Richards counted the days to go home and begin her married life, Mooney continued to socialise and made a close friend: Rita. Rita Romelli was a frequent host of social evenings and was also a dancer, actress, teacher and later a key figure in the Harlem Renaissance. A New Yorker born and bred, she trained at the American Academy of Dramatic Art under its founder, Charles Jehliger.[122] She took a minor role in *The Living Corpse* by Tolstoy staged at the Civic Repertory in 1929; thereafter, all archival traces of Rita Romilly relate to teaching. Mooney referred to her simply as 'a beautiful girl named Rita Romelli'.[123]

In his biography, McGlone assumes that Rita Romelli became (on her marriage) Mrs Milton Kick Erlanger, the woman to whom Mooney's autobiography is dedicated.[124] The erroneous conflation is understandable; the editor's footnote, referring to Mrs Milton (Kick) Erlanger as a 'close friend and patron' is placed between the names of the two women.[125] But they were not the same woman. Kick Erlanger was a wealthy heiress, a friend of Seán O'Casey and later of Ria Mooney. Mooney and Erlanger had a relationship that lasted their whole lives, with Erlanger eventually providing Mooney with the funds to retire comfortably from the theatre.

However, the clarification of this detail still doesn't bring any further light on the matter of Mooney's intimate relationships. There is no evidence that her friendship with Romelli, or Erlanger, developed into a sexual relationship, or indeed is there anything to suggest that it was only platonic. She clearly remembered Romelli distinctly, and with much affection. Her relationship with Kick Erlanger was intimate, loving and became over the years vital to Mooney's happiness. Anything else is speculation.

Without Richards' company, Mooney threw herself into life at the Civic with her new friends and colleagues, spending free time drinking coffee or eating cheap meals in the Childs restaurant next door to the theatre. As well as her friendship with literary manager Helen Lohman, Mooney was close to scenic designer Aline Bernstein and her assistant Irene Schariff. Bernstein was 'plump, mature and well-corseted' with 'straight grey hair which she wore parted down the front.'[126] In 1926, she had become the first woman to join the Scenic Artists' Union of the US. As well as discussions about theatre design, Mooney jested with Bernstein about searching for a wealthy male suitor. Yet, she was surrounded by same-sex arrangements.

According to McGlone's survey of Mooney's life, the troupe was rumoured to be a 'den of lesbianism'; *American Mercury* critic George Jean Nathan called the group the 'Le Gallienne sorority'.[127] Le Gallienne had been living in an apartment on 11th Street with leading actress Jo Hutchinson (recently separated from her husband) for over a year when Mooney arrived. The other actors called the couple 'The Botticelli Twins' and not even their own mothers objected to the arrangement.[128] Leona Roberts (Hutchinson's mother) was a member of the core company and Julie, Le Gallienne's open-minded mother, shared their flat for months each time she came to visit.

After her first season, Mooney returned to Ireland for the summer break; but in 1930, she decided to forgo the trip home. As well as working with the Arden theatre group in Philadelphia, she spent one dissolute weekend with friends in Greenwich, Connecticut. McGlone asserts the details of this scene have been left 'purposely vague' in the memoirs.[129] The episode, though not recounted in detail, is tinged with nostalgia and magic; yet its inclusion in the memoir—otherwise so impersonal—lends it a gravity that cannot be ignored.

With little memory of events during daylight hours, Mooney focuses on the night-time adventures and one particular bacchanalian scene. Walking through the woods around the home of Richard Chanler, close to midnight, 'they' came upon a clearing. By a river, a picnic meal illuminated by a log fire was coming to a close:

> They sat in twos, making love between sips, or in groups, having loud and fierce arguments while they drank and nibbled food—and each other. From a large flat rock overhanging the river, naked figures were seen for a moment as they shot through the light in dives that engulfed them in the black waters. Everywhere were the sounds of laughter, arguments, corks popping, bodies splashing into the water, mingling with nature's medley of night sounds.[130]

Exactly who were the 'we' that took that moonlit walk? Was this 'scene of revelry' a party exclusively for women? Was Mooney only an observer of events? McGlone asks these rhetorical questions and decides that the scene 'might have been extracted from popular novels of the period' but was 'out of character' for Mooney.[131] Yet, it may be that it is 'out of character' only for the persona created in her memoir. As referred to above in relation to her friendship with Romelli, Mooney's sexuality has always been opaque. McGlone never addresses the issue directly, but it appears vital to draw attention to the social forces acting on Mooney at this point in her life, encouraging her to break with Irish models and follow her own desires.

Ria's autobiography is reticent in relation to her relationships with men, but there are the accounts of others to support the veracity of rumours. And regardless of the nature of the relationships, working and living with this circle of lesbian women had a profound impact on her life. As well as attracting the attention of Nazimova and Le Gallienne in her first season, the CRTC files demonstrate that in the years that followed, Ria Mooney would be swapping in and out of roles with Josephine Hutchinson and with Glesca Marshall (who went onto become Nazimova's long-term partner). She was not just around these same-sex relationships, she was at the nexus of the 'sewing-circle' (Nazimova's term for lesbian circles).

That same summer Ria socialised in Greenwich, Josephine Hutchinson was divorcing her husband, Robert Bell, and the New York theatre scene was agog with rumours about Le

Gallienne's involvement in the closed divorce proceedings. The divorce was held in open court in Reno, with no other parties named and the estranged couple remained always on good terms.[132] But damage was done by malicious speculation: *The Daily News* published a photograph of Le Gallienne with the headline 'Bell Divorces Actress, Eva Le Gallienne's Shadow'.[133] 'Shadow' was then an insinuation of lesbianism.

More pertinently, the future of the Civic Repertory Company was in serious doubt, with financial strain heaped on Le Gallienne's already-struggling shoulders. Mooney could have been worrying about her future, seeking parts outside the company or looking for other work; instead, she focused on the magic of her new social life. Spending one night in a guest room belonging to Madame Rubinstein, Mooney slept in a comfortable bed in a room scented with sandalwood, under a roof that rolled back to expose the night sky. Looking up at the stars, she discovered that soft glitter was falling slowly from them and melting into the darkness.[134] Despite the struggles behind and the unknown future ahead, a 27-year-old Mooney reached out in blissful joy and wonder, trying to catch fireflies.

While on tour with *The Plough and the Stars* in Chicago in the 1920s, Abbey actor Michael Scott chose to visit an exhibition of French paintings in the Wrigley Building and Ria Mooney joined him. As she wandered along beside her friend, Ria's attention was captured by a 'glimmering object' in the distance.[135] Transfixed, she abandoned her companions and moved towards the torpedo-shaped piece of metal. The sculpture, by Brâncuşi, was titled *The Golden Bird*, although there was only the suggestion of a beak and tail in the silhouette that sat on a rough-hewn geometric base. Mooney studied this one piece for the rest of the afternoon, in awe of 'the artistry that made this piece of shining metal a thing of movement, exhilaration and truly great beauty.'[136]

She wasn't new to the art world; at the age of 19 Ria had joined the Dublin Metropolitan School of Art on a whim and spent two years studying drawing and painting. There, she realised 'the meaning of hard work and the satisfaction to be derived from it.'[137] While she continued to act in amateur dramatic groups in the evenings, she gave up her office job to create a studio in Anne Street with five other students. Ria specialised in embroidery, the others in leatherwork, design and figure work. Only on Lennox Robinson's request to appear at the Abbey in 1924 did she subsequently abandon the artists' collective. Mooney's introduction to the modern art movement in that Chicago museum was a world away from those days embroidering in the chilly Anne Street studio, but both ignited her sensitivity to shape, light and colour.

In New York, when moving into her apartment on 13th Street, Ria and her flatmate took advice from Irene Schariff (the Civic Repertory Company's assistant scenic designer) on decorating the humble walk-up. They stained the floor black and used rugs of cheap felt, covering the couch with royal blue sateen behind cushions of red, yellow, green and black.[138] In their design, they mimicked the dark blue walls and oiled timbers of Le Gallienne's exceedingly more luxurious home. All were following the fashions in Greenwich village at that time, but Mooney's insistence on a vivid colour scheme is central to her dramatic vision.

Helen Lohman, of the Civic Repertory Company, would subsequently take Mooney to see and hold two more pieces of Brâncuşi's work. The same Madame Helena Rubinstein who offered fireflies in Connecticut introduced Mooney to the work of Picasso, engendering a life-long passion for his Cubist work. In Dublin in the 1940s and 1950s, Ria was a frequent visitor to Waddington's small gallery on South Anne Street to buy art in the meagre weekly instalments that she could afford.[139] This acutely colourist sensibility was developed in her work as the Assistant Director with the Civic and would come to fruition in her work with the Abbey Experimental Theatre in Dublin in the 1940s.

Given this sensibility, it is no surprise that in her own writing Mooney often reverts to memories of colour to illustrate scenes. A lengthy expedition to the Aran Islands in 1930, during a holiday at home, forms an interlude in the story of her career. On the island, Mooney spent time with documentary filmmaker Robert Flaherty and Tom Casement, brother of Irish patriot Roger. As they sailed between the islands on a still June evening, the sun 'began to tip to the west'. She sketches the scene: 'Silver and black were the colours on our right, pink and blue above our heads, crimson and gold on our left.'[140] Wherever she went, Mooney drew strength and life from the colour and artistry in the world around her.

Mooney returned from a summer of stock theatre and heady socialising in 1930 to one more challenging season at the 14th Street Theatre. The Civic Repertory Theatre Company began the theatre calendar with a reprised production of *Romeo & Juliet*, an established success; but both Le Gallienne and Hutchinson were ill: tonsillitis and appendicitis. Aline Bernstein was struggling with personal difficulties. A leading actor left after an offer from a theatre 'uptown'. New productions were quickly cancelled and in an uncharacteristically downbeat mode, Le Gallienne wrote in her diary of 'Bad days—tiring, wearing days.'[141] She was no stranger to long periods of depression and had been known to find solace in alcohol, but during the day Le Gallienne continued to rehearse and make business plans. Others noted how her figure grew ever slighter and her eyes more enormous.[142] When she gave her usual performance of *Peter Pan* at Christmas, soaring across the auditorium on a wire, her breathing was laboured and her body feverish.

The apprentices in Dore Boylston's fictional Stuyvesant Company gradually become part of company life and come to understand the backstage atmosphere. Budding actress Carol observes:

> [I]n light plays, requiring little emotional acting, the backstage mood of the company was gay and relaxed [...] sometimes an actor going on stage was unable to stop laughing and had difficulty with his lines. In other plays the mood was tense and serious; there was no joking or conversation in the wings [...][143]

As 1930 came to an end, the real Civic Repertory Company were caught between an atmosphere of festive celebration and intense stress over Le Gallienne's physical state and emotional fragility. Any hope that the rest over the holidays would restore their director's strength faded in January when she was confined to bed with bronchitis. Le Gallienne handed over rehearsals to her old teacher, Constance Collier. Collier began directing *Camille*, while Le Gallienne learnt her lines and prepared for her starring role in bed. It is characteristic of Mooney that she reminisces about the gems of wisdom she learnt watching Collier direct rehearsals, without ever recording any tension around the arrangements.[144]

Despite Le Gallienne's frailty, *Camille* transpired to be the Civic Repertory Company's biggest hit. Brooks Atkinson announced in the *New York Times*: '[I]t is a major hit that turns 'em away at the box office.'[145] Atkinson described the atmosphere inside the theatre as electrifying: 'The excitement leaps from row to row like an electric spark.'[146] The critics may have thought Le Gallienne and her company were back on form; the actors knew better. At some point, Le Gallienne gathered her cast and crew backstage to share a major decision. She was taking advantage of the current success to close the theatre on a positive note, planning to take a year off to recuperate and plan for the future. The financial problems had not gone away and the depression was worsening all over America, but Le Gallienne would not step away from 14th Street under a cloud. She was determined to retain the impression that her talent and vision were undimmed.

Mooney never says that she was shocked at the closure of the Civic Repertory Company. Records show that she was there for the final gala week of performances, celebrating with the company and the group of apprentices. Nazimova returned briefly to appear in two performances of *The Cherry Orchard* and they also staged *Peter Pan* and *Romeo and Juliet* before closing with *Camille*. While some of the company would find work with a tour of *Alison's House* by Susan Glaspell, others were offered a $50-a-week retaining fee to return in 1932. Ria was not in the first group, and letters to friends in Dublin don't mention any retainer. News may have filtered back from Paris, where Le Gallienne was staying, that May Sarton had been offered the job of salaried director of the Civic Repertory apprentices when the theatre reopened.[147] Mooney was working on other plans, holding fast to the belief her future was in New York. She set to work with an actor friend on a dramatic adaptation of Brontë's *Wuthering Heights*. Shelah Richards received a letter from her friend and told Denis Johnston the news:

> Ria Mooney has written saying she and Grupke are starting theatre life on Broadway (!) and she is to be managing this that and the other including reading of plays and would you send 'Moon'?[148]

Mooney was seeking to produce Johnston's play, *The Moon in the Yellow River*. The identity of 'Grupke' is unknown, mainly because the plans came to naught. When word came in the new year that the touring Abbey company needed a player, Mooney packed up her 13th Street home, planning to join them in Georgia. It was then that Cheryl Crawford, casting director of the New York Theatre Guild, contacted her, offering her a role.[149] A future in New York was a distinct possibility, but Mooney elected to hold the promise of secure work and return home. She was weary of struggling for work or was eager to share her skills in Ireland; perhaps both.

Dublin, again

To follow in full the chronology of Mooney's career following her return to Dublin from the Civic Repertory Company in 1932 is confusing and difficult; it entangles distinct threads of her work. For over three decades, Ria Mooney was a central figure in Dublin theatre life: acting, directing and teaching. She was a working professional, immersed in the day-to-day grind of the theatre. Yet, to consider all of her acting roles during those decades would not prove particularly illuminating. Instead, I'd like to follow two specific trajectories in her artistic work that she kept distinct but in careful counterbalance.

On the one hand, Ria continued to appear on the main stages of the capital's theatres in traditional conservative drama, such as plays by George Shiels and Lennox Robinson. Initially, the Gate Theatre fulfilled her desire for leading roles. She subsequently returned to the Abbey Theatre, taking roles in plays by new female playwrights, Elizabeth Connor and Teresa Deevy. At the same time, she pursued her interest in mentoring young actors and in working with drama of a more experimental form than ever before seen in Ireland. In her memoirs, Mooney refers in a self-deprecating way to 'my little Experimental Theatre'.[150] In fact, the project, which she began with senior student at the School of Acting Cecil Ford in June 1939, was a major innovation in Irish theatre. Setting these two tracks of Mooney's career side-by-side, studying them separately while allowing them to reflect back on each other, brings us closer to an understanding of the theatre that drove and sustained her, spiritually and financially.

There is a photograph of Ria, dressed as Rosie Redmond, on stage with Seán O'Casey during the dress rehearsal of *The Plough and the Stars.* Her skirt reaches below her knee; she wears thick tights and flat shoes, with a tartan shawl around her shoulders. For the modern spectator, there is nothing sexual about this prostitute, except for the coy smile the actress is giving the playwright, who has autographed the memento for her. He says: 'Be clever, M'girl, & let who will be good.'[151] In September 1969, Mooney returned this photo to the O'Casey Estate, and it was placed in the Berg Collection in the New York Public Library. Holding the original photo in my hands, I see that there is a well-worn thumbtack hole in every corner. This photo was not framed or stored in a dust-free album, but was tacked to the bedroom wall, to the mirror in a dressing room, or to any available surface. Always visible, always close, it was a talisman to remind Mooney of her experiences as Rosie Redmond, and the journey it had set her on.

That photograph, and other items in her personal archive, were packed up in the bohemian walk-up in Greenwich and brought back to the bedroom she shared with her sister in her father's house on Dublin's southside. Retracing that path to the Abbey's backstage door was not a joyous reunion or comforting transition for Mooney. But beneath her warm, open nature and child-like idealism, she had a resilience earned during *The Plough and the Stars* and compounded as she walked the streets of New York after the Civic Repertory closed, looking for work. At various times in her career, Mooney's insecurities about her talents would re-surface and threaten to overwhelm her, but an enduring belief in her craft, coupled with economic necessity, drove her on.

The memoir, *Players and the Painted Stage*, contains only two references to intersections between Mooney's family and her work. The first is her father's anxiety during the riots during *The Plough and the Stars.* The second is her sister's weeping after she saw Mooney perform at the Abbey after her return from New York in 1932. Almost 30, with a figure that had always been womanly in its curves and a face that was always mature if elegant, Mooney was cast as the 16-year-old schoolgirl Ducky in Robinson's drawing-room comedy, *The Far-Off Hills.* After the curtain came down, Mooney returned home to her father's house to find her sister crying with shame and disappointment.[152]

The Abbey directors often put adult women into the roles of children and teenagers. Such casting was judged to be a necessary practice to maintain the ensemble nature of the company, and it also connects to the amateur beginnings of the theatre. The preposterous practice was not confined to Ria Mooney: in 1935 the *San Francisco News* reviewed Brinsley MacNamara's *Look at the Heffernans* and spoke of the 'lamentable casting of Maureen Delany [sic.] as a bold, young girl.'[153] While there is no evidence actresses objected, the reaction of Mooney's sister shows that the absurd nature of the casting did not go unnoticed by the audience. Mooney's telling of the event in her autobiography cleverly displaces any personal shame onto her sister, allowing her to make the point without appearing to judge. She didn't give up the part: that wasn't an option; nor was objecting or making a complaint. In Ria's account: her sister cried; she resolved to find other opportunities.

After that reprise of Ducky and other similar roles, Mooney was weary of playing parts for which she was unsuited and also, perhaps, of being infantilised by the Abbey directorate. In September 1933, a chance came to work with Hilton Edwards and Micheál MacLiammóir at the Gate Theatre and she grasped it. In their rehearsal room at the top of O'Connell Street, she found the magic that had exhilarated her in New York: 'There was the 'poetry' of theatre [...]

the same escape from dull reality; the same magic windows on to different places, people and periods.'[154] The Gate offered international plays and elegant roles like Lady Precious Stream in Hsiung's work of the same name and Gwendoline in Wilde's *The Importance of being Earnest*. As McGlone observes, for the first time ever, Mooney had 'an entire season playing romantic parts.'[155] MacLiammóir saw something in her that the Abbey directors didn't; in fact, he saw something she had trouble seeing in the mirror. The woman MacLiammóir remembers is unlike the dumpy persona she repeatedly presents of herself:

> Small, with night-black hair and long, slow-glancing green eyes, she had [...] a curious intensity like a steadily burning inner fire, and her acting was poised, shapely and full of intelligence.[156]

This intense woman was not only focused on acting; at some point she presented the adaptation of *Wuthering Heights* that she had worked on in New York with fellow actor Donald Stauffer. MacLiammóir read it, and was stunned, declaring it 'by far the best I had ever read' and noting how it 'preserved the essence of Emily Bronte's mind into the few feet of the Gate theatre.'[157] He cast Mooney as Catherine Earnshaw, taking the role of Heathcliff for himself.

Huge success was close, but fragile self-esteem again threatened to mar her performance. Mooney believed that she was far from 'an ideal Catherine' on the basis that she was simply 'too small' and also struggled with the fact that she knew every line and comma in the script.[158] As she had with Le Gallienne, Mooney drove herself on relentlessly, a perfectionist intent on securing the right interpretation of each line and each gesture. Her discipline was a gift but it could be a noose, strangling her instincts. It was MacLiammóir who nurtured and supported her. He coaxed her to focus on one line, one objective, one scene at a time, and he eased her back into an assured performance.

The production was revived in February 1935, when the *Irish Independent* critic 'D. S.' noted that, 'Miss Ria Mooney has by a series of slight alterations considerably improved the original adaptation of the famous novel.' He also gave the acting honours to Ria, and believed 'her Catherine Earnshaw is greater than Emily Bronte's.'[159] The *Irish Times* reviewer that saw the revival echoed D. S.'s view that Catherine overshadowed Heathcliff in every scene, saying Mooney gave 'a performance of quite remarkable force, and in the course of it she never seems to strike a wrong note.'[160]

Nurtured in the rehearsal room, praised by the critics, exploring her full potential, little could tempt Mooney away from the Gate. Except, perhaps, for one thing: another approach by the Abbey Theatre. During an 'At Home' social soirée in 1934, Abbey Theatre director and poet F. R. Higgins gave her the news that they were recasting the repertoire and would like to include her. The offer to entice her included leading roles and top salary, although initially she would perform with the second company, as the first company was on tour. Mooney later claimed that this opportunity came at a time when she was 'temporarily annoyed' with the Gate directors, but this may have been a retrospective rationalisation of her decision.[161] Her devotion to the National Theatre never wavered.

The second Abbey Theatre Company

Buoyed by her success at the Gate, Ria now felt she could confidently contribute her experience to the National Theatre. She came back to the Abbey with the expectation of being a romantic lead, albeit in the No. 2 company, but it was not long before she was reminded that some of the Abbey directorate would forever consider her 'the Abbey whore'. Ethel Mannin later noted this jibe, which she saw as simply 'good-natured'.[162] However, the identification of Mooney with the playing of prostitutes and other unrespectable women would continue to shape her career at the Abbey.

One of Mooney's first castings was in the role of Mrs Katharine O'Shea in W. R. Fearon's play, *Parnell of Avondale.* In this, she was asked to perform one of the most notorious women in Irish history: an English-born divorcée who had a public affair with Home Rule champion Charles Stewart Parnell. The affair led to the downfall of the nationalist political leader in the 1890s, and many continued to believe that O'Shea was a spy for the British government. Parnell's enemies gave his lover the name 'Kitty O'Shea', because 'Kitty' suggested a shortening of Katharine, but was also English slang for prostitute. Dismissing once again the scandal and hearsay, Mooney immersed herself in the text and her role. Research included visiting Avondale House, Parnell's ancestral home, with Fearon. She sensitively observed the house and its inhabitants:

> We waited for 'the girls' in an over-furnished drawing-room ... There were dance programmes with pencils attached, paper fans, paper chains, antimacassars on all the many chairs and sofas, and photos in frames all over the room. Several of these photos were of the great Irish Leader, but there was none of Mrs. O'Shea.[163]

The 'girls' were the two mature Miss Parnells, who still lived in the Victorian stone house in the undulating Wicklow hills. This once grand home now, for Mooney, 'seemed to reflect the fortunes of its owners'.[164] The grounds were uncared for, the staff ageing, and the inhabitants refusing to live in the present. Both of the 'girls' were disgusted at the sympathetic presentation of Mrs O'Shea in the play and looked on Mooney as a person with 'rather bad taste'.[165] They made it clear that they could not understand how a respectable Irish woman would play Mrs O'Shea. Mooney notes with a touch of humour: 'at least they presumed I was respectable'.[166] For her, notions of respectability had come to mean little. It was always about interpreting the part the author had created, giving the character dignity and emotional truth. Lennox Robinson, as director, cast an actress he knew would relish the complexity of the part rather than worrying about the historical reputation.

The opening scene of Fearon's play focuses on the first meeting of Parnell and Katherine (Kitty) O'Shea. Ria wore a nineteenth-century-style dress in black velvet and chiffon that she had designed, and Denis Carey played Parnell. From that first meeting, the action shifts to William O'Shea's discovery of his wife's affair and the play concludes with Parnell's downfall. As Mooney observed, the love affair takes precedence over the politics in Fearon's plot.

The *Irish Times* reviewer on 2 October thought the play a 'gallant failure'. He said that Carey's 'physique was rather against him' in the role but he was 'competent' while Mooney was 'excellent'.[167] All of the critics seemed incapable of seeing past the portrayal of Parnell as something other, or something more, than a patriotic political leader. A young actress in the Abbey Experimental Theatre attended and was mesmerised by Mooney's performance. She remembered: 'The play itself was little more than documentary, but their portrayals carried it to a revelation of passion seldom seen now.'[168] In Fearon's second version, Mrs O'Shea's part was reduced and Parnell made the central feature.[169] Mooney was disgusted that the part became nothing more than 'a dressed dummy'. She believed Fearon destroyed good drama for a political argument and points out, 'This production was quite unsuccessful.'[170]

Making it grand for Teresa Deevy

In the spring of 1935, a thin, severe-looking woman arrived off the train from Waterford and headed for the Abbey Theatre. She reached the theatre just in time to take her seat before the orchestra finished and the curtain rose. Any excitement she'd felt on the journey dissipated rapidly in the half-empty audience. Teresa (Tessa) Deevy was there to see the first performance of her one-act play, *The King of Spain's Daughter* and was accompanied by her sister, Nell. Yet, the programme notes didn't match the script she'd submitted and the characters that appeared differed fundamentally from those she'd created.[171] Teresa continued to watch. She watched facial expressions, physical gestures and movements, both of those on the stage and in the audience around her. Where possible, she read the lips of the performers. The words were her own, but the intonation indecipherable. Despite how intently she watched, her deafness meant that Teresa Deevy could never understand all that was going on around her.

Although she'd been submitting plays to the Abbey for over a decade and had shared first prize in the Abbey Theatre new play competition in 1932, the Waterford native had thought carefully about attending that performance of *The King of Spain's Daughter*. She wrote to her friend, fellow writer Florence Hackett:

> I'm afraid now I shan't be up to see it in Dublin. Fares are so high, and the play is so tiny a thing – Then it would mean staying a night or so in Dublin – all runs to so much money.[172]

When she changed her mind and did travel, it was a distressing experience:

> The house was wretched! You could count the people. I think the production was good, but the producer's interpretation of the play was very different from my conception of it.[173]

Producer Fred Johnson had eradicated the 'gay air' that had been central to her composition. The 'light-hearted youth' she'd called Jim Harris was now a cruel, careworn man and Mrs Marks 'a weary apathetic woman, beaten by the world' while she had envisioned 'the big genial mother sort'.[174] For Deevy, the only source of solace was that when the central figure, Annie Kinsella, appeared on the grassy roadside: 'She was good, very good.'[175] The romantic dreamer, Annie, was aged 'about twenty' and wore under her dark shawl a red dress.[176] The actress didn't have the golden hair Deevy described in the script: she was played by Ria Mooney.

Frank O'Connor, writer and board member, had been interested in Deevy's work since her early submissions. After she wrote *Temporal Powers* in 1932, O'Connor sought Deevy out in the lobby of the Abbey to tell her: 'I was enchanted by the technique of your play, its delicious invention and steady, perfectly controlled progression, its masterly climax without a hint of theatre.'[177] Deevy relied on her sister Nell to interpret. She had been deaf since the age of 20 and although her lip-reading was proficient, her work is marked by an abiding fascination with how people consistently try and fail to fully comprehend each other. In the early 1930s, she wrote to a friend to commend a play (unnamed) she'd read. In setting out the elements she views as key to its power, it gives an insight into her sense of drama: 'first of all delight in the atmosphere – the delicious turn of their talk – the absurdity and reality of them all.'[178] True dramatic conflict, as she sees it, is in the 'action of the soul.'[179] In writing *The King of Spain's Daughter*, Deevy focused on the 'April day atmosphere' and on holding the absurdity and reality of Annie Kinsella in careful balance.[180] Johnson eradicated the first, by changing the setting to the summer. Annie's spirit was left to Ria Mooney to portray. Joseph Holloway, who attended the opening night, was uncertain about the play, saying it had 'an unusual theme'.[181] But Holloway was convinced that it was Mooney's acting which 'made it seem almost a masterpiece' as she 'revealed all the depth of feeling.'[182]

As always, Mooney committed herself to interpreting the character as conceived by the author. The difficulty with playing Annie Kinsella, a woman forced to choose between indentured labour in the local factory and marriage, is that she is consistently nothing except inconsistent. In fact, the entire script of *The King of Spain's Daughter* tends so much towards hyperbole that it's difficult to read it as a serious situation. Annie is incapable of remembering accurately the bride she has just seen:

> ANNIE: It was in pale gold I saw her.
>
> JIM: *(Furious)* An' in shimmerin' green, an' in flamin' red, an' in milk-white when it will suit you![183]

Annie's whimsy often slips into ignorance, and her fanciful imagination into deceit. So much so that, on reading, one can empathise with Jim's impatience and her father's anger. However, all indications suggest that it was Ria's subtle talents that gave the character such presence. Her work on Bernard's *L'Invitation Au Voyage* meant that she understood how to work with an apparent absence of drama. Schooled by Le Gallienne in observing the slightest shifts of humour, in tracing emotional shifts in gear so that they flowed effortlessly, Mooney was one of the few actresses that could bring a sense of coherence to the role.

Given this success with Deevy's material, it may have been expected that Mooney would be cast as the leading lady in Deevy's next play, *Katie Roche*. However, in 1936 she was cast as the 'odd little' unmarried woman Amelia Gregg, who is 'something over fifty' and lives in fear that her brother will marry and she'll be left homeless.[184] The title role was given to Eileen Crowe and the part of Stanislaus Gregg, her new husband, to F. J. McCormick. The casting is noteworthy because it gave the role of a young single Irish female seeking independence to a married woman: Eileen Crowe was married to devout Catholic, F. J. McCormick. On stage, the Abbey directorate could be seen to explore ideas of female independence. But it was always in the context of male decision-making power and sheltered by the off-stage reality of the institution of Catholic marriage.

Katie Roche explores the same subjects as *The King of Spain's Daughter* in a more protracted form. As the play opens, in the home of Amelia Gregg, the servant Katie is contemplating entering the convent. At the same time, she wavers on the idea of marriage to a number of different men. Katie's social position is more complicated than Annie Kinsella's because of her parentage: her mother was unmarried and the identity of her father remains a mystery to her for most of the play. Stan's proposal of marriage comes with the confession that he loved her mother. As in *The King of Spain's Daughter*, there is futile and endless vacillation between choices, none of which offer Katie any kind of meaningful future.

> KATIE: *(goes to him).* Is it me to be the woman behind you? A help at your work? Is that what you want? *(Eager.)*
>
> STAN: You might indeed: you very well might *(so condescending that she is repulsed).*[185]

Amelia Gregg functions only to point up the other option to Irish women: unmarried, she manages her brother and the house like his mother. The spinster sister both welcomes the new wife as an ally and fears her as a competitor with the power to put her out of the house. Often, Amelia and Stan speak of Katie as if she is a recalcitrant child:

> AMELIA: No,—but I mean, she does her best. She's a brave little soul.[186]

In the play's final moments, when Stan has ordered Katie to accompany him to Dublin and she is 'bitter' and 'full of self pity', it is Amelia who urges her on. She encourages her to be brave, insisting:

> AMELIA: [...] If you're brave, you can make it grand.
> My dear, you must![187]

Katie leaves 'exultant' and 'almost gaily', while Amelia is left to watch her from the doorway, as if contemplating the misery of her own predicament in comparison.[188]

Katie's triumphant departure with her violent husband has always drawn the focus of readers and critics. It can be overlooked that, in performance, the final image left by Deevy is: 'AMELIA stands at the door, looking after her.'[189] With Crowe and McCormick in the wings, Ria Mooney held the stage. As the unmarried, solitary Amelia, she was left to contemplate the position of Irish women, their lives, their options and their capacity to 'make it grand'.[190]

Deevy travelled to Dublin in March 1936 to spend a few days in rehearsal with the Abbey company before *Katie Roche* premiered. She thought the new English producer, Hugh Hunt, to be young but full of enthusiasm and was struck by the industry and friendliness of the cast. Once the play was 'safely over' she could reflect on the whole experience and told Florence Hackett in April: 'all this looks as if you are right in saying that "Katie" is my best.'[191]

Mooney had inhabited the romantic idealism of Deevy's heroines and she also knew the harsh reality of the treatment of Irish women. Despite the play's success in Dublin, it wasn't popular with American audiences. The reviews from 1937 suggest, not that they were disturbed by the patriarchal violence of Irish society, but that they failed to grasp the issues at stake and the subtlety of Deevy's writing. Ria was ordered by director Ernest Blythe to direct the play in 1949, and in a neat reversal of history she cast Eileen Crowe (the original Katie) as Amelia Gregg. In that instance, the nine-week run was a success, making Deevy 'feel like a millionaire for the time being.'[192] Mooney, then the theatre's Director of Plays in English, described it as a 'beautiful play,' which she always thought of with 'tears in my heart.'[193]

'Actress Attracting'

The Irish Modernist poet Denis Devlin has a poem, initially entitled 'Actress Attracting', in which he beautifully captures the sense of performance:

> The rite
> Unrolls with the casual necessity of a bullfight;
> Pinned on the Euclidean frame
> Of the stage, night after night,
> Always our sentence and remand the same.[194]

Devlin, five years younger than Ria, was the eldest of nine children. He started writing poetry while a student in UCD, before he earned himself an international bureaucratic career, travelling the world with various presidents. He continued to write and publish his poetry.

There is a marked juncture in Irish literary history from 1934 when Samuel Beckett, writing under the pseudonym Andrew Bellis in *The Bookman*, drew a battle line in Irish poetry. On the one side were the antiquarians or 'twilighters', including Yeats and F. R. Higgins. On the other were the erudite young men with new ideas, including Denis Devlin. It speaks so beautifully to Ria's artistic sensibility, poised between the two traditions and equally conversant with both, that she had a relationship both with the dashing upstart Denis Devlin and, later, with F. R. Higgins.

According to the editor of a collection of his letters published in 2022, Sarah Bennett, Devlin began a relationship with Ria Mooney sometime in 1937. Bennett surmises they were introduced by Devlin's sister, Moya, an actress in the Abbey company from 1935–9, as Devlin subsequently used his sister to deliver letters to Ria. By March of that year, he was sending her 'My love and inmost thoughts' and there's even a poem, never published, specifically addressed to her entitled 'A Loving Argument', which begins: 'My temperate south / What summer have you lit in me?'[195] The letters show that during the summer months, Ria was up and down to the family cottage in Annamoe in Wicklow. Sometimes Devlin was with her and sometimes he was at home, cursing the distance and the lack of public transport to the isolated cottage. She was busy with the new Experimental Theatre, staging work with her industrious charges, but it seems the couple were together as much as permitted—Jim Fanning of Birr Little Theatre hosted him when she was performing there.[196] Early the next year, Devlin told her he was still thinking about her often: 'You come to my mind very vividly in odd places such as the Fun Palace bus stop.'[197] Outside the amusement arcade on Burgh Quay was the bus stop where Ria waited to go home. But as summer gave way to autumn in 1937, Ria was not hanging around at Dublin bus stops. She said goodbye to Devlin to travel with the Abbey company to America, under the management of F. R. Higgins.

Interlude

The American Tour of 1937/38

I'm going to stop time now and go down a trapdoor in both of these life stories. Bear with me. Or don't, travel on to the rest of Aideen's story or Ria's story and come back to this section later. This syncopated beat explores in detail the personalities involved in the Abbey company's tour of America of 1937/38, and the impact it had in America, in Dublin and, most significantly, on the lives of the women who were involved in it.

In Sumner House, on the corner of College and First Avenue in Claremont village in California, I first encounter Elbert Ambrose Wickes. I am staying in the Victorian building, with gables, bay windows and autumnal colours, built for the Reverend Sumner and his wife in 1887. Claremont is a toy village: symmetrical streets with symmetrical flowerbeds in the front gardens of low, adobe houses. My bones chilled from a day working in the dark, cool shade of Special Collections, I emerge from the Honnold/Mudd Library of Claremont College bleary-eyed and dozy to be assaulted by the heat of the day: over 100 degrees. And the question that follows me back to Sumner House: Did Elbert Wickes want to end up here?

The context of encountering the archives has become inseparable from the research. It's becoming more and more compelling to know: Is this where he chose his papers (personal and business) to be stored in perpetuity? Claremont is idyllic. It's serene and secure, steeped in learning, in wealth and privilege. Wickes served in World War I. He lived through the Great Depression of 1929 and then World War II. Leaving his wife to raise their two sons, he toured the world promoting and introducing celebrities like the Water Follies to the world. When he launched *The Blue Book of World Celebrities* it made his name, but his firm frequently teetered on the verge of bankruptcy (some of the difficulties exacerbated by the Abbey company). By the early 1940s, he was staying in the Hotel Lincoln in New York City, trying to rescue his livelihood while a secretary back in the office on Boylston Street in Boston was fending off creditors and making his excuses to clients.

Wickes emerged as a 'bit player' while I was researching in the National Library in Dublin. Operating on nothing more than a hunch, an instinct that this 'bit player' had had a pivotal role at a crucial moment, I got myself to Claremont University. There, I slowly began to grasp the complexity of this project. Scanning and noting is one thing, but it is a process to transform the ephemera into a text that can be read and to arrange the evidence into a life. It is a creative act to transform these papers into a character. Yet 'creative' suggests an instinctive and free-flowing act, when often this is something closer to interrogation. It's an ongoing list of questions; it's using the evidence to build theories and finding theories to test the evidence.

I finally identify Wickes in photographs: tall, broad-shouldered and hefty (not fat) with a thin-lipped smile and a laugh in his eyes. He often wears a fedora hat and a heavy coat. Although in the files from his Boston office there are stacks of press photographs of the Abbey company, there are few photographs of him. Piecing together the events of his life may be possible from his letters, his diaries and his press interviews. Constructing a personality from such scraps, with barely a hint of his personal circumstances, is more difficult.

The solid, squat lettering of an American typewriter stacks up into the columns of the office inventory that was compiled on 18 November 1938.[1] The underlined headings give it a frame and the careful numbering and dating provide ballast. It all builds up into something that Mr E. A. Wickes can walk right into. While I want to wander, admire the colours and feel the heavy brocade of the fringed table covers, the legal team are waiting impatiently in reception.

It is November 1938 and an office inventory of the rooms (307–311) at 729 Boylston Street, Boston, Massachusetts, is required for the purposes of a legal case. Miss Gertrude Lamothe, a permanent fixture in his office, is tapping away at her typewriter and answering the phone to make apologies. As the lawyers sit in the walnut chairs of the reception, they can flick through the photo album on display. In sumptuous purple with gold lettering, it's full of souvenir photographs from *The Plough and the Stars*. If they tire of admiring the young ladies of the cast, they can peruse the window cards advertising Eleanor Holme and the Water Follies, Fritz Leiber or even the Abbey Theatre Players, of whom they have probably heard. Lou Alber would have mentioned them as he detailed Wickes's ongoing work with the Irish theatre company that are taking up so much of the partnership's time although they are not making any money.

In Wickes's private office, he sits behind a walnut roll-top desk in a mahogany swivel desk chair. He tips his cigarettes into a walnut ash stand and talks into a leather-covered Dictaphone on the desk. A Steiffel & Freeman iron safe with a combination lock stands sentry in a corner and the smaller mahogany tables display a range of bric-a-brac: bronze bookends, a brass Chinese opium pipe, a paperweight shaped like a dinosaur from the American Museum of Natural History, a glass paperweight, a pipe rack with three pipes and a silver Cup that was a prize in a golf championship. In the heap of items behind the door are an umbrella, a cane, a raincoat, an office coat, a briefcase and one piece of aeroplane luggage (weekend size). There are more framed photographs (41) than books (35) but only one of the framed photographs stands on the desk. From this vantage point, it's not possible to see if the photograph is of his wife and young sons or of an Irish theatre company.

The legal case has been trundling on for a while. In July 1938, Wickes had no choice but to contact his old friends in the Abbey Theatre management and tell them of the difficulties the partnership was undergoing. He dictated for his loyal secretary, Miss Lamothe, a letter addressed to 'Fred' (F. R. Higgins). It said:

> I have sufficient understanding of human characteristics to know that we are all compounded of many moods and characteristics and my attitudes toward any weaknesses in others is one of sympathy and compassion in the hope that similar sentiments will be extended toward me in any weaknesses I may have. But in a business sense, I am terribly afraid of Mr. Alber's stability. Any man can suffer financial reverses. But what is important is how he handles himself. In the last six years, his record is astoundingly filled with fraudulent checks, unpaid hotel bills, unhesitating borrowing of money in large and small sums from any and every source with extravagant promises and then complete disregard of statements made, refusal to answer letters and failure to pay.[2]

Wickes wasn't exchanging idle gossip. He goes on to detail the statements he has gathered, from a woman who gave Lou Alber money and checks in the middle of the night in a New York hotel to prevent his arrest, from The Copley Plaza hotel in Boston who were still seeking payment from unpaid bills and from the Vanderbilt Hotel in New York who had successfully sued and got a settlement of $600. There was also the case of the husband who was threatening to find and violently attack Mr Alber for money he'd borrowed from his wife, with no prospect of repayment. Wickes was, charmingly and cleverly, fighting to keep the Abbey Theatre as a client. Their tours had not been particularly lucrative for him, but the company had won a place in his affections. In his entreaties to the Abbey, his own loyalty and support for the company can be traced.

It was Mr Lou Alber, 'pioneer in the lecture-bureau business', who founded the company, inviting Wickes to promote a Chicago art project sometime before 1920. They subsequently merged to form The Alber-Wickes Bureau. In the summer of 1934, 'Smilo' (as Alber affectionately called his partner) headed to Europe to sign up new talent. In London that summer, he was to renew his acquaintance with Winston Churchill. In Dublin, he conferred with W. B. Yeats and Lennox Robinson and previewed the Abbey Theatre's new repertoire. He also met with poet F. R. Higgins, who spent six years on the board of the Abbey. He was a broad, striking-looking man with lank black hair that constantly fell over his eyes and a ruddy face. Wickes had boarded the ship to Europe from New York 'armed with a fountain pen, a thick sheaf of contracts and several hundred thousand dollars in guarantees'. Press agents and flashing cameras recorded his departure 'to hunt big game with a fountain pen'.[3] In fact, the Abbey needed the American tour far more than Wickes needed them—touring was providing a much-needed stream of income.

Pre-tour advice from Elbert A. Wickes

Prior to the 1937/38 Abbey Tour, Wickes had cabled to advise that the Abbey company either provide a reduction in terms or a repertoire of new plays.[4] Frankly, he had told Higgins that 'normal theatrical promotion in the ordinary show sense is totally inadequate and unsuitable for the Abbey Players' and that there was a need to focus on finding an audience of those 'who are of the calibre to be Abbey enthusiasts'. Wickes pointed out that there would be a falling off in audiences 'without at least two strong new plays'.[5]

His private correspondence with Boss Shields at the same time was more positive, although the advice remained the same. Shields suggested that the Abbey company appear in only larger cities and run the plays a week at a time to reduce the extensive repertoire of the company. Wickes wasn't convinced although he said: 'With the right plays, sparkling and punchy and new, (if there are any such), I would not be averse to trying out the idea.'[6] With laid-back charm, he set out in stark terms the practical realities of the tour:

> And Boss, if I may use American slang: Have a heart! A study of the data on the last tour shows as I remember it, (I'm not looking it up), that about two towns lost for every town that broke even or paid a profit and that I was very lucky to come out with a little profit at the end of the run.[7]

The Abbey Board decided to consider their position and didn't formally respond to Wickes and his advice. Getting nervous, he sent a telegram to Higgins:

> No letter appreciate knowing developments sincerely trust Abbey will remain loyal to me since my courage and management gave opportunity show their great ability to America appreciate your conferring directors report results.[8]

At an early evening Board Meeting in July, the Abbey Board discussed arrangements for the social outing to Horse Show Week and a play called *Nostalgia* that had been submitted by a Miss O'Callaghan. They then came to discuss arrangements for the American tour. Walter Starkie proposed a motion that Higgins be given sole charge of the company's tour in America at a salary of $150 a week with $25 for expenses. They also dismissed Wickes's advice and agreed to hire another theatre promotion company: the Grisman Organisation. For road management, they engaged the Shuberts. Despite Arthur Shields's reservations, they prepared to leave for an American tour without Wickes.

The Abbey company attended a luncheon in the Hibernian Hotel on Dawson Street to launch the new US tour in the autumn of 1937.[9] There was a second official send-off at Westland Row train station, when they departed on the train for Belfast. On the platform, director Hugh Hunt gallantly presented each of the ladies with a bunch of flowers.[10] They posed for photos and waved goodbye tearfully to family and friends. In Belfast, they would alight the awaiting ship without any marked ceremony.

Sailing away

> O'Connor, Mooney and Mulhern are walking the decks like Russian peasants with kerchiefs over their heads. Delany [sic.] is sitting reading with sunglasses. Craig and Crowe are in their cabins, not too well.[11]

F. R. (Fred) Higgins was the most pugnacious of all the Abbey directors. He could be witty and amiable but was always suspicious, constantly forming one firm alliance while he betrayed another. He rapidly set out to dislodge Lennox Robinson and become Yeats's successor himself, building an intricate maze of intrigues around him. Frank O'Connor described Higgins in his autobiography, *My Father's Son*: '[He] criticized [O'Connor] to Yeats and Yeats to [O'Connor] and Robinson and Hunt to anyone who would listen; but he could not fight. He saw secret agents everywhere ...'[12] After he nearly missed the train departing Dublin, Higgins's moods and dramas continued on his Atlantic crossing. The narrow boundaries of the imagination of this strident, arrogant poet are betrayed when he attempts to describe the ferry that brought them to board the liner, and falls back on provincial Irish scenes, describing the tender next to the Samaria as being like 'an apple woman's stall under Nelson's Pillar.'[13] Vacillating between indulgence in hot seawater baths nightly and then turning his nose up at the whole atmosphere of the ship as 'stinking with swank', he turned down an invite from the President of the dining hall to sit with the Abbey company instead, and then later dismissed the actors as snobs. He said: 'My task in America will be a heavy one and [the actors] can give me little help.'[14]

It wasn't long before the wind was picking up over the Atlantic, and the members of the travelling company were doing their best to avoid nausea. They spent the afternoon watching the horse racing, with wooden horses and mock bookies, on the deck, and then dressed for a 'carnival' dinner. When they arrived in the dining room, the tables were strewn with balloons, bugles and lutes. The women wore the headdresses of Indian chiefs.[15] O'Connor, Mulhern and Mooney sat together for the meal, separate from the elders of the company, away from the stiff manners of Higgins and the small talk of the older women, Maureen Delany and Eileen Crowe. Together, they drank and ate, and danced when the meal was over.[16]

Higgins had little but disdain for most of the actors, telling his wife: 'They are really laughable in their snobbery, style and behaviour—all except Paddy, Delany [sic.] and Mulhern and Dossie—I talk to these most of all—the others only annoy me.'[17] Maureen Delany was a large-framed comedienne originally from Kilkenny; in size alone her presence on the stage was immense.[18] Dorothy Dayton described her in the *New York Sun* in December 1934 as a 'witty and altogether delightful spinster', who, off stage, lived alone and had a deeply superstitious streak.[19] Higgins wasn't the only one to pair Frolie with Delany. On tour, American newspapers speculated that should Delany stay in Hollywood to pursue a movie career, Frolie Mulhern could move into her substantial roles.[20] The women shared a talent for comedy, but, if others expected it, there's no evidence Mulhern wanted a future similar to that proffered by Delany. In his free time, Arthur Shields used the gym, 'pulling artificial rowing boats, punching the ball and what not', and he also went to the library and played cards with Higgins.[21]

That sea crossing to the US was a particularly choppy one, often rendering the actors bedbound with nausea. In one letter, Higgins described to his wife how he visited the actors in their sick beds and then: 'Dr Higgins and Nurse Mooney (she was the only woman who survived) went upstairs and [...] played House, the boat still heaving.'[22]

Ria Mooney continued to walk the decks and play cards with Higgins, while the others struggled. She impressed him with her strength of mind, her focus and poise. Higgins was delicate and paranoid; he feared being away from home and doubted his ability to cope. Ria, on the other hand, was at ease with travel and used to making the best of strange surroundings. The Atlantic crossing wasn't new to her; she believed fresh air and exercise on board were cures for nausea. Regrettably, her reaction sometimes came later. In a cottage on the Aran Islands after a similarly choppy crossing, Ria woke at 4am to find the whole building heaving and became violently ill.[23] Outwardly strong and worldly, Mooney's turbulent moments were private and solitary.

Aideen and Frolie shared a cabin and Higgins and Ria came to see them huddled in their beds. Frolie was 'staring as if her eyes would next come up' and Aideen had 'gone [as] white' as May's pet cat.[24] The worst of the seasickness passed, but the carnival nights and long days of walking the decks (with moments of shark spotting) did become tiresome for all. They were relieved, at the end of September, when calm conditions created the perfect afternoon for their 4pm arrival into the port of New York.[25]

Hotel Edison, Broadway

Broadway was the first stop on the tour. Higgins commanded two rooms on the 12th storey of the Hotel Edison, just off Times Square on West 47th Street. O'Connor and the others were escorted by bellboys to rooms on another floor. The bedrooms were small and some of them dark. Each had a mahogany desk and a bathroom with an American-style 'tub'. Sash windows opened onto the street and the noise of traffic, crowds of tourists and the occasional wail of a siren created a constant bass line of noise. The hotel was decorated in Art Deco style, with angular lines, gold, deep reds and blues running through the lobby to the restaurant, where guests were escorted up shallow steps to their tables. At the top of 22 storeys was a roof garden, with a breathtaking view of the surrounding skyscrapers and river.[26]

Teresa Deevy had always hoped that one of her plays would be brought to America and the success of *Katie Roche* in Dublin led the board to choose the play to open the US tour in New York.[27] But the subtle exploration of female independence was not popular with American audiences. The New York newspaper, *Daily Mirror*, was quick to pick up the error of that decision, reporting on the Abbey's 'half-hearted struggle with Teresa Deevy's shadow of a play *Katie Roche*, which they unwisely, we think, chose to open their current repertory engagement here.'[28]

It was at this point that Ria Mooney took ill and went to bed in the Hotel Edison. She had dyed her hair, and it seems she hated the result. While Denis Devlin wrote to say it was 'foolish of you', he does assure her she will look 'much more distinguished and lovely in silver – or silverblack'. Devlin was sympathetic and sorry to hear of her illness, in that 'big can of a hotel and lonely too.'[29] Aideen and Frolie had discovered dancing and nightclubs, Boss was trying to help Higgins with plans, and Ria was in bed writing to Devlin of the 'verminous company' she was travelling with.[30] *Katie Roche* was replaced with more crowd-friendly fare, and full details of the failure on Broadway never reached Deevy.

Higgins, already under strain from the business of the tour, wrote to his wife:

> For the past two weeks, Ria Mooney is very sick. Doctors attending here. (Lucky for me she is not in *The Far-Off Hills*, which is now in its third week.) She has gone completely limp and the [d]octors cannot make out what is the matter.[31]

Medics failed to diagnose anything; the illness may not have been only physical. The city had a difficult history for the actress and now she struggled to cope with it. MacLiammóir had nurtured her in Dublin but there was no such support now. Higgins couldn't support Mooney, nor could the other actresses, who had no understanding of the fear that seized her on arrival back to the place where Le Gallienne had affected her confidence so badly. When she managed to get on stage, Ria was nothing but miserable about her performances. Decades later, on 1 September 1953, she recalled the time and confessed to friend Theresa Helburn: '[A]ll the complexes I developed at the Civic Rep Theatre came crowding down upon me.'[32]

Aideen wasn't cast in *Katie Roche*. The failure and rapid removal of Deevy's play from the repertory was no loss to her; its hasty replacement brought her onto the Broadway stage sooner than expected. The social life in New York was busy and exciting. Giddily, Aideen wrote to her sisters of how they performed on Saturday night and then danced all night. On leaving the nightclub, she and Frolie realised there was no sense in going home before the Sunday sermon and they went straight to 4am mass.[33] She was enamoured with one particular dance: the 'Big Apple'. She found it 'really intricate and quite mad'.[34] But by the end of November, Aideen was weary, running short of money and trying to settle into some kind of routine. She took a week of early nights and spent time in her room writing home to catch up on her sister Eileen's wedding plans. The rain outside was horrendous, but her hotel room was so hot from the central heating that she slept with no bed covers.[35]

Christmas approached and Aideen sent her sisters stockings. Friends at home weren't forgotten: a book on Van Gogh (including 30 plates of his work) by Walter Pach, an expensive gift, was dispatched back to Anne Yeats.[36] Aideen was eager to get on the road again: it was cheaper and more fun than long stays in one city.[37] But questions around the viability of the tour, particularly the west coast section, were starting to surface.

Higgins's sole reason for taking on the management of the tour had been to impress Yeats with his capabilities, but now he wasn't coping well with the stress of travelling and managing a cast and crew. From a stifling hot room in the hotel, where he'd had two extra tables moved in to accommodate the papers, plays and all that he had to attend to, he confessed only to his wife, 'My temper is unbearable, my nerves are shattered.' He goes on:

> Last week—I thought I was going mad—I got hysterical and had a few bad fights from sheer

nerves. Boss gave me a few doses of bromide to calm my nerves and it worked wonders. This week I'm calmer—but very worried with this awful rush, bustle and responsibility.[38]

Higgins bustled on through Christmas with the aid of Boss Shields and packed up for the road with the company.

With all of the anxious planning and scheduling, the performing, the socialising and the dancing, there may have been no time, or little interest, in following political events at home. There is certainly no reference to it in any letters home. But on 29 December 1937, Bunreacht na hÉireann (Ireland's Constitution) came into operation. It had been passed by referendum in March, and now the Irish Free State was succeeded by Éire (Ireland), a sovereign, independent, democratic state. The document, authored by Éamon de Valera with support from leaders of the Catholic Church, inserted sections on the role of women in Irish society, and their position within the home, that are contentious to this day.

By January the company were in Toronto, where the temperature plummeted to 20 degrees below zero. In seven days, they performed seven different plays and on the Sunday, they began a 15-hour train journey to Chicago. Business at the box office still wasn't improving and the actors didn't even know how long they'd be in Chicago.[39] Houses were not good. A critic for the *Philadelphia Record* complained about 'a brogue thicker than a London fog' and pronounced, 'The Abbey Players, it seems to me, try too hard.'[40] An article on the dramatic pages of the *Boston Sunday Post* on 16 January 1938 also supported Wickes's wisdom. Commenting on the paltry audiences during the Abbey Theatre's three-week residence in The Copley Theatre it said:

> It may be well, furthermore, that some people stayed away who might have gone if the repertory had been brightened with some brand new plays. Whatever the reason, the crowds who came were pitifully small, though this is one of the best acting companies in the world, unique and extraordinary of its kind.[41]

The Abbey Theatre needed Wickes's expertise and the copy of this article in his papers suggests he was watching their progress.

Higgins was avoiding all correspondence from Dublin, where the Abbey Board were furious that they were not being updated on progress. Frank O'Connor, in his autobiography, remembers this time from the perspective of those still producing plays in Dublin.

> In America Higgins dropped the company altogether, and all the news we could get of them was from American newspapers, which described furious scenes between rival lawyers. Higgins simply ignored our cables, though after a month or so I got one report from him which was a masterpiece of wild humour, but told me nothing that we really wanted to know.[42]

He divulges the attitude of the Board to those who were in America: 'We merely wanted someone to keep that wretched touring company out of our hair while Hunt went on with the real business of the theatre, which was producing new plays.'[43] Shortly after they arrived in Chicago, the company learnt that both the Shuberts and Grisman were pulling out for financial reasons, leaving the West Coast stage of their tour in danger of being abandoned. They were all staying in the Hotel Sherman, a 1600-room hotel located in the centre of the theatre district. It also housed a vibrant nightclub famous for its jazz music and a restaurant called *The College Inn*. While the players continued to perform, Higgins flew back to New York to enter negotiations with another producer and the actors were on edge for two days. Back in New York's Hotel Edison, business arrangements for the tour were being made and unmade. Unless the business issues were resolved, the company would be sent home without delay.

Nobody appears to have informed the Abbey Board, but Higgins met with Wickes. When, months later, Higgins was safely at home in Dublin, Wickes reminded him of that meeting and said:

> I took over, not because I had any expectation of making any worthwhile profit. Naturally I hoped to. But I greatly doubted it. But I took over because I can truthfully state that I have felt and do feel a great responsibility for the Abbey Theatre prestige in this country.[44]

A deal was done in that stuffy hotel room in New York, and a new contract between Wickes and the Abbey was signed on 19 February 1938. When a telegram from Higgins arrived in Chicago announcing they should prepare to leave for San Francisco, the company celebrated all night.[45] Management of the tour on the West Coast had been taken up by Elbert Wickes, and he would accompany the company on the lengthy train journey to the west coast.

While the actors were feted and fed off stage by audiences, the critics were wearying of the performance style. It had been observed that, 'The Abbey Theatre players are as standard as the nationally advertised brands of cigarette'.[46] The company played to meet expectations. Audiences dictated shows from the repertory, and actors, in their individual performances, went out of their way to please in the anticipated manner.[47] Popular success had come, some felt, at the expense of artistic ideals.

Heading his article, filed from Pittsburgh, *Erin Go Blah*, infamous critic, George Jean Nathan, attacked the histrionic acting style he saw on stage. Actors were playing lines purely for comedy and consciously playing the 'Irishness' the audiences came to mock. Nathan remembered how the Abbey Theatre had once been one of the finest acting organisations in the world; it was now a 'caricature of its former self'.[48] Irish elements of the scripts were 'accentuated in theatrical delivery or consciously stylised for them by the Irish performers'.[49]

Aideen, as the female ingénue, watched as other company members mugged at and bantered with the audience, often reducing serious plays to farce. Performing each night became a riotous and hilarious game, a game that could continue afterwards in the green room or in the nightclub. The careful pitching of tragic dialogue and deft physical characterisation that she had developed in London and under Hunt's direction was being eroded by the 'improvised self-mocking, meta-theatrical, exaggerated performance style'.[50] Her craft was also being eroded by sheer exhaustion, but the travelling had to continue.

On their final Saturday night in the Grand Opera House in Chicago, the company played *The Playboy of the Western World* with *The Rising of the Moon* before packing up the sets, props, costumes and their own belongings to go straight to the train station. The train was held for them, and they collapsed into sleep once they'd settled into their sleeper carriages. They arrived in Saint Louis for a brief stint the next day at 7.30am. It was a Sunday, but they were performing that night.[51] St Louis was dreary and damp. The performances were poorly attended and there were flurries of snow to contend with. A doctor prescribed liver extract for O'Connor's stomach and dismissed the New York doctors' diagnosis of something more serious. Before they knew it, they were back on the train heading for the west coast. Aideen always found it difficult to sleep on the trains and now she was contending with stomach pains. On one journey, she remembered:

I didn't sleep all last night. It is a very rocky route and the train swayed and swerved and banged and clattered and stopped with a jerk and started again. It was impossible to sleep. Frolie came into my berth and we giggled and looked out of the window for hours until Boss heard us and ordered us to go to sleep. Then we were called at 5.30 this morning for customs inspections.[52]

Aideen had full responsibility for costumes. They had to be unpacked and re-packed for customs checks and again for the dressing rooms.

She awoke at 6am in the wilds of Colorado, and could see out the window from her pillow: 'It was glorious. We were going through prairie lands, the sun was just up and the whole thing looked like a technicolour movie.'[53] After an early breakfast in the dining carriage with Ria Mooney, Arthur Shields, Elbert Wickes and Maureen Delany, she settled down to write letters until they reached a stop where they could alight for some air and exercise. She captures the company in their idle hours:

> ...in the distance are the Rockies with snow-covered tops. Oh, Boy they look grand. The Co. are in various attitudes around the coach. Frolie is writing letters, Joe is wandering about, Austin ditto, Boss is cleaning his typewriter, the stagehands are in a huddle with Elbert. Eileen is still in bed while the others are in the diner having breakfast.[54]

There were unscheduled stops, when landslides blocked the train lines, and breaks in 'depots'. If the train pulled up unexpectedly, some of the actors got out to climb around and take photographs, passing time until the blockage was cleared. At depots, they rushed out to buy sweets and magazines, or to walk around. One photograph shows the company hanging around on a platform.[55] The sun is shining; Joe Linnane sits on the edge of the platform with Frolie on one side and Aideen on the other. She is demure, her legs neatly folded under her. Frolie sits with her legs apart, feet on the sleepers. She wears dark sunglasses and is laughing or telling a joke. Shields sits at a polite distance away. May Craig, Maureen Delany and some of the men stand around behind them, as if they're pacing, eager to get going. The family nature of this Abbey company is captured so eloquently in these images of 'down time'.

Frolie and Aideen still found a huge amount of excitement and delight in their travels. O'Connor told her sister, 'Frolie and I are still getting along together,' but added, 'We have a few rows now and again but we always make it up in no time'.[56] When they reprised their roles in Robinson's *The Far-Off Hills*, one reviewer commented that Mulhern was 'not quite so little now' and was displaying 'her indisputable development as a comic actress'. Her figure had expanded with new curves; she wore slacks and sunglasses off stage and was becoming known for her lampooning of famous figures. Aideen was noted to be 'still little' and a 'juvenile joy'.[57] When they performed the comedy in Toronto a journalist reported that the actresses playing 'the fun-loving younger sisters' were 'both bewitching and perfect foils for one another.'[58] If Mulhern was feeling frustration at playing a girl almost half her age, there was no sign of it on stage. The same high-spirits and youthful exuberance that they shared in their real hotel rooms enchanted audiences.

Even in the heated carriages of the reputable trains, the journey to the West Coast was an arduous and tiring trek. For days on end, they crossed deserted prairies, brown and dry as far as the eye could see. Often the company slept through the night and found that either there remained no sign of any living soul or that the season had changed entirely overnight. When the trains broke down or a customs check was required, the actors got out and wandered around to stretch their legs and try to pass the time. Sometimes, they were stranded for hours. High up in the Sierra Nevada mountains, there was snow heaped on the tracks. The train trundled and shook over the precarious trestles that carried the tracks over the gaping ravines. From the observation car, the players watched the trucks crawl along in front of the train, tapping the slender supports to ensure they were secure. Wickes is a recurrent character in Aideen's letters. Higgins had opted to stay in New York; Wickes had slipped easily back into his role as mentor and friend to the Abbey Theatre.

Years later, Frank O'Connor asked Arthur Shields for advice on dealing with the players. Shields had learnt much from Wickes and his short advice to O'Connor was:

> Treat us as though we were children. [...] Nice children, of course, children that you're fond of, but not as grown-ups. And for God's sake, whatever you do, don't praise us. That drives us mad.[59]

Andy Oakley, writing for the San Francisco newsletter *Wasp* in a column entitled 'Showtown—Showing Steeptown How', had privileged access to the Abbey company. After the St Patrick's Day performance at the Curran Theatre on Geary Street, Wickes invited him backstage. He met Shields 'and his compatriots' and accompanied them to the Bohemian Bar where they all toasted the Saint with Burke's and Bushmills.[60] Wickes initiated and guided this carefully planned PR exercise, of which the actors happily partook. Oakley explains to his readers why the celebrations were particularly boisterous: '[They celebrated] the more heartily since saloons are closed on the snake-chasing Saint's holiday in Dublin, for obvious reasons.[61] Elbert (as Aideen called him in her letters) was popular with the whole company, but Boss Shields became a particularly close friend and confidante. From Dublin, Shields continued through the 1930s and early 1940s to send Wickes news of the Abbey's fortunes. He told him, 'And so we will go on, one week up and one week down.'[62]

When the Abbey was on a down week, Boss wanted nothing more than to share his problems with Wickes, saying: 'I would love to sit in that Greek café and talk things over with you.'[63] He disliked the idea of touring in America without Wickes's supervision and must have supported Higgins wholeheartedly when the fraught managing director decided to seek his help. With Wickes, Shields shared details of his personal life. He told him in 1937, 'Between you and me, I want to get away from this place and I see in this a slight opening.'[64] Shields's affair with Aideen O'Connor had been made public a few months earlier; both needed to get away.

In the correspondence between the two friends from the early 1930s, Boss always sent his regards to Mrs Wickes and the two boys. Wickes had married Helen Kahle from Lima, Ohio in New York City in 1919, shortly after his return from World War I. They had Thomas two years later and Philip Mccutcheon three years after that. But by 1930, the US Federal Census shows that Helen was living in Los Angeles City with three lodgers (all of whom were teachers) and her two sons. She provided an estimated date of birth (about 1900) and gave herself the title 'Head of the Household'. Wickes found another family in the Abbey company.

While there is a hint in a later letter from Aideen, there is no other evidence that Frolie Mulhern had a relationship with Wickes. Frolie left no correspondence and her remaining family know nothing of the romance. There is nothing in Wickes's official papers. Except for one photograph: The *only* photograph in Wickes's papers that is not an official press shot. Taken from the 'sidewalk', the photographer has turned the camera up towards the fifth or sixth floor of a hotel room on the corner, possibly the Hotel Clark in Los Angeles. A beaming Frolie, in a short-sleeved dress, is hanging out the window as if having a conversation with the photographer. To Frolie's right, further back, the head and shoulders of Wickes are visible. He may be smiling; his expression is unclear. It may be nothing, or it may be the only tangible evidence of a love affair that ended when Frolie got back from the US.

Wickes's business papers contain all of the press releases and prepared statements for the Abbey's tour. This is the Abbey company that Wickes worked hard to present and to re-present, as opposed to the reviews and reports that finally ended up on the pages of the press. His 'spin' lifted and transformed the fortunes of the Abbey company in the US. He did not only work with words. The detailed business records show that he was intimately involved in the practical aspects of the production. All the financial records, balancing box office takings with company wages are in his handwriting. He kept notes of the duration of each act of each of the plays in the repertoire, so that an evening's entertainment could be rearranged at any time to suit the audience or a cast that were prone to illness. (Ria Mooney couldn't perform in New York; Aideen O'Connor had to have a doctor called several times between Canada, Chicago and St Louis.) When P. J. Carolan became fatally ill with TB, it was Wickes who pencilled out his name and replaced it with Barry Fitzgerald, who had been summoned from New York to cover his parts. There is no evidence to show where Higgins was staying at this point, or what business he was doing.

Spirits picked up considerably when the company reached San Francisco and then the sun-soaked, star-filled city of Los Angeles. They were staying in the Hotel Clark, downtown. Hotel Clark was opened as a 'luxury hotel for the corporate traveller', with the novelty of a private bathroom for each room. It rumbled and shook with a regular rhythm from the subway station directly across the road. The trip to Erlanger's Biltmore Theatre could easily be made on foot, a few times a day and back home at night. Wickes and Shields, sometimes accompanied by their lady friends, trotted down Hill to Pershing Square, and turned right to cross over to Olive Street. Despite civic attempts to improve it, Pershing Square was a haunt for degenerates at night and masses of filthy pigeons during the day. But looming over it, the gilded exterior glinting in the sun, was the extravagant Biltmore Hotel, and on the side of that was the Biltmore Theatre, managed by Erlanger.

With the exception of the interference from the trolleys, trundling and whistling past on the street outside, it was a comfortable and glamorous theatre to watch the Abbey in any of their daily performances from 28 March to 2 April. They performed on a wooden stage, in a 40-feet wide proscenium arch to a capacity of 1,640 seats. The interior of the theatre was in tones of blue and antique gold. The walls were painted a rather dark ultramarine which was repeated on the asbestos curtain design of a galleon, with a map of California in one corner and undertones of dull maroons, greens and browns throughout. In the auditorium, two large carved wood lanterns were suspended above the boxes and there was a chandelier, containing over 200 electric lights. Draperies covered large areas of the auditorium for acoustical as well as decorative purposes.[65] According to the financial records of the Biltmore Theatre, the Abbey company took in $10,000 at the box office in their first week and $9,000 in their second.[66] This was exactly $1,000 less than their 1935 visit.

The Abbey actors were invited to meet producers and film stars at all the big studios: 20th Century Fox, RKO and Paramount. There were pool parties and charity luncheons and outings to the beach. There are two photos of a lunch in Paramount Studios from April 1938: one in the Shields archive in Galway and one in the Wickes papers in Claremont, California. Seated at a table, backs to the camera, are all of the actors. They are seated as three couples: Aideen

O'Connor and Arthur Shields; Frolie Mulhern and Elbert Wickes; Ria Mooney and Fred Higgins. The rest of the company are at the other side of the table. Most of the actors (particularly those without children) were being tempted and enthralled by the prospects of film work. From the initial disappointment of the flop of *Katie Roche* in New York, Wickes had turned things around until there was endless sunshine, star-filled parties and some good reviews.

After the 1938 Tour

After the Abbey company sailed back to Dublin in the spring of 1938, Wickes spent a busy two months putting his books in order for audit. He wrote privately to Higgins (rather than the entire Board) to share his idea of 'giving a complete financial analysis with a record of the disastrous losses I suffered'. He decided it was unnecessary to set out the losses as, 'I don't believe any such details are necessary for you and [the Board of Directors] have the figures of the attendance and you know the situation.'[67] Yet, despite the financial disappointment, his devotion to the Abbey company remained steadfast. He goes on to speak of the management of the Abbey Players. For him, it had been:

> A source of personal pride and interest on my part, perhaps comparable to the devotion and interest of you gentlemen of the Board of Directors. Their work over here during the various tours earned extraordinary approval from the critics, which was carefully nourished by personal attention to and endless conferences with the critics in every city.[68]

The financial losses concerned Wickes less than the artistic life of the company, or what he calls 'another highly important phase' for the Abbey. He believed that the Board would comprehend 'the necessity of so completely understanding them and their work'.[69] While the Abbey Board had sent the company on tour seeking to improve its finances, the American producer was now asserting the importance of the tour from a cultural and national perspective.

Miss Lamothe, in the office in Boston, kept a manila file: *Stories: Agents File 1938*. Among the carefully worded stories describing the Abbey Board of Directors as 'men, notable in Irish literature and capable of dramatic enterprise', is an interview with F. R. Higgins. Wickes's prowess is perhaps most evident here, set against the stubborn egotism of Higgins, who sneered at a journalist, saying: 'Broadway audiences enjoy the most appalling trash and enjoy it heartily.' Having singled out San Francisco and Los Angeles playgoers as 'the best in America for intelligent reaction', he tells the American public that their theatre would be better placed if there were 'less money and more brains.' Wickes jumps in to rescue the situation. With a jaunty tone, he speaks of 'the great vogue for the theatre' and how Americans are being 'exposed to culture on a scale unduplicated anywhere in the world'.[70] He puts an optimistic gloss on Higgins's comments and somehow sets up the Abbey Theatre Company as both an entertaining treat and a cultural panacea especially designed for the American audience.

In the summer in Boston, Wickes found himself battling with Lou Alber and the lawyers, and he never gave up trying from afar to secure the Abbey Board's loyalty. Lou Alber had by now begun his campaign to secure the Bureau's most lucrative client and had sent numerous letters to the Abbey board seeking to represent them on their next tour. Shields repeatedly stepped in to recommend that they remain with Wickes, pointing out that not only were they more likely to be successful, but that he 'always played decent'.[71] Wickes told Higgins in that letter from July 1938 where he outlined the problems with Alber:

I am desirous of standing solely on my own merits in a constructive sense. I am not desirous of achieving anything through attack on someone else. Therefore I have written you and the Abbey Board on the merits of my own situation.[72]

From 8 to 20 August 1938, the Abbey Theatre hosted what Hunt later called in his book, *A Festival and a Farewell*, as Yeats made his last appearance on the Abbey stage.[73] During the day, there were lectures on the history of the theatre and exhibitions, while the actors were busy rehearsing and performing. Seventeen plays in total were performed over the 12 days and the ongoing problem of Wickes and Alber was far from the minds of the Abbey directors.

But when business resumed after Yeats's death, in February 1939, Higgins sent a polite note to Wickes's Boston office. He asked Wickes to 'save us serious inconvenience' and remit the $1,800 that had been promised in May 1938 as the final payment due to the Abbey for that tour.[74] Wickes had promised payment by October, but nine months later it had still not arrived and the auditors had requested it. The same month, Shields also re-connected with his old friend 'after many months of glorious memories and remorse' and provided more details for the increasingly anxious Wickes, writing to him on Abbey Theatre letterhead.[75] Despite suggestions from Shields that the Board were considering a further tour in 1940/41, neither Alber nor Wickes secured the business. The outbreak of World War II and other domestic considerations meant another tour didn't materialise, and neither did the remittance of $1,800 to the Abbey.

The Elbert Wickes first encountered, behind his walnut roll-top desk in his mahogany swivel desk chair, tipping his cigarettes into a walnut ash stand and dictating another letter to the dependable Gertrude Lamothe is older now, weary and hassled. There is evidence that Wickes went to New York sometime in 1940. He secured a room in the Hotel Lincoln for a long-term stay, spending the days looking for business while Miss Lamothe managed the office in Boston, keeping the lawyers at bay.

The initials of 'GL' for Gertrude Lamothe are the reference on each of the letters sent from Wickes to the Abbey board and to Shields, dating back to the late 1920s. Boss asked for her often; she assisted with the inventory and kept immaculately organised files of correspondence, press material, promotional material and photographs. And then, unexpectedly, she slips out from behind the neat initials and has the last word on the entire matter. She wrote a letter of resignation to Wickes on 22 March 1941. In a startled scrawl, he notes on the top in pencil: 'Monica, you will read with interest. Please return at once. EAW.'[76]

Miss Lamothe assures Mr Wickes that she has left his office in good order, and says, 'I've had a reason for trying to keep my affair in the 'dark' but since it popped out ...'[77] The 'affair' is her engagement with a railway engineer, a respectable man with a good inheritance, allowing her to become a married lady of leisure. She addresses Wickes as 'lordy mister man' and reveals:

> If it were not for the great happiness ahead and a feeling of security for my remaining days, I imagine I should have felt a greater tug at the heart-strings, for as you say, with all the ups and downs, I've kept at it, and tried to always give my loyal support, no matter how I felt about things that disturbed.[78]

Like the photo of Frolie, the letter is a curious fragment, a startling revelation of a personal relationship amid the stack of business records. There is no record to elucidate the 'things that disturbed her'; it is only evident that another figure of support and friendship was lost to Wickes. She concludes:

I'll be seeing you, if you ever do get back, and needless to say I'm wishing you success and a quick solving of your problems. Would have liked to have been here when it happened, to cheer. But I'll be thinking of you just the same.[79]

She would not be there to welcome him back to Boston, and never again would Wickes welcome the Abbey Theatre Company to the US. But Miss Lamothe had seen Wickes turn around his own fortunes and those of his clients many times. Throughout his life, he supported and inspired others with his practical management, positive attitude and ambition. She had faith that his sojourn in New York would bring a resolution to the temporary issues because all his business difficulties were only temporary; it was only ever a matter of time before things turned around for Elbert Wickes.

Chapter 3

Ria Again: After the 1937/38 Tour

With F. R. Higgins in New York

On boarding the liner to travel from Belfast to America with the Abbey company in the autumn of 1937, Ria hung over the railing on deck with producer F. R. (Fred) Higgins. Three convoluted paragraphs follow this scene in the memoir, as Mooney tries to convince the reader that their relationship was a familial one, through mutual relations in Trim, Co. Meath.[1] It's an attempt to persuade the reader, and possibly herself, that her connection with this married man was innocuous. It was more than that, although the exact nature of the relationship is for only them to know. Writer Mervyn Wall and Val Mulkerns described their relationship as an affair; if it wasn't romantic, it was intimate and meaningful to them both. In an appendix to the volume, Higgins' place in her heart is revealed: he presented her with a silver ring sometime in the late 1930s. The poem attached to the ring includes the line: 'For her, this ring; to keep the artist mind / The stamina of Ireland, upon her hand.' In her own admission, Mooney wore the ring like a wedding troth until the metal wore away.[2]

When she left for New York, Ria was still in a relationship with Denis Devlin, but it appears the love affair didn't endure the distance. Her travels across America, and ongoing deliberations about staying there or coming home, contributed to the breakdown of the relationship, although his loss of interest and rude behaviour seems to have been the deciding factor. From a new post in Rome, Devlin penned a tardy response to a letter from her. The relationship was definitively over, but he apologises for his insensitivity and alludes to the guilt he felt after the fury she had shown him.[3] Again, we only glimpse Mooney's passion and fury at a remove: there is no evidence of what she said, or how she shared her feelings, but he acknowledges that it was fair of her to be angry with him.

In the collection of books bequeathed to the National Library after her death is a book of Higgins' poetry entitled *Arable Holdings*. It is inscribed: 'To Ria, in a Californian twilight, as a memory of our American tour.'[4] He offered her comfort, it seems, in the twilight of their visit to California during the spring of 1938. The poem he wrote for her during that American tour, 'A Wish for Ria', hung on the wall of her hideaway cottage in Glencree, Co. Wicklow for decades.

While Higgins was dour, rude and often spiteful, Mooney had a child-like frankness. She had an easy manner with strangers and the ability to make friendships and to foster them. At the same time, she was erudite, educated in European theatre and versed in American literature through her exposure to the Harlem Renaissance. Higgins was a neo-romantic poet with little practical theatre experience. It may never be possible to fully explain an intimate relationship between two historical figures, but there's no doubt that Mooney was a useful tool in Higgins' machinations.

Frank O'Connor was content to have Higgins out of the way for a period, but the company did return from the American tour, with some success thanks to the intervention of Wickes. The board cemented Higgins' position of authority the following September by appointing him as managing director. Yeats had left for France and Higgins' appointment heaped more pressure on his shoulders, creating more paranoia and spite for him.[5]

Since her appearance as Rosie Redmond, Mooney was detached from the other devout Catholic actresses and actors. Now she had been brought on tour with the first company, having been on stage with the second company for over three years, and she was outside of the tight-knit circle. Although close enough to be privy to what was going on with the individual actors, Ria did not have allegiances to any of them. Such knowledge of personal details and company gossip was the kind of information prized by the paranoid Higgins. At the same time, her intimacy with the man the other actresses openly despised cut her off from close friendship. Mooney was content forever situated somewhere on the outside of the group, and it came to suit her professional interests; it also suited Higgins to have her there.

Elizabeth Connor, Una Troy and *Mount Prospect*

In May 1940, Mooney spent a morning trying to write a letter to playwright Una Troy. Una Troy had a number of identities. To some, she was Mrs Walsh, wife to the GP in Clonmel in Tipperary. To others, she was the banned novelist Elizabeth Connor, with avid readers across the UK and Europe. To her family of artist relations, she was Una Troy: the name she was given at birth. Mooney was writing to Troy to thank her for the gift of an evening bag. *Mount Prospect: A Tragedy in Three Acts* had been staged at the Abbey Theatre weeks earlier and Mooney played the central role of Mrs Kennefick. After throwing away two drafts, she wrote the following:

> You really are much too generous because I feel, honestly and truly in debt to you for having written it and to Frank Dermody for fighting for the part for me. It's meant a very great deal to me, I haven't had such compliments since I was in the Gate, in fact, numbers of people had forgotten I could act until they saw me as 'Mrs K' – so it's I who should send presents.[6]

Despite the usual mannerly gratitude of an actress to a playwright, there is pain in her admission that others had forgotten her skills. Some quality of this playwright's work captured Mooney's latent talent and re-inspired her; the play, and its provenance, offered her something vital.

The adjudicators of the Abbey Play Competition that year were George Shiels and P. S. O'Hegarty, assisted by Brinsley MacNamara. According to the *Irish Independent*, the first prize was shared between a W. D. Hepenstall (from Greystones) whose play, *Today and Yesterday*, was a comedy of modern Irish life and Connor's *Mount Prospect*, a tragedy of middle-class life in an Irish provincial town.[7] Connor travelled from Clonmel to accept the prize and she had lunch with Lennox Robinson in the Unicorn restaurant the following day. Although the prize of £50 was shared equally, some weeks later, on 12 February 1940, Robinson corresponded privately with Connor to say:

> [I]t should of course have the whole prize, but we Directors preferred to leave the judgment

Headshot of Aideen O'Connor in the 1930s. T13/B Shields Family Archive, James Hardiman Library Archives, University of Galway.

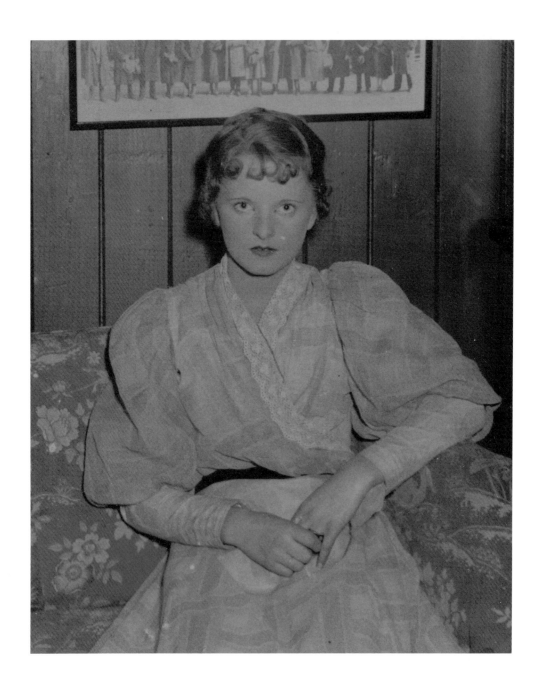

Aideen O'Connor in the Abbey green room *c.*1933. T13/B/130 Shields Family Archive, James Hardiman Library Archives, University of Galway.

Aideen O'Connor with Arthur Shields in *Shadow and Substance* in January 1937. T13/B/007 Shields Family Archive, James Hardiman Library Archives, University of Galway.

Frolie Mulhern on stage, unidentified play. T13B Shields Family Archive, James Hardiman Library Archives, University of Galway.

Headshot of actress Frolie Mulhern. Family Collection, courtesy of Helen De Geus.

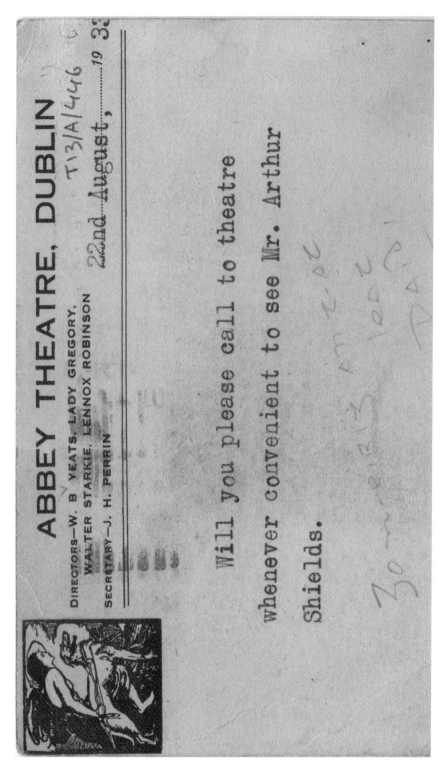

ABBEY THEATRE, DUBLIN

DIRECTORS—W. B YEATS, LADY GREGORY,
WALTER STARKIE, LENNOX ROBINSON
SECRETARY—J. H. PERRIN

T13/A/446

22nd August 19 33

Will you please call to theatre

whenever convenient to see Mr. Arthur

Shields.

Postcard from the Abbey Theatre to Aideen O'Connor 1933. T13/A/446 Shields Family Archive, James Hardiman Library Archives, University of Galway.

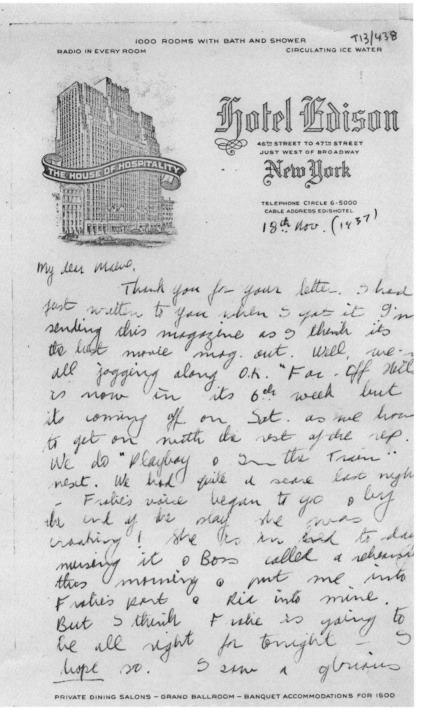

18th Nov. (1937)

My dear Maeve,

Thank you for your letter. I had
just written to you when I got it. I'm
sending this magazine as I think its
the last movie mag. out. Well, we're
all jogging along O.K. "Far · Off Hill"
is now in its 6th week but
its coming off on Sat. as we have
to get on with the rest of the rep.
We do "Playboy" & "In the Train"
next. We had quite a scare last night
– Frolie's voice began to go & by
the end of the play she was
croaking! She is in bed to-day
nursing it & Boss called a rehearsal
this morning & put me into
Frolie's part & Rie into mine.
But I think Frolie is going to
be all right for tonight – I
hope so. I saw a glorious

Letter from Hotel Edison, Aideen to Eileen O'Connor, 1937. T13/B/438 Shields Family Archive, James Hardiman Library Archives, University of Galway.

be yourself, because 'yourself' is a very charming, generous, honest person — you needn't be ashamed of it, and have no reason on earth why you should want to hide it — let's see more of it, because well like it!

Now maybe, I'm all wrong about you and this letter has been no help at all — If it hasn't you'd better look me up in the Peacock (6.P.M – 7.P.M) during the week of July 27th!

Again many thanks for your letter — and come back to School!

Sincerely
Ria Mooney.

Letter from Ria Mooney to Lilian Roberts *c.*1936. Lilian Roberts Notes 3. Private Collection, courtesy of Finola Finlay and family.

Ria Mooney and Christine Hayden in the world premiere of *Parnell of Avondale* by William Fearon, Abbey Theatre, 1934.
Photo: Herbert W. Lewis. 1934 Parnell of Avondale 01 / ATDA 2235_PH_001 Courtesy of the Abbey Theatre Archive.

Ria Mooney as Mary Cavan Tyrone and Vincent Dowling as Edmund Tyrone in the Irish premiere of *Long Day's Journey into Night* by Eugene O'Neill, Abbey Theatre, 1959. Photo: John Sarsfield. 1959 Long Days Journey 01 Courtesy of the Abbey Theatre Archive.

Ria Mooney as Hannie Martin in the world premiere of *Lover's Meeting* by Louis D'Alton, Abbey Theatre, 1941. 1941 Lovers Meeting 01 / ATDA 1755_PH_001 Courtesy of the Abbey Theatre Archive.

Scene from *The Far-Off Hills* by Lennox Robinson. Left to right: Frolie Mulhern, Eileen Crowe, P. J. Carolan, Maureen Delany, Aideen O'Connor. Unidentified photographer. Elbert A. Wickes Papers: Theatre Impressario (1884–1974). Claremont Colleges, Honnold/Mudd Special Collections, California.

Lunch in Paramount Studios, 1938. Left to right: Elbert Wickes, Ria Mooney and F. R. Higgins, Maureen Delany. Unidentified photographer. Elbert A. Wickes Papers: Theatre Impressario (1884–1974). Claremont Colleges, Honnold/ Mudd Special Collections, California.

Left to right: Joe Linnane, Aideen O'Connor, F. R. Higgins, Frolie Mulhern, Arthur Shields *c.*1937. T13/B Shields Family Archive, James Hardiman Library Archives, University of Galway.

Abbey Theatre Company on train tracks, US Tour 1937/38. T13/B/326 Shields Family Archive, James Hardiman Library Archives, University of Galway.

Abbey Theatre Company in New York, 1937/38 Tour. T13/B/317 Shields Family Archive, James Hardiman Library Archives, University of Galway.

Abbey Theatre Company in Philadelphia, 1934/35 Tour. T13/B Shields Family Archive, James Hardiman Library Archives, University of Galway.

to other people and so could only accept their opinions. [...] I think you have written a tremendous play. Your woman in it is as great, and greater, than Strindberg's *The Father*.[8]

Robinson was already concerned about casting the eldest son and, according to Mooney's May letter, Dermody had to fight for Mooney to have the role of the family matriarch. (There were actresses closer in age to the character, such as Craig and Delany.) But with parts assigned, the play was staged for the first time in April 1940. It drew good houses and played for a second week. *London Tatler* attended the premiere and deftly summarised how the play 'deals with a kind of female Tartuffe in the Irish bogs' and had 'set Dublin talking.'[9] In attendance that night were Lord Longford (of the Gate Theatre) and his wife; Brinsley MacNamara; the painter Charles Lamb (a relative of Connor); the Lennox Robinsons, 'an interesting pair'; Higgins and Mrs George Yeats, 'Dublin's most inveterate first-nighter'.[10]

Much of the talk about the play centred on the fact that the play was based on a novel banned in Ireland by the Censor. (It was subsequently published in England.) All of the action takes place in the drawing room of a grand house—Mount Prospect—in an Irish provincial town. Robinson believed the playwright captures 'all the quality of snobbish, country, county Cork.'[11]

The first scene stages the reading of Mr Kennefick's will, when they learn the house is to be shared by his second wife and stepson Rex with his children from his first marriage, Peter and Mary. Early on, Mrs Kennefick reveals her attachment to her home:

> Mrs Kennefick: I was so proud when I came here first as Edward's wife—as you know, Kate, I was past thirty and not handsome at my best and it seemed as if God had forgotten me. And then, after all, he made me Mrs Kennefick of Mount Prospect. This house has been my home for so long—I've worked and cared for it for twenty-three years—I feel it's alive with me...[12]

Gradually, the strange tendencies of Peter and Mary become apparent and the audience is left guessing to the motives of all involved. Sharing the house, as Mr Kennefick wished, seems an impossible resolution. Mooney's character is a pious member of the Legion of Mary and the Vincent De Paul Society, who rules her children with medicine, egg flip and her domineering presence. In the novel on which the play is based she openly declares: 'I could never live out of Ireland, Rex. My kind would never get on away from here.'[13]

While Peter struggles to run the solicitors' office inherited from his father, Rex is carousing. Peter insists Rex is lazy and useless; Mrs Kennefick argues Peter works too hard and needs to find help. She embodies practical sense and maternal devotion. Mrs Kennefick always knows what is best for her step-children, as she alone holds the secret of their inherited madness. Tensions rise when word reaches Mount Prospect that a girl in the village is pregnant with Rex's child, although she had been dating other men in a bid to conceal her state. Yet, contrary to the conventional ending in which true motives may be revealed and evil forces ousted, things take a different turn. The pregnancy subplot is neatly sidestepped with a timely motorcar accident, so that all focus remains on the family unit. Hugh Hunt called Deevy's Ireland a 'twilight world' of romantic female dreamers, but Connor's Irish countryside is a place as black as night.[14]

Reading the plot of her banned novel, *Mount Prospect*, alongside the play reveals the highly accomplished nature of the adaptation, dramatising material that could be staged without scandal while still holding an audience's attention. Her subtle touch shapes each of her female characters into fascinating individuals: strong, dynamic women. In each case, there is a marked gap, a dramatic space, between who they are and who they purport to be. Early in the play, Mrs Kennefick confesses to a female friend the strain of motherhood: 'Sometimes I get so tired, thinking of others... But I shouldn't say that.'[15]

In the novel, Mary is a married woman who has left Mount Prospect with her husband. Her marriage is unhappy, however, and she realises that the feminine ideal she has worked to achieve bores her husband. She has an epiphany: 'At least, she knew now that she could make no change in her husband; she could change only herself.'[16] After much thought, Mary decides there is only one remedy for her 'agonizingly dull' union: 'She must, of course, commit adultery.'[17]

Marital infidelity and female emancipation of any kind are excised from the play. In the stage adaptation, Mary is a fragile girl, almost a prisoner at home. She wants to become a doctor and tells Mrs Kennefick:

Mary: I could you know, Mother. I got my Matric at school and it would be quite easy – ... I want to go away. I want a life of my own.[18]

Despite opposition, Mary does talk back to her stepmother. Unlike the idealistic and hopelessly imaginative heroines penned by Deevy, Connor writes wise and cunning women, who see boundaries that can be gently poked without full transgression. At one point, she shares this exchange:

Mrs Kennefick: You're not fitted for this world, child.
Mary: Who unfitted me?[19]

At the same time, the violence of the novel is tempered for the stage. In the book, Peter kills Rex in a clear display of the 'strength of insanity'.[20] When they gather at his bedside in the final scene, Mrs Kennefick is convulsed with grief and 'Mary reeled, swayed and leant heavily on the bed.' The final order is then a maternal plea driven by love, grief and desperation, and delivered in 'a croaking whisper': 'Mary ... take your ... hands off the ... white quilt.'[21]

In the play, Peter taking out his rage on the drawing room furniture is the most violent section of the action. Mrs Kennefick watches from aside, calm and stately. In the final line of dialogue before the curtain falls, she requests the drawing room door be closed lest the servants overhear. From page to stage, there is a clear shift in emphasis from female desire to social propriety. Connor couldn't stage female emancipation, but she presented female power in a form palatable to the Abbey directorate.

The theatre critic from the *Irish Times* was stunned by 'the grip and compulsion of the moving and very human story' on 23 April 1940 and hoped the production signalled 'the rebirth of the serious play in the Abbey Theatre.'[22] Gabriel Fallon thought Mooney's performance 'one of her best' but had misgivings about the character of Mrs Kennefick, describing her as 'almost fully drawn and nearly credible.'[23] Robinson's reading of the character (quoted above) is more astute: she is a complex, unflinching portrait of an Irish woman in full control of her home, her family and her future. The audience's sympathy for the widow is manipulated by the playwright at every step of the action.

Mount Prospect is a dark and eerie thriller, a morbid analysis of Irish small-town society and a callous dissection of the Irish mother figure. While Elizabeth Connor would go on to future success with her novels, it is a huge loss to the National Theatre that she shifted her attention from the stage. She understood that the stage of the Abbey Theatre was not a space for the things she wrote about in her fiction: female emancipation, infidelity and power. Mary Kennefick can meddle with such issues because she will be declared 'mad' at the end of the play.

The part of Mrs Kennefick presented Mooney with a challenge worthy of her talents, and she rose to it. For a role of similar stature, she had to wait for Mrs Tyrone in Eugene O'Neill's *A Long Day's Journey Into Night*. That production opened in 1959, but there would be challenges in a different form before she returned to the stage as a performer.

Experimenting with form

In the autumn of 1935, Ria Mooney was appointed as Director of the Abbey School of Acting. Robinson's alcoholism had become intolerable, and M. J. Dolan had previously been in charge but was replaced by Mooney.[24] Given her history with the school and her experience in New York, it was a position to which she knew she was ideally suited. It also brought in an additional salary, while she continued to perform with the company on the main stage.

After rehearsing during the day, Mooney tramped down the stairs to the Peacock Theatre, the smaller studio on the same site as the Abbey, to lead classes. She began the term with high ideals, some of which were lost in the daily toil necessary to keep the school operating. In February 1936, she presented to the board her new scheme for the school, which included classes in the theory of acting, the practice of acting and a separate class for the juvenile leads.[25] The scheme was unanimously accepted, as was her proposal that Sara Payne (with a musical accompanist) give a class once a week in rhythmical movement.[26]

Frank O'Connor would repeatedly interfere in her work, but Mooney dismissed the intrusions to focus on recapturing the respectful observation and gentle mentoring that she had experienced at the Civic Repertory in New York. Students, she insisted, should be allowed to feel their way into parts. They should be allowed to experiment with every kind of role, even those that may not ostensibly suit them.

In a step outside of O'Connor's comprehension, Mooney directed her charges with what she termed 'poor movements', or inadequate staging and gestures. This was based on the theory that their conception of the character could not then rely on outward gestures or movements. The student had to focus on fully inhabiting the mind of the character. Once completely secure and confident in the interior life of the character, Mooney would assist the young actors with natural and minimal movements.[27] In her memoirs, Mooney reiterates her belief that while only the 'original creator' could give somebody talent: 'If you couldn't teach to act, you could teach someone HOW to act.'[28]

It is the highest tribute to her work during those long evenings that not only did many future stars of the Abbey stage emerge from her tutelage, but the enthusiasm and professionalism of her charges engendered a company. Adopting a logo that merged the traditional Irish wolfhounds with a modern, geometric form, in 1937 Mooney's students formed AET: the Abbey Experimental Theatre.

The concept of an experimental theatre group at the Abbey had been in the air for some time, but it was only in the spring of 1937 that the idea took formal shape. Mooney learnt that a senior student at the School of Acting, Cecil Ford, was organising rehearsals at night with the intention of a public production. At first, Mooney believed the endeavour was premature but she was won over by Ford's enthusiasm and industriousness. Together, director and student came to agree on a scheme for staging plays by foreign authors that were not welcome at the Abbey. W. B. Yeats thought of the AET as a theatre that would 'try out' plays rejected by the Abbey.[29] Robinson later dismissed the plays staged by the AET as 'not impressive' but said that at least 'the Theatre has never been guilty of quenching young talent.'[30]

The students of the Abbey School financed this experiment themselves. Each student was a shareholder in the Society, with small weekly contributions constituting a share. They produced the plays, designed their own sets, made and painted the scenery and, when necessary, created their own costumes. Front of house, they ran the box office, the pit café, and they ushered people to their seats. The directors of the Abbey chose the plays and provided the Peacock Theatre free of charge. Hugh Hunt and Mooney also had a right to veto productions that didn't meet a certain standard. (There is no evidence Hunt ever got involved.)

A photograph of the AET Group during the production of *Harlequin's Positions* shows a total of 58 students with a vast range in age: 37 men and 21 women. There was a small managing committee, comprising six students and Ria Mooney. One of those serving on the committee was a married woman with a young family at home (Josephine Fitzgerald); another a young lady with an ordinary day job (Shela Ward). George Yeats spoke of them all affectionately, urging her husband to send a telegram to wish them luck: 'The 'Experimentalists' have been working with the enthusiasm of fanatics and the sense which fanatics do not usually possess.'[31]

The students directed the first productions (in April 1937), but in 1939 Mooney took on the direction of Jack Yeats' *Harlequin's Positions.* Ian R. Walsh proposes that this production of the first play of the well-known artist was approved by Higgins after the death of W. B. Yeats.[32] In fact, weeks before the death of his brother, the playwright was in contact with Mooney about the production, or a possible one. Jack Yeats sent her notes of scenes while working on it, with the disclaimer: 'They are probably much too elaborate, though they may be of use as suggestions.'[33] He continued to send letters of inquiry, but rehearsals did not begin until April 1939. The following month, he added some lines to the script. Four times he attended rehearsals, 'each time with more respect for the way the company carried the days along'.[34]

Harlequin's Positions ostensibly presents a conventional 'stranger in the house' plot, but it works in a radically different mode. It's a dramatic piece wholly dependent on images rather than words, very much in the modernist style, and thus it appealed directly to Mooney's sense of colour and shape. From the first reading, Mooney felt Jack Yeats 'could have contributed as much to the Irish theatre as he did to Irish painting.'[35] The students were encouraged to restrict their movement as much as possible and to speak the words with 'intelligence and conviction.'[36] The playwright himself believed that 'acting' in the traditional sense would be fatal to the script. Instead, 'dialogue must flow from one actor to another each becoming nothing but an agent and putting all of Yeats into his words.'[37] The dialogue should be nothing but words; the expression only that of the dramatist.

Mooney was a conduit between the playwright and cast. Both writer and actors needed confidence building as well as a disciplined hand. As she introduced the students to a text they had never seen the like of, she had to endow them with the techniques and assurance to work in this radically new mode. Simultaneously, she worked with Yeats to ensure her interpretation of the work was to his satisfaction. Meanwhile, she assured the Abbey directorate of an upcoming success. Performing this balancing act between all involved, there was little time to consider critics' opinions. In the event, the *Irish Times* journalist treated it as a showcase for the Experimental Theatre actors, saying 'It gives nearly every member of the cast the opportunity of playing a leading part in at least one of the five acts.'[38] He lamented that parts of the play 'might have been better in the hands of more experienced performers,' and opined the play was 'a strange piece of material.'[39]

McGlone describes how, following the death of Yeats, Mooney and 'her poet stood together now at the head of the Abbey.'[40] While this image of Higgins and Mooney is attractive, it has no basis. Mooney moved around behind Higgins, perhaps whispering in his ear while they spent the day in Glencree or gently leading him in different directions with a prepared argument and presentation of a particular script, but she was never fully visible to those watching Higgins's strategic manoeuvrers. At the age of 45, Higgins took ill while at a meeting and was transported to Jervis Street Hospital, where he died on 6 January 1941. The chief mourner at his funeral was his wife, well known harpist, May (Beatrice) Moore.[41] Ria had lost another mentor and ally.

Mooney's powers of persuasion at the Abbey, particularly after the death of Higgins, had their limits. When she directed Jack Yeats' play *La La Noo* in May 1942, the production would have only one performance to prove itself. That Sunday night, the curtain rose to show a dingy bar where seven women had gathered to take shelter from the rain. Coming from the nearby athletic sports, these women meet a strange man and the publican. There is much of the traditional 'peasant quality' familiar to the Abbey audiences in *La La Noo*, but also many departures from this style.

The colour scheme of the set is distinctive. The bar and dresser are 'dingy blue', at the window hangs a 'dingy claret-coloured cotton half-curtain', and the door and outside shutter are 'green'.[42] Seven women, ranging in age from 19 to 45, advance to the bar where two men sit. Yeats has not only considered the physical aspects of each woman, but he includes notes on colour: one wears 'heather tweed' and another a 'grey felt hat'. The publican has a 'slightly blue chin' while the stranger drinking with him has a 'red-grey moustache'.[43]

The traditional tale that seems to be opening up slips rapidly into something closer to absurdism. The dialogue does not advance the plot; it hinders it. Some commentators have called Yeats' drama 'pre-Absurd' on this basis.[44] The women have meandering discussions about American hats and bald men. The men's conversations about motorcars, bicycles and submarines have only the most tenuous of connection to the action. At the same time, Yeats meditates on the moral issues brought up by World War II, through the musings of his characters:

> 1st WOMAN: [W]e are getting into the way of thinking very little of a life. Holding it too cheap.[45]

And later:

> STRANGER: The world away from us this day is full of terrible cruel things.[46]

Mooney's attraction to the piece is evident—not only in the colour-scape of the set, but in the painterly arrangement of the women on every entrance, and the gentle, abstract progress of the plot with its modernist agenda. Much of Jack Yeats' philosophy on drama is captured in one line of dialogue. The '5th Woman' declares: 'Dreams don't go by contraries. They speak the truth.'[47] However, much of the audience was confused by the ending, which presents the senseless death of the stranger as he tries to drive the others away.

If Jack Yeats' drama was 'dream-like', his concept of drama was concrete. Mooney had artistic vision; she understood his theories, appreciated his art and her devotion to his work was steadfast. Despite its reception, Yeats knew how hard she had worked, without support from Abbey directors. In a letter to Mooney dated 3 February 1944, he said: 'I do certainly know that it was yourself who interested F. R. Higgins sufficiently in *La La Noo* to put it on.'[48] The morning after the premiere, Jack Yeats sent Mooney a note from his Fitzwilliam Street home:

> Thank you very much for the production you made of 'La La Noo' to say the play got 'every chance' is not quite enough – you added to it. Anytime the opportunity comes I would like you to say to the company that I believe every one of the players made the play.[49]

He insisted the play had been given every opportunity, but he knew it hadn't made an impression on the board or on the audience, who were baffled. Jack Yeats told Mooney on 3 February 1944 that he believed:

> any audience, whose skulls weren't filled with crumpled cellophane alone, and were well shepherded into a not-too-big theatre would get entertainment out of any of my plays – that were produced as well as *La La Noo* was produced.[50]

Mooney could not change the contents of skulls or convince in any other way than honouring the script in production. She also had to recognise that the limits of her influence in the National Theatre were becoming apparent. The following year, Jack Yeats' play, *In the Sand*, was rejected and she could do nothing for it. It was finally staged by the Experimental Theatre group in 1949 and was not professionally produced until 1964.

Ria Mooney always responded respectfully to strong leadership. Seán O'Casey, Eva Le Gallienne, W. B. Yeats and F. R. Higgins: All recognised the talents of this thoughtful, hard-working actress and were treated with veneration in return. Ernest Blythe, however, who replaced Higgins as managing director of the Abbey Theatre in 1941, tested her patience and sapped her usually boundless energy. Under him, she entered a period in her career of gradual and painful disempowerment. Blythe was an ex-Minister of Finance, who earned the position at the Abbey as a result of his securing the theatre's annual subsidy. But he had little time for the poetry of theatre that Mooney prized; he was intent on using the theatre to resurrect Irish as the national language. He viewed the Abbey as 'an instrument of national defence.'[51]

The general gloom of World War II and the Irish Emergency was extending over Dublin, and now when Mooney escaped to her hut in Wicklow at the weekends it was to grieve in private for Higgins. Although she struggled through a few productions under Blythe, both as director and performer, she was ready to leave the institution. A chance came when the managing director of the Gaiety Theatre decided to start his own acting school and Mooney applied for the position.

A portrait of Louis Elliman, once the managing director of the 1200-seat Gaiety Theatre at the top of Grafton Street, still hangs above the stairs leading to the dress circle. The glass cover catches the light of the chandeliers and almost obscures the thin face and bald head of the painter's subject. Elliman has an aquiline nose and wears a suit more suited to an undertaker than a theatre mogul. This serious expression challenged Mooney while it also promised full support for this venture. Soon, she was auditioning 500 applicants for the group of young performers that would be exposed to her techniques for mentoring talent.

Although her account shows her a touch resentful of being pressurised to show results sooner than planned, Mooney rose to Elliman's summons and staged a full-scale production of Heijermans' *The Good Hope*. She had been cast in this play at the Civic Repertory, and again would draw on Le Gallienne's technique and the confidence this experience gave her. There were two casts under her direction: one performed for the Sunday matinee and the second for the evening performance. To cater for the students without parts in the main show, she directed Robinson's one-act play, *Crabbed Youth and Age*, to be performed on the same day. After her retirement, Mooney still could not conceal the delight she felt when Elliman chided her for putting professionals on the stage and claiming they were amateurs.[52]

Mooney's workload was continually dictated by her desire to express her creativity while also earning enough money to sustain not only herself but now her family dependents also. She lived at home with her widowed father, and an aunt that had joined the household. Thus, while running the Gaiety School of Acting she accepted work from Roibéard O'Faracháin and Austin Clarke in their Dublin Verse Society. The position was effectively a stage manager, blocking movement, and it increased her workload further. But with much of her days spent drilling young actors in movement, she was happy to work solely with language and verse in this additional task.

As a director, Mooney's visual sense had always been primary. This period of working intensely with actors and verse drama reinforced her understanding of how actors use rhythm and voice. Mooney had learnt vocal technique directly from W. B. Yeats, when performing his verse dramas, and now she had the maturity to reflect on his teaching. Yet, it seems inevitable that she would quickly grow restless with the strict form and leave the Society (newly christened the Lyric Theatre).

Once again, time away from the Abbey Theatre seems to have given Mooney time to heal. With the war finally over, life promised better things. MacLiammóir and Edwards re-staged her adaptation of *Wuthering Heights* at the Gaiety and two years later, she was asked to direct the London production of O'Casey's new play, *Red Roses for Me*. To date, she had directed only three professional productions on the Abbey main stage and a number of student productions. Bronson Albery, who had come to Dublin to engage a director for *Red Roses for Me*, may have seen a burgeoning talent. Alternatively, he may have noted that she was one of the few people prepared to work with the playwright.

Mooney's devotion to O'Casey had not wavered since he assisted her stint looking for work in London in the 1920s. Now, she took to corresponding with him regularly by letter and eventually visiting his family home in Devon to discuss her ideas for staging *Red Roses for Me*. Working patiently but determinedly with him to make cuts in the script and to inculcate the cast in the uncompromising expressionism of some scenes, she was largely credited with the success of the play. It ran in London for 17 weeks. Mooney became annoyed by a lack of discipline among the actors as the run progressed, but the production established her as a director of note. Doors may have been opened in the UK by the success, but Mooney had an agreement with Elliman. She returned to Dublin to stage another version of *Red Roses for Me* at the Gaiety Theatre.

In 1947, Mooney had a delight tinged with nostalgia when an old charge from Le Gallienne's company of apprentices arrived in Dublin for her new cast. Burgess Meredith, now an American star of the stage and screen, had been cast in the leading role in *Winterset*, a play by Maxwell Anderson. His glamorous wife Paulette Gordon accompanied him to play opposite him. Also turning up for rehearsals under her direction at the Gaiety were her old mentor Micheál MacLiammóir and seasoned actor Anew McMaster.[53] She was finally granted casts and production budgets worthy of her experience, but in her memoir, Mooney gives the impression that she was not overly enamoured with her new powers. Instead, Ria enthuses about the latest developments in light and sound technology.[54] Immersed in the process, she had little time to reflect on her achievements. And as always with theatre, the pleasure of a successful run ended all too soon, leaving her once again at a crossroads.

Burgess Meredith wanted to include Mooney in his plans for a theatre company in Hollywood, while the Ensemble Theatre in London had sought her out as a potential teacher of acting with the responsibility of directing every third play. She had established an international reputation, but Ria knew both the thrill and painful reality of such tenuous offers; and she was no longer young enough to live on gin and chocolate as she had in her early adventures. As she pondered this dilemma and the potential implications of leaving Dublin, the Abbey Theatre entered stage left once again, this time in the person of Roibéard O'Faracháin. Mooney always clung to the narrative of the theatre that had compelled her from a young age. She had affixed a narrative of magical import, of real significance, to the Irish National Theatre. She sought to position herself as a part of that tradition and that story no matter how grim the reality.

O'Faracháin had no post to offer Mooney when he approached her. Indeed, the board were seeking a Director of Plays fluent in the Irish language; but the notion of Mooney leaving the country to use her talents elsewhere left them disgruntled. The board somehow agreed to offer her a position, most likely consenting to Blythe's demand that it be a holding position until an Irish speaker presented himself. For Blythe, hiring Mooney was a strategic move to assist in silencing the criticism appearing in the newspapers in 1947. The minor scandal followed in the wake of Valentin Iremonger's outburst from the stalls of the Abbey about the quality of the productions. Blythe insisted years later that Ria had been the instigator, telling this to Vincent Dowling, who was then on the Players' Council.[55] Blythe advised, 'Grasp the talon and the bird is lost!'[56]

To those looking on, Mooney's work in the theatre was all-consuming, but she did have a family life few knew about. As her father and aunt grew elderly, she arranged a house move to a small new home in Goatstown, a suburb in the shelter of the Dublin Mountains on the south side of the city. In October 1953, Mooney told a friend in an exasperated tone, 'I am the MAN of this household.'[57] To use 'this' rather than 'the' may suggest there also was a 'household' where she was not the decision-maker: the Abbey Theatre.

One may speculate as to Blythe's true motives in offering Mooney a position, but in retrospect it seems she had no intention of taking any post other than Director of Plays in English at the Irish National Theatre. Thus, in January 1948 she once again walked through the lobby of the Abbey, to take up the role. Mooney shows gratitude for 'the privilege of working for my own country', although she henceforth worked for the Abbey directorate, something arguably different.[58]

While she was 'the man' at home, at the theatre, Mooney remained the quiet and unassuming if secretly furious 'little woman', doing her best for productions between the Irish-language pantomimes that had become a staple of the repertoire. She fought to maintain artistic standards without any support—practically or emotionally. Mooney's days were long and full, but seldom joyful. The day, or night if she had to watch a performance, ended with the long bus trip out to Goatstown. There, she was called on to be the cheerful, practical provider. One of her business letters, sent to New York in April 1955, had already been used as a shopping list on which she reminded herself to bring home coffee and fruit cup. At weekends, if time and weather allowed, she would potter in the garden.

After a fire at the Abbey Theatre in the early hours of 18 July 1951, a crowd gathered to survey the charred remains of the building. Among them was a weary, disillusioned and openly upset Ria Mooney. She trudged through the stalls, looking at the burnt-out roof and scorched walls. To Mooney's dismay, some of the theatre staff gathered accused her of predicting the disaster, of foreseeing the destruction of the theatre, like a witch.[59] Her memoir recounts this anecdote with obvious pain, yet in some ways Mooney was a soothsayer and visionary. The old building had been a vital part of her life; its current state was destroying her.

That day brought excruciating pain for all she'd lost, but Mooney recognised the potential for new life to rise from the ashes. That night, she performed in the Peacock Theatre. May Craig was not available to play Mrs Gogan, and Mooney replaced her. The audience loudly applauded the gallant cast in their makeshift costumes on the cramped stage. Afterwards, they drank champagne brought by a relative of Lady Gregory.[60] That night, Mooney was determined, positive change was coming.

After the fire

In 1953, a letter from an old colleague in the New York Theatre Guild, Theresa Helburn, arrived at the Abbey. It was a business letter for the Director of Plays in English, requesting a script by Louis D'Alton. One evening, miserable but buoyed by nervous exhaustion, Mooney responded. In comparison with the guarded prose of her memoir, the letter is an insight into her personal thoughts. On 27 October 1953, Mooney wrote:

> I wish you'd let me work for you in New York, our National Theatre is so hopelessly mismanaged that it is the grave of all one's hopes; ideas are smothered at birth and to speak the language of the Theatre is to be looked upon as an arty person with grandiose ideas – for six years I have been as a voice crying in the wilderness. It would be heaven to have a School of Acting in New York.[61]

At this point, the Abbey company had taken refuge in the Queen's Theatre. (This supposedly temporary arrangement would last for almost 14 years.) To Mooney's despair, the repertoire was full of plays that were 'monotonously alike'.[62] Helburn's polite reply quietly killed the idea of Ria returning to New York. On reflection, Mooney told her: 'As a matter of fact I'd DIE from the strain of life in your enormous capital. How you stand the pace I do not know!'[63] The women continued to correspond, Mooney delighting in the connection with the international theatre world, and happy to share her 'Paris plans'.[64] O'Casey's *The Plough and the Stars* again was providing a joyous challenge. She was directing a production that would open the Paris Festival in May. Blythe had even been persuaded to allow Michael O'Herlihy to design new sets. To be working on a 'good' play, Mooney told her friend in April 1955, was 'a holiday for all of us!'[65]

The production in Paris was more than a holiday: the Abbey company received third prize in the festival, behind China's Opera de Peking and Brecht's Berliner Ensemble. European newspapers contained positive reviews, but Mooney returned to the Abbey after this exhilarating reprieve to find that Dublin audiences thought little of the prestigious award and the status it brought.

Still striking as Mary Tyrone

Ernest Blythe was delighted to bring back Frank Dermody as company director, in place of Mooney, in the spring of 1959. It was not an act of chicanery; Mooney conceded the position for something more valuable: the role of Mrs James Tyrone in Eugene O'Neill's play, *Long Day's Journey Into Night*. After years of pressure from Mooney and from the ambitious young actor Vincent Dowling, Blythe conceded to stage the play. He thought the project a harmless caper, which at worst could temporarily distract from his own agenda. With no understanding of the devotion of this small team to the epic family drama, he indulged the actors, hoping to benefit from the deal in the future.

The text demanded a 13-week rehearsal period, extended from the usual 12 days that had become management (or Blythe's) policy. Six days a week, three to five hours a day, the cast rehearsed. Dowling remembers:

> Even after the official rehearsals, in pubs or restaurants or walking the streets, afternoons, evenings and even nights, TP [McKenna] and I and often Philip [O'Flynn] went on teasing out this long, tightly woven, profoundly personal, painful material of O'Neill's with Frank Dermody.[66]

While the men paced the streets together, reciting O'Neill in the pubs and dark streets around Dublin, Mooney worked alone.

Mrs Mary Cavan James Tyrone, the mother, is 54 years old. She has a face that is 'distinctly Irish in type' and is 'still striking'.[67] In her memoirs, Mooney devotes less than a page to describing the challenge of the part. She recalls attending to practical production work in the mornings, before rehearsing for the afternoon and then memorising lines until late into the night. In private rehearsals at home, it took two and a half hours to speak the lines on cue with a friend. While recording the practical facts, the ageing actress says nothing of the physical and mental struggles during the production that many others in the cast remember.

Mooney studied O'Neill's description:

> Her voice is soft and attractive. When she is merry, there is a touch of Irish lilt in it. Her most appealing quality is the simple, unaffected charm of a shy convent-girl youthfulness she has never lost—an innate unworldly innocence.[68]

But this charm is laced with 'extreme nervousness', much of which the character carries in her hands. They are knotted with rheumatism 'so that now they have an ugly crippled look'.[69] Mrs Tyrone is ever conscious of and humiliated by her fingers. As well as the lengthy monologues to memorise, with the melodious vocal work she was known for, Mooney tried to perfect the physical characteristics of a morphine addict, focusing on how she held her hands to conceal their deformity. Such delicate work she had seen before; this echoes Le Gallienne concealing her burnt hands on the stage over 25 years before.

Dermody never stopped making demands of his male actors, tirelessly working on movement, on the poetry of the text and on finding the perfect stage images to carry the story over the four and a quarter hours running time. With Mooney, he worked differently: 'He gave her notes and direction quietly and privately, in deference to her age, her sex and her position as producer of the Abbey.'[70] Dowling does not countenance that Dermody may have been acting in deference to her experience and acting skills. Dermody worked with her as she had mentored others: quietly, respectfully.

For the first time in many years, Mooney was an ordinary cast member. The detached, disciplined persona she had developed as director began to come away as she increasingly relied on her fellow actors. Some came to her Goatstown home to help her with line runs; others gently supported her backstage during the run when she was struggling with dialogue and with nerves. The actress Kathleen Barrington recalled (in an interview with McGlone) how marvellous she was in rehearsals, how magical to watch while reciting lines, but how on stage some discomfort set in.[71] Her old insecurity, her faltering belief in her skills when the audience sat on the other side of footlights had never gone away. Old age, weariness and the impatience of the young men around her exacerbated the problem. Her terror that her performance wouldn't be 'perfect' haunted her.

Despite the 6.30pm curtain-up and a running time of over four hours, the audience was prompt and attentive at the opening performance in the Queen's Theatre on 28 April 1959. The *Irish Independent* admired all the cast, saying Mooney used her voice 'beautifully' and was 'superb in the nervous desperation and moving in the final witlessness of the mother.'[72] But rather than breaking new ground, the Abbey was seen to be ploughing 'rather poor soil'.[73] *Long Day's Journey Into Night* was replaced on 11 May with John Murphy's *The Country Boy*. Somehow, Mooney had found time and mental energy to direct this new play while spending over four hours on stage each night.

In one of the audiences for O'Neill's epic play was an engineering student who was spending too much time hanging around in the drama society of University College Dublin. Patrick Laffan was stunned by the production: the mammoth text performed without cuts and the mesmerising lead actress. Even this inexperienced student recognised while these weren't 'the starriest actors', something special was happening at the Abbey; it was a major breakthrough for the institution. For Laffan, 'the sheer sincerity of the production was compelling.'[74]

Laffan had no idea that night that when the play would be revived three years later, he would be in the wings. He joined the company in the summer of 1961, auditioning for Blythe and Mooney less than a week after his graduation. For the Dublin Theatre Festival in 1962, there was a revival of *Long Day's Journey Into Night*; it was to be performed at the Queen's Theatre on alternate nights for two weeks. Mooney would still be the small, feisty woman Laffan remembered watching from the stalls, but this time he would be prompting her from a hidden spot in the wings. Indeed, he would be *trying to* prompt her, as she flailed desperately with lines and cues. It was often impossible to save her, even with his presence stage left and a stage manager prompting from stage right.

During that revival, the character's extreme nervousness began to seep into real life. Somebody noticed that Mooney's balance was unsteady as she blocked scenes with the director. There were rumours of a fall from the stage when she appeared using a cane to help her walk, although nobody ever asked the question directly. McGlone interviewed a number of actors with vivid memories of the production. The accounts vary in their depiction of her state; many return to the one word: vulnerable.[75]

In the three years after the Irish premiere of *Long Day's Journey Into Night*, Mooney directed six new plays at the Abbey. Nervous anxiety was now causing her increased spates of memory loss and she was notably weaker and openly disillusioned. Her isolation was compounded by tensions backstage: the actors were moving towards a strike, demanding more money in tandem with an improved artistic regime. The newly-established Players' Council sought more contemporary plays with longer rehearsal periods, and some of the most influential members thought little of Mooney's old-fashioned discipline. There was a malicious complaint that 'she couldn't direct traffic'.[76] But there was still work for Mooney to do and her sense of theatre remained impeccable.

Discovering *The Enemy Within*

With his usual distaste for anything slightly unconventional, in 1962 Ernest Blythe passed off to Mooney a new play entitled *The Enemy Within*. She had been repeatedly overlooked as a director for new productions and had chosen to bear the slights to her reputation with silent dignity. Despite her frailty, when she read the script by first-time playwright Brian Friel, Ria was captivated by the tale of St Columba and his struggle to choose between the monastic life and his home. Mooney was amongst the first to identify the talent of one of Ireland's foremost playwrights.

The Enemy Within stages an imagined life of St Columba and some of his faithful followers in Iona in 587AD. With warmth and wit, it puts modern dialogue into the mouths of these mythic figures. Although it didn't achieve the same level of popular success as Friel's later play, *Philadelphia, Here I Come*, it bears the marks of a growing dramatic consciousness: fluid dialogue, compelling characters, and emotional ambition. The action is gentle; the drama is in the conflicts between the characters. Mooney cast Ray MacAnally in the lead and assembled a strong team of male actors around him. She arrived into the 12-day rehearsal period knowing that some of those actors (such as Dowling) had little respect for her methods, but she was intent on honouring Friel's work.

Laffan, who appeared in one scene of that production, remembers Friel as a well-heeled schoolteacher with an acerbic wit, driving the entire cast around Derry in his posh new motorcar.[77] Mooney didn't accompany the all-male company on that tour to Friel's hometown. Laffan also remembers the script as being 'kind of perfect' and the cast were deemed 'outstanding' by critics.[78] Although he felt the play had weaknesses, the *Irish Press* critic was adamant on 7 August 1962: 'Ria Mooney's vigorous direction also helps to make this play one of the most adult and interesting the Abbey has given us recently.'[79] 'Adult' and 'interesting' were features that drew Mooney to plays.

The final production she directed at the Abbey in 1963, *Copperfaced Jack* by John O'Donovan, was plagued by rows about unauthorised script changes and a general disrespect for the author that smacks of Blythe rather than the ever-courteous Mooney. Hugh Hunt claims she had a nervous breakdown; it's not clear how he adduced this, there is no behaviour or evidence to support it.[80] At age 60, Mooney resigned from her position of Director of Plays in English, when her 'way at last became clear'.[81] This carefully chosen phrase conceals the truth, but personal friends believe that Mooney finally retired only when she had secured money from an old friend in America to support herself.[82]

Mooney now lived alone in Goatstown, infirm and increasingly reclusive. Having awoken from 'the nightmare' of her last few years at the Abbey, she spent time writing her memoirs.[83] Sporadically, she attended the theatre, where she was amused by the huge number of production staff listed in the programmes. The Abbey's new building she thought: 'functional—and quite without character'.[84]

All her life, the theatre was Mooney's home; now it offered no solace. In fact, nothing did. In July 1969, she wrote to Mary O'Malley of the Lyric Theatre in Belfast, telling her of the death of Mrs Kick Erlanger. She told her, 'I don't know what I would have done without my friend in America.'[85] Grief-stricken, Mooney wrote to O'Malley: 'I have lost all desire ever to take part in any performance, in any capacity.'[86] Old friends and colleagues did their best to help, but her health deteriorated rapidly and Ria Mooney died on 3 January 1973. She left behind her memoirs, completed but unpublished.

The closing scene

There was a party hosted by Mrs Martin Beck in an apartment on West 55th Street in New York in June 1956, with Mooney as the guest of honour, accompanied by her friend Mrs Milton (Kick) Erlanger. Mooney was spending a month's holiday in New Jersey. These women had known each other since their 30s, when Mooney's artistic consciousness had started to take shape. This time, the 53-year-old Mooney, a successful director, arrived in New York by airplane. Yet despite the external changes, Mooney believed: 'Women will never change. The fashions may change but women won't.'[87] She often sought in her New York circle affection and warmth that energised and rejuvenated her, something no longer available to her at the Abbey. As Mooney told Helburn in June 1956:

> I can't tell you how happy I was to be back [in New York] again. How all that warm friendship one receives in America lifts and enlarges the spirit. My debt to your country increases with the years.[88]

For the women in Mrs Beck's house that evening, it was a time to catch up, to remember old times and share new plans.

There is a temptation to trace the origins of Mooney's theatre work to one artistic theory, but in fact there are several. From Yeats and the Fay brothers, she understood the work of Andre Antoine's Théâtre Libre and the style of performance in place at the foundation of the Abbey. Working with Le Gallienne and Nazimova, she gained a firm grounding in Stanislavski, a theoretical basis adapted by the Civic Repertory Theatre. Le Gallienne combined Stanislavski's system with the semi-religious artistic principles of Eleonora Duse. Although Le Gallienne intimidated her, Mooney learnt much from her. Duse championed the destruction of the ego, the complete abandonment of the personal to allow the body to serve a higher power on the stage. Ria Mooney followed that path. She also admired the ideals of the Civic Repertory: the notion that everybody, regardless of financial circumstances or social status, had the right to access art and theatre of the highest quality and to appreciate its beauty.

With Le Gallienne, Mooney trained as an implicitly feminist director and teacher, guiding and mentoring others to come to their own understanding of their craft and aiding their individual creation of characters. Like her mentor, Mooney implemented a professional rehearsal process with well-honed technique, intellect, empathy and respect at its core. The failure of this regime at the Abbey Theatre arguably is more revealing of the artistic environment there under Blythe's management than of Mooney's skills. Outside of Ireland, her direction of O'Casey's *The Plough and the Stars* in 1955 was so esteemed that it put the Abbey Theatre in the same rank as the Berliner Ensemble.

Mooney brought back with her from the US a firm grounding in Stanislavski technique along with a clear understanding of the European philosophies of acting and her work also bore the mark of Le Gallienne's strident feminism. She did her utmost to impart these ideals in Dublin, where it was permitted. While it is not appropriate to deem her the first Artistic Director of the Abbey Theatre, as the title did not exist during her tenure, in practice Mooney was the first feminist director at the Irish National Theatre. To date, this contribution to Irish theatre history has never been acknowledged. Female artistic directors Lelia Doolan and Garry Hynes would follow in her footsteps, both with a clear understanding of what Mooney had aimed to achieve with her directing and teaching and where she had met resistance within the institution.

At the same time as she developed her acting craft, Mooney increasingly drew on modernist aesthetics and abstract art. She was a radical modernist in her art and her thinking; few in Dublin understood this mode at that time. She always moved enthusiastically into the future holding firm to the principles she'd adopted in her youth. By day, she worked with Irish dramatists and actors steeped in conservative drama and by night, she rehearsed with niche groups exploring experimental modes. Out of this dense complex of influences, she drew an aesthetic of beautiful simplicity.

It is characteristic of Mooney that the only documented evidence of her theories is found in personal letters she wrote to students. In 1936, she wrote to Lilian Roberts and urged her, 'If you are going to be an artist—you must be yourself!'[89] Ria recognised something of herself in the young Dublin girl:

> We happen to be the type of person whose sensitivities make us self-conscious in the way that is bad for acting; because we tighten up on emotions, and work exclusively with our minds ...'[90]

She told her: '[I]t's through years of heartbreak, discouragement, and hard work that I've come to learn what I now know —'[91] Encouraging him to continue to work on his talent, Mooney wrote to actor Pat Laffan on 25 June 1962 in a letter he kept in a private collection:

> Follow your instinct and listen to criticism, then try to analyse that criticism in stage terms. Work, so far as acting is concerned, is learning lines, moving easily and naturally in character and <u>RELAXING INTO THE PART.</u> Stupid people often make better actors than the more intelligent because they are less likely to work too hard on analysing character and leave their acting to instinct.[92]

This simplicity of method can be traced directly to her casting as Rosie Redmond in *The Plough and the Stars.* Above all else, Mooney sought to understand, inhabit and honour the minds of individual women:

> I knew how women behaved when they wore these [costumes], what they wore underneath or if they wore anything. Best of all I believed I knew what went on inside their heads.[93]

Stanislavski believed: 'empathy can be a more powerful prompt to creativity than personal emotion.'[94] Ria followed this teaching. Knowing what was going on inside the heads but also feeling what was going on inside the hearts of Irish women, everything else became possible for Ria Mooney.

Chapter 4

Aideen Again: After the 1937/38 Tour

In a room in the Courtyard Marriott hotel in Culver City, Los Angeles, one balmy August evening, Christine Shields shows me the diaries her mother, Aideen, had kept sporadically between 1939 and approximately 1945. Christine has set up her laptop on the desk, showing me where she has started transcribing the notes as the thin, fragile diaries are starting to wear and the ink to fade. She is recently retired and has set herself this task. I help her decipher some of the scrawls; she knows many of the words before I do. She has some questions about the Abbey I can answer; Christine has many answers for me. It is Christine who explains her mother's alcoholism, how the family had known of it, how it progressed and how the family (as well as the local parish priest) tried to stop the secret drinking that eventually took over her life.

The journals are some of the few items Christine Shields did not include in the bequest to the Hardiman Library. She also kept some jewellery, inexpensive but pretty. I hold in my palm the delicate pendant Aideen once wore. My heart beats faster as we sit together on the bed and start to leaf through the journals. They aren't fulsome, vivid descriptions of scenes as her letters had been. They are short, personal notes–mainly recording dates and appointments. Christine is gracious enough to let me check dates and places, and to show me moments where Aideen's mood and state of mind is clear. Christine explains that the Shields Archive, now in Galway, was collected by a number of women: Lini Saurin, a sister of her father's, as well as Laurie Shields, her stepmother, who moved to Ireland in 1972 to write a book about Arthur Shields that was never published. I feel as if I'm being handed a baton, asked to pick up a trail. Sitting there, with the journals in my hands, is the moment I begin to believe in the presence of ghosts.

We made plans that evening, Christine and I, and we kept them. As well as a visit to her mother's grave, and to that of Sara Allgood, we went to the homes she'd lived in. We had a special dinner in Aideen's favourite restaurant, Musso Franks on Hollywood Boulevard. We celebrated her mother, and Aideen's friendships and family. There is no doubt that this life story comes with a tragic ending; it is a story of potential and of loss. And yet, I hope this chapter serves as an example of how fragmentary archives can be re-constituted, to allow a narrative to be drawn or created. Moments of vitality and pure joy can be found in the letters and photographs; we can choose to focus on these.

During the period of travelling with the Abbey company from autumn 1937 to June of 1938, Aideen's letters display a contentment that eluded her in Ireland. In San Francisco, she found serenity. The harbour reminded her of Cobh, and after the fog and snow of St Louis, everything radiated with the West Coast sunlight. Her stomach cramps had settled; a doctor had diagnosed a pulled muscle and provided medication. They arrived in The New Olympic Hotel late at night and she woke the next morning to streams of sunlight coming through her window and the prospect of a week's rest before they performed again.[1]

Ria and Frolie were occupied elsewhere; Aideen refers to 'the boys and myself' in her jaunts to the beach and the countryside, or exploring the city.[2] Arthur Shields was never far away. The other 'boys' were company members Joe Linnane and Austin Meldon. They all shared a cable car to Fisherman's Wharf, wandered around Chinatown and for dinner had chicken chow mein, cold pork with ginger and fried rice. There were cocktails, as well as Chinese wine and tea. Going to see the cartoon *Snow White and the Seven Dwarves* for the first time, Aideen was the beautiful lady at the centre of this circle of charming men.

Her letters to her sisters from this time give no intimation of a relationship with Shields. O'Connor told her sister that she was contemplating marriage to a responsible lawyer that offered her a luxurious life. This Boston lawyer was called Madison and she said: 'I'm not in love with him. However, my last love affair was so disastrous to all concerned that possibly I can get along without love this time.'[3] Off stage, O'Connor adopted a casual, comfortable look, wearing slack suits with sandals and ankle socks. She described one 'natty get up':

> I wear my new slack suit, which consists of a very fine worsted material in purpley navy, the slacks are beautifully fitting and have a concealed zipper down the side, a pleat in the back and a buttoned breast pocket. The pants button on the top. It's a cute idea and they're awfully comfy. I'm wearing a red cowboy handkerchief round my neck and red ankle socks (no stockings or girdle etc) and red and green and blue sandals and ditto ribbon in my hair.[4]

One morning, she got up early and went out to buy an adornment for her room. Then she retreated there to write letters and enjoy the view:

> This morning I went out and bought bluebells, hyacinths, daffodils and marigolds – 4 large bowls full for 75c. My room has two big windows and the sun pours in. I can look right across the bay from where I'm sitting now. There are ships passing all the time.[5]

The emotional turmoil and public shame of the previous spring was behind her; she was a successful actress considering a life in Boston as a lawyer's wife.

While Aideen relaxed with Shields and the others, Frolie Mulhern accompanied Ria Mooney on a sight-seeing excursion to a Chinese Temple. When they arrived, led by a sweet Chinese girl called Rose, and saw the High Priest with his 'shabby coat and shabbier cap', they realised this was a performance of its own kind, but handed over their dollars anyway.[6] Joss sticks were lit before colourful images and gods invoked in a strange tongue; the Irish women kept their heads down, resisting the urge to laugh or cough in the air thick with incense. Eventually, the High Priest rose from kneeling and opened scrolls, at random, to read passages aloud in Chinese. He exchanged words in a grave tone with Rose before the ritual concluded.[7] Outside, Ria pressed Rose for an explanation of the message. In curiously-accented English, the girl reluctantly revealed that the High Priest had foretold of Mooney's death within a year. The girl was sad; she held out her hand. Ria laughed loudly; Mulhern joined in. Both believed the High Priest was nothing but a 'money-making racket'.[8]

From the relaxed sunshine of San Francisco, the company travelled by train to the dry heat of downtown Los Angeles. With Wickes now at the helm, the one dark cloud that hung over them was the ill health of actor P. J. (Paddy) Carolan. Carolan was suffering from TB. As his condition worsened, he began to drink heavily. O'Connor told her sister:

Paddy is all right when he's sober but at times it's been grim. It's awfully hard on Dossie and Boss who have to do his work. I'm afraid he's quite hopeless – nothing seems to have any effect on him.[9]

By the time they checked into the Hotel Clarke in downtown Los Angeles, it was evident that Carolan was not going to recover—from his lung condition or alcoholism. His surrogate family rallied around and all of the actors contributed what they could afford to pay for a special train compartment so he could travel home comfortably. They agreed to keep this private until his family were notified and arrangements made. Aideen then wrote to her sister to say, 'We did all we could for him'.[10] The company waved off the thin, dejected man with real grief; they had done all they could to stop him drinking. Aideen watched, it seems, with a sense of incomprehension of such a struggle with alcohol.

The women took every available opportunity to sunbathe on the roof of the Hotel Clarke. In the evenings, there were parties in Hollywood. On consecutive nights in April, the Abbey company visited RKO and Paramount studios. They had already been hosted at 20th Century Fox. It appears all of the actresses were offered screen tests and promised work, but Aideen wasn't as naïve as she had been on her earlier tour. She guarded herself against disappointment. It was clear to her how all of the studios were 'retrenching like hell' and she doubted if her screen test would materialise.[11] Aware there was a strong possibility that 'when the tour will be over they just lose interest', she determined to finish the tour and then return to London to look for work.[12] Lying on the sun-drenched hotel roof, recovering from another party, O'Connor was considering Boston, Hollywood and London—but not Dublin. There was no future for her there, professionally or personally. Yet she took the boat back with the company, bringing with her a small trousseau for her sister Eileen's June wedding.

Frolie goes back to Enniskillen

Despite the fact she had left Elbert Wickes behind, Frolie appears to have settled back into the Abbey Theatre more easily than her best friend. Aideen's dispute with her father continued to rage after her return; she had to seek somewhere else to live. Frolie was welcomed back to Ailesbury Road with open arms: there was teasing about her wearing slacks and she unpacked presents of candies and toys for her brood of nieces and nephews.[13] She also visited family in Enniskillen and stayed there for some time, 'renewing old friendships and adding, if that were possible, to her widespread popularity.'[14]

Frolie continued to get comic roles in new productions at the Abbey. Aideen wrote to Choate of seeing Mulhern appear in a new play by J. K. Montgomery called *Heritage*, declaring her friend's portrayal as a movie-struck servant to be 'grand'.[15] Mulhern continued to smoke, drink and entertain endlessly with her uncanny impressions, but some of those around her had come to know that she was weak and attending a doctor.[16]

In early October 1938, the Abbey company began rehearsing *Pilgrims*, a play by a first-time playwright, Mary Rynne. Educated in London but now living in Clare, Rynne was a prolific fiction writer before she began writing for the stage. Frolie was cast as Kitty Brady, who enters in the first act of *Pilgrims* 'amidst applause from outside. She is a pretty, giggling small-town Miss; even in her uniform she looks "dressy".'[17] Kitty is a society girl, who joins a pilgrimage to Italy hoping for a miracle: to pass the matriculation exam she has failed three times and so be able to enter university. Her petition is not granted; they learn that only the first visitor to the shrine will be successful. Kitty Brady doesn't gain exam success but is pleased by the male attention she receives during her travels and is married off to the 50-something Captain as the play ends.

In the final scene of *Pilgrims*, she and the Captain that led the pilgrimage have an exchange:

> KITTY.   I do very well on my own.
> CAPTAIN. You don't. You couldn't. You need protection, assistance, gentle correction—[18]

Frolie had traditionally played comedic roles, but here there was a definite suggestion that she would not, as others suggested, follow in Maureen Delany's footsteps. Instead, she was showing her ability to play the romantic heroine or to give a fresh interpretation to the depiction of young Irish women. As with many of the plays of the time, the females were to be disciplined, brought into line by their prospective lovers. Yet Frolie (like Deevy's heroine Katie Roche) was pushing gently at the boundaries of the role with her lively and spirited performance of the maturing woman. Her dramatic range was broadening. The *Irish Independent* critic singled her out saying, 'I have never enjoyed Frolie Mulhern more than I did in her study of Kitty.'[19] Aideen did not have a part in *Pilgrims*.

The following spring, Frolie was approached by Arthur Shields about taking a role in a New York production of Paul Vincent Carroll's new play *Kindred*. He noted: '[Frolie] is very keen to work in the States again.' He was certain that if Mulhern got a firm offer of work that she would go back.[20] Yet, as time passed, he worried about her strength and noted her family appeared intent on keeping her at home.

One newspaper cutting in her scrapbook gives a unique glimpse of Mulhern as an, 'accomplished diseuse,' in her family hometown of Enniskillen in August 1939.[21] There, she performed in an evening of vaudeville entertainment, of 'mystery, music and mirth' where her dramatic talents 'charmed and pleased' the local audience.[22] At the packed event, in aid of the parochial bazaar, Mulhern was obliged to recite 'no fewer than six pieces,' with her 'imitation of the dialect and mannerisms of the people of home and foreign countries being exceptionally clever.'[23] Her touring of the US left a lasting impression and in her own way, she introduced Wickes and her other American friends to her family.

An emergency approaches

By the end of the 1937/38 tour, Aideen determined, 'I shall take a room somewhere in Dublin if Daddy wishes to keep up his attitude towards me.'[24] Her father was furious with what he thought of as unseemly behaviour: her relationship with an older, married and Protestant man. Higgins had also taken against the actress, mainly, it appears, for her off-stage behaviour.[25] In the Abbey Theatre minute books from March 1939, Higgins informs the board that he has written to Phyllis Ryan and encouraged her, with the promise of a possible small contract, to come back from London.[26] Later, he reveals she will now be playing 'most of the parts previously played by Aideen O'Connor, she will be constantly in work for many weeks to come'.[27] Aideen would not be in work. She was also left without an income. In the preparations for the Abbey Festival scheduled for August, she was cast only in a small role in *The Well of the Saints* by J. M. Synge. After years of growing exposure and popularity, O'Connor was returned to the unspeaking chorus.

Coinciding with Horse Show Week, the 12-day Abbey Festival in 1938 presented 17 plays to an audience drawn from America, Britain and the Continent as well as Ireland. During the day, the

Gresham Hotel on O'Connell Street hosted lectures on the theatre and its dramatists, along with exhibitions and manuscripts on view. The *Spectator* journalist visiting from the UK was so bored that he didn't stay to see Shields reprise his role as Christy in *Playboy of the Western World*, which concluded the programme.[28] He went to the Gaiety instead. Dent also described the premiere of *Purgatory* as 'an unsmiling symbolical fragment that gives us parricide and filicide cheek by jowl'.[29] Neither the *Spectator* journalist nor the Abbey directorate seemed to know or understand the meaning of Yeats' play.

At an open lecture on the work of W. B. Yeats in the Gresham Hotel on a Wednesday afternoon, the actress Shelah Richards stood up in the audience. The lecturer was F. R. Higgins and a Reverend Connolly (Head of English at Boston College) had asked a question from the back of the room about the symbolism of *Purgatory*. Robinson, the chairman, deemed it an unfair question to pose to Higgins; Richards disagreed. According to the *Evening Herald*, she pointed out, 'He had put his question with great courtesy and sincerity, and as he genuinely desired information, he should be answered.'[30] Higgins did not give an answer, either as to what Yeats meant or what he himself thought the piece to mean.

Many members of the company were at the lecture. In watching Shelah Richards confront Higgins, Aideen would have seen an established, professional actress take on a man whom she detested but had to be seen to obey. Richards' social standing meant that she had the power to speak out in a way O'Connor was denied, and here she was, openly challenging Higgins to interpret Yeats' work. If Aideen did wish to emulate the confidence of Shelah Richards, she was acutely aware of their class differences. Where Aideen had written a letter to the board apologising for behaviour deemed insubordinate (and still lost her secretarial post), Richards could have her say, flounce out of the hotel and drive herself home in her sports car to her large house in Greystones.[31] Richards would go on to become a successful theatre and radio producer, yet she already spoke like somebody with influence. She had money and she had social status both from her wealthy Protestant background (of Anglo-Irish ascendancy) and through her marriage to barrister and playwright Denis Johnston. Richards herself once wrote, 'We were born respectable. We can't be anything else.'[32] Lower-middle-class women such as O'Connor, without financial independence or a family name deemed respectable, were at a distinct disadvantage in such power relations.

Aideen appeared in a minor role in Synge's play *The Well of the Saints*; the bit-part was a step back in her career. She would soon be considered too old for the juvenile parts for which she'd become known. The other women continued in their careers much as before; obstacles were being put in the way of Aideen O'Connor's progression.

Two months after the August festival, Aideen's role in *The Far-Off Hills* was given to newcomer Phyllis Ryan. Frolie Mulhern had been refused a contract by the board on the basis that she was 'not sufficiently useful' but had retained her role as the other sister, Anna.[33] At 18, Phyllis Ryan was more suitable for the part than either of the other two women, yet it was a slight to push Aideen out in this way. Frolie was in an awkward situation, yet her career was too important to refuse the part. She giggled and conspired with Ryan by candlelight in the bedroom setting.

Both Aideen and Shields were excluded by Higgins from a trip to Cambridge in April 1939. Furious, O'Connor told an American friend, producer Eddie Choate, 'I don't know when I'll be playing again […] Higgins appears to hate me with a deadly hate!'[34] While she tried to remain polite, the strain was showing. She declared, 'One of these days [my tongue] will come unstuck and I'll tell Higgins what I and the rest of the world think of him—and be fired forever from the Abbey!'[35] There's desperation behind her fury. Her patience with Abbey management was wearing thin, and she was increasingly unhappy in Dublin.

Staying with Anne and Mrs George Yeats in Rathfarnham one Sunday night, O'Connor told Mrs Yeats 'very solemnly' that 'Mr Higgins has a very good business head.'[36] While to her superiors, she remained polite and respectful, Aideen had good reason to detest the man. Higgins' rancour could have been due to her relationship with Shields, or her earlier perceived insubordination, but other evidence suggests Higgins had a strong streak of misogyny.[37] His relations with the male actors were strained, but there is no evidence that he bullied them in the way women suffered from his mistreatment.

Higgins revelled in his power over these women, his ability to dispense with them at will, and he took any suggestion of insubordination as licence to make their working lives impossible. His relationship to the men suggested similar callousness, but he did not view them as dispensable and he relied on certain men, including Shields, for support. Aideen tried to co-operate, but the relationship with Higgins never improved. Ultimately, he was always in control and he used his power to push her out of the company and thus out of Ireland to find work.

The 1938 Abbey Festival ended with a large, relaxed party backstage at the theatre after the curtain came down on a performance of *Shadow and Substance*. The members of the company acted as hosts and hostesses, greeting guests and offering raffle tickets for sale before inviting them to find a spot to sit in the green room. The 'intimate meeting' let friends mingle with the directors and the actors on the stairs backstage or in the offices and green room upstairs.[38] When called upon, P. V. Carroll made a speech 'with a few touching remarks' about the departed Paddy Carolan.[39] The company observed a respectful silence, remembering their dear friend and the difficult scenes on tour as his illness progressed. After the raffle to raise money for the benefit funds, the company carried on dancing and drinking and talking theatre until the early hours. Few knew that, amid the riotous jollity, Aideen O'Connor and Arthur Shields were planning a new life together.

Some weeks later, Shields arranged a meeting with W. B. Yeats in the Hibernian Club on Stephen's Green and explained his dissatisfaction with the theatre, along with sharing details of his personal life.[40] He had been offered a role on Broadway. Yeats assured him there would always be a place for him in the Abbey but advised him to go. In October, Yeats left for France. The same month, the London *Times* announced that Shields and O'Connor would be travelling to New York (along with Shelah Richards) to appear in *Spring Meeting*, a play by M. J. Farrell and John Perry.[41]

At the point of their arrival in New York with the company for *Spring Meeting*, Shields was a respected actor but Aideen was struggling to move out of ingénue parts, despite her noted talent. He played a faithful servant who first appears in Act 3 of the play; Baby Furze (played by O'Connor) was at the centre of the plot. The lovers may have been looking forward to spending Christmas alone in their lodgings in the Whitby building, but they would be chaperoned by Shelah Richards, also in the cast. The three Irish actors worked throughout January with director John Gielgud, learning the witty text penned by a smart, publicity-shy female writer based in Ireland called Molly Keane (She used the pen name M. J. Farrell).

A few weeks into the popular run for *Spring Meeting*, these three Abbey stalwarts saw a newspaper feature they didn't approve of. The article referred to the 'all-British' cast of the play. Shields penned a letter setting out their patriotism and clarifying that a certain number of the actors were 'citizens of the Irish Free State' and therefore 'IRISH, not English.'[42] There's a jovial tone to the letter, signed by Shields, O'Connor, Richards and also actor Denis Carey. They identify themselves as Abbey actors and stress that the letter was written for the purposes of 'clarification, not rancour'.[43] Their assertion of nationalism is perhaps less surprising than the loyalty they express to the Abbey Theatre.

Mere days after that letter was published, the three actors and friends heard the news of the death of W. B. Yeats. He had died in France, with his wife George at his side. In their rooms in the Whitby building, looking out on the lights of Broadway, they waited for news from home of funeral arrangements and tributes. All three feared for the future of the Abbey Theatre under the tyranny of Higgins; not one of them would return to perform there. Far from the mourning in Dublin, they continued to perform. Aideen O'Connor was a professional and she would not let down Philip Merivale, the producer who frequently sat in on rehearsals and often took her for dinner.[44]

The successful production transferred to The Little Theatre in February 1939. Spring was creeping up Fifth Avenue, blossoms were braving the cold air in Central Park, and the fashions began to change. The theatre's *Fashion Report* described how 'chiffons wisped airily up and down the aisles', silk wraps reappeared, and 'prints and lighter colours' had begun to appear.[45] Some of the women wore opera-length gloves in black kid and bright-colored evening gloves. For up-to-the-minute accessories, women wore pearls twisted high around the neck, and headdresses of ivory lace 'like a Martha Washington bonnet'.[46]

This was the stylish audience that came to see *Spring Meeting*. The production's scene design, depicting the interior of the Furze household in Woodruff, Co. Tipperary, was lavish and Aideen's part was fun. But O'Connor knew Equity restrictions would limit her time in New York. Shields was supporting his wife at home and she didn't earn much, so money was scarce.

As Shields' new partner, Aideen O'Connor had learnt not to show insecurities. She gave the impression of being a strong woman not to be cowed, but she knew of Shelah Richards' friendship with Mac (Bazie Shields) and of Richards' own marital difficulties. The programme notes joke of Johnson's inability to pin down his wife; in fact, the couple were already living separate lives. He was in another relationship. Richards had two children and aspirations to become a director. Minutes before the curtain went up, Aideen and Shelah came together and took positions on the stage for their opening scene. It opened:

> Seated on the stool L.C., JOAN FURZE is trying an enormous Dorothy Walker model on to BABY FURZE, who is standing L. in front of her. They both seem despairing. BABY can see herself in a long mirror which is leaning against the table behind the settee.[47]

Baby (O'Connor) scowls at her appearance in the mirror, disconsolate at the ill-fitting and out-of-fashion evening dress. Joan Furze (Richards) fusses around the dress with pins and scissors, trying to make the best of it. Joan is the 32-year-old daughter of the penurious Sir Richard, who manages the household. She is bitter about her life: 'Never a drink or a party. Nothing but doing the flowers and fighting with [Aunt] Bijou and growing older.'[48] Both girls are victims of their father's stinginess and rudeness, but Baby retains her youth, energy and determination to find a different life for herself. Tiny Fox-Collier arrives hoping to marry her son Tony off to Joan for her inheritance of Woodruff, but Tony falls for Baby. Meanwhile, Joan's relationship with the family's groom is ended by her father.

Baby is the most innocent and yet most dynamic member of the Furze household. She charms and flirts her way through life in Tipperary, cheerfully manipulating servants and her father to get her way. When her spinster aunt insists that no lady looks for a husband, she responds: 'I think of it often and I want one, and I'll have one too.'[49] Tiny Fox-Collier describes her as 'entirely undeveloped mentally' and notes she has 'a brogue you can cut with a knife'.[50] But she seduces Tony with her beauty and wit, and by appearing in the sitting room wrapped only in an eiderdown. Aideen O'Connor's sexuality was not just on open display; it was the punch line of jokes. At one point she asks him, 'What do you think I am – a child on the threshold of life?' Tony responds, 'I don't know what you'd do on a threshold. You're wonderful in a hay loft.'[51]

On stage each night, O'Connor was the pretty coquette, nipping sips from her father's brandy glass and cadging money to pay for cigarettes. The play allowed her to declare, and enjoy, her sexuality, and to perform being of a social class where she could talk openly without fear of financial or other penalties. After the curtain fell, the actress was weary from stress. The awkward circumstances with Richards, career issues, and money problems were strains on her relationship with Shields. She was coming to accept there was no future for her on the Irish stage. But for all the worry, there was a vibrant group of theatre people in New York. Notes in her journals show a life packed with rehearsals, dinners and parties. They mention meetings with Iris Whitney and a new friend called 'Kay'. As life became more complex for Aideen, a New Yorker called Kay Swift swept into her life, like the rousing chords of a Broadway show's opening number.

Kinship and friendship

The relationships between all of these women, both in the company and with other women in theatre they encountered, were key networks in their lives, regardless of their relationships with men. O'Connor defined herself by her position in the middle of her two sisters and the tempestuous nature of her friendship with Frolie Mulhern showed their intimacy and reliance on each other. At the same time, the attitude of the older women towards the young novices was a crucial dynamic in the company. (This includes Bazie's attitude to Aideen as well as Aideen's treatment of Phyllis Ryan.) Much like the character of Amelia Gregg in Deevy's play *Katie Roche*, they formed a model of respectable Irish femininity showing women how they could 'make it grand'.[52] The elder generation often deplored the younger women's behaviour, which they viewed as rebellious or simply unseemly. Female friendship is a crucial feature of the biography of any woman, and O'Connor's connection with Kay Swift is fascinating for its apparent unlikeliness, its obvious strength, and for its indelible mark on O'Connor's personality and her conception of herself as an actress and a woman.

Kay Swift was a Broadway composer, a divorcee, and a busy socialite. This small, elegant lady with dark, carefully-coiffed hair and huge eyes 'always wanted the works, every minute' and felt entitled to have it.[53] She had an infectious energy, living constantly to the rhythm of her first Broadway hit, aptly titled *Fine and Dandy*. Swift and O'Connor had little in common in terms of background, but they shared a love of drama and an understanding of complicated love affairs. Swift had a long relationship with the composer George Gershwin; she assisted him in composing the musical *Porgy and Bess*. The Abbey company saw this musical staged in San Francisco during the early 1930s.[54] However, there's no record that during her first tour in 1934/35, O'Connor saw this work, or that she met Swift. Gershwin's unexpected death in July 1937 was well publicised, but his union with Swift was never official. The women were most likely introduced around 1938 by Swift's new beau, radio star and old acquaintance of the Abbey Players, Eddie Byron.

For all her verve, Swift's life had been beset by vicissitudes. After her father's premature death, she supported her mother with her musical talents, teaching and playing. Marriage to banker (and sometimes lyricist) James Warburg brought a luxurious standard of living, but she abandoned this and gave up custody of her three daughters to continue her musical work and relationship with Gershwin. She was now living alone, composing music for a number of organisations, including the New York World Fair scheduled for 1939. While she rarely stopped working on her musical compositions, she relied on her girlfriends, most especially businesswoman Mary Lasker, for emotional support. She kept Sundays free for 'our good Sabbath gab fests, settling our lives [and] we've really made more progress at that on Sundays than any other days.'[55]

Both O'Connor and Swift had ambitions for career success with a man they adored by their side. Swift repeatedly threw over money and security for passion and excitement. Yet while O'Connor despaired in private, Swift kept her mood light and her hopes high. There was always the prospect of another tune, another paycheck and another lover. Swift always had enough money for a visit to the hairdresser: 'No doing of own hair by this hand', and a Sunday always involved a couple of her favourite 'vod-tons', either out or at home with friends.[56] Swift was, in fact, something of a 'Pollyanna', endlessly positive, an attribute that would infuriate and bolster O'Connor in equal measure. The 'disappointment adjustant' Swift believed she had inherited from her mother served her well and brought joy to those around her; O'Connor lacked such a genetic gift.[57]

Spring Meeting ran at The Little Theatre until the end of February 1940, so that O'Connor was still performing in the city during one of Kay Swift's most dramatic social evenings. At Hampshire House, the 37-storey luxurious apartment building south of Central Park, Mary Lasker was living and working on her design business. Lasker held a cocktail party: a habitual event that ended with guests sodden with drink and emotionally spent after a night of heated arguments and passionate encounters. That evening, Lasker ended her relationship with a married man the women called 'Fiend' to protect his identity. Swift had taken a 'horrible beating' emotionally when Byron dropped her unceremoniously, but that night she met *Time* magazine writer Charles Wertenbaker.[58] O'Connor remained sorry that Swift and Byron had parted ways, but the women's friendship endured.[59]

O'Connor returned to the UK for more auditions after the run of *Spring Meeting* finished, but Shields stayed on, trying to make connections and get further work on Broadway. He met businessman Eddie Choate, and together they set up a production company and secured the rights to produce Paul Vincent Carroll's new play *Kindred*. O'Connor spent more time in England, where she met up with Hugh Hunt and auditioned where possible.[60] With Higgins pushing her out, she had no choice but to seek other work, and in May 1939 she had an interview with the producers of the Shell Theatre in London. There was the prospect of a part in *French Without Tears*, a new comedy of manners by Terence Rattigan. O'Connor had perfected an English accent that would suit this caper, set in a French boarding house. She spent the little money she had travelling to London and finding accommodation, but nothing came of the meeting.[61] When Shields finalised the deal for *Kindred*, he wired with the news. O'Connor rushed back to Dublin at the earliest opportunity. She was staying at her father's house in Ranelagh when she expressed her relief to Choate: 'We're both absolutely thrilled to bits.'[62]

Dublin was miserable. The weather was wet and gloomy and 'There is a very worried look on everyone's face in the streets. [...] There is talk of nothing else but WAR'.[63] *French Without Tears* was a huge success in London; O'Connor watched from afar as Kay Hammond and Rex Harrison went on from the Rattigan play to bigger and bigger success. Carroll's play *Shadow and Substance* was staged again in May. Management at the Abbey Theatre was hoping to capitalise on its earlier popularity even though Hunt (the original director) had left the country. Perhaps to replicate as much as possible the original cast, O'Connor was asked to reprise her role as Thomasina and she appeared with the rising star, Cyril Cusack. At the Dublin theatre, the ignominy of her affair and her public behaviour still lingered. Carroll joked with her about a play he was writing about 'a nice little teaser … with a nose like yours.'[64]

If not rehearsing, O'Connor spent time typing letters in the office or reading in the green room. Eager to get back to the US, to be with Boss and to escape her strained family situation in Ranelagh, she enquired in letters to Eddie Choate about a role in *Kindred* for herself. At the same time, she promoted Frolie Mulhern's talents and added: 'She has a very conservative and religious family and they refuse to believe she wants to go to America again. […] Poor old Frolie–she's longing to go!'[65] O'Connor hated the thought of leaving her best friend behind and continued to coax Mulhern to leave with her. Shields also discussed with Choate the possibility of Mulhern playing the character of Primrose in their first venture, although he revealed, 'The only thing that worries me about her is that she is not very strong.'[66] O'Connor wanted Mulhern with her because she knew that without a confirmed role or money, travelling to the US was going to be a challenge. Requests for a role are repeated breezily, but there's real fear Shields would leave her behind in O'Connor's letter to Choate in May 1939: 'Boss and I have no money whatsoever! … Don't worry about me as I can wait a few weeks longer until Boss earns some money in Hollywood and then sends for me.'[67] O'Connor was now consumed with possible career moves. Hunt was considering staging *Kindred* in the UK and there was a production of Carroll's *White Steed* opening in Glasgow. Both plays were familiar to the actress, and she had Carroll's approval. Hunt suggested there might be a part for her in a UK production, or O'Connor heard of the production and suggested it herself. She was ready to grasp at any part to leave Dublin, but she wouldn't return to England without the blessing of Shields and Choate. One night, desperate for a plan, she sent a telegram:

> Hunt definitely offers part Steed August. Sorry to rush you. Please cable decision re my last letter. Love Aideen.[68]

She may have been hoping to push them into action with news of the UK production; the action rebounded. Choate sent a polite note:

> Their production definite. Mine Not. You make decision. Best Eddie.[69]

Despite her diligence and talent, apparent confidence and headstrong manner, such decisions left her floundering. After impassioned and lengthy discussions about the future, Shields arrived in New York without his partner.[70] On midsummer's day, Aideen took a train to Cork. The Abbey Theatre was, as usual, closed for the month of July. In Cork, she could stay rent-free with her mother's family at 4 Graham's Terrace in the port village of Cobh, from which boats left regularly for America. She had run out of friends to rely on in Dublin.

Preparing for New York

Graham's Terrace has an iron gate, closing it off from the road. The terrace is carved into the hillside; the row of houses hangs precipitously over the steep incline down to the sea. It was a mature, respectable address, halfway between the port and the cathedral perched at the top of the hill. O'Connor could look down on the harbour from her window. It reminded her now of the wharfs of San Francisco, filling her with nostalgia in the same way that in San Francisco she was once nostalgic for Cobh.

Number 4 Graham's Terrace was a place O'Connor associated with the long, lazy summer days of childhood. Now she was 25, and her mother's family knew of the dispute with her father and the unsavoury love life of the actress. She often found herself trapped in the grim light of the house. After months of travelling independently, being toasted and feted, O'Connor was reduced to unpaid housework and childminding. Occasionally, she managed to find a quiet corner and a few minutes to herself to write letters. She sent a note to Choate:

> I had to cable Boss on Sunday about coming earlier. I've struck a bad patch at the moment! I'm here with my mother's people and Uncle Dick arrived home unexpectedly [from military service] and is very ill ... It's frightful. I have to look after the child (who is a fiend) and do all the meals – sit with him for hours on end. He just stares at me without uttering a word. Yesterday I thought I was really going mad.[71]

Shields had learnt to fill his days with calming activities when he wasn't working; he loved his vegetable garden, collecting stamps and reading about trains or talking about them with his son, Adam. O'Connor never had such serenity off stage and the tedium of housework only exacerbated her temper. She said: 'Nothing ever happens in Cobh. Even Atlantic fliers going astray land at Galway—but perhaps the German fleet will anchor in the harbour and that would be news.[72] Away from the career opportunities of Dublin and London, her anxiety intensified and she pleaded with Choate, 'You won't stop writing to me, will you, just because Boss will be in New York?'[73]

Aideen thought the monotony of the house and her daily tasks would kill her and was desperately lonely for her theatre colleagues. Often, when she wrote to Choate, O'Connor had a headache and was feeling physically ill; she may have begun drinking in private to relieve her suffering. Her only valid excuses to leave the house were to attend mass or confession in the Cathedral, or to visit her old friend Sister Mary Monica in the Sisters of Mercy Convent.

Sister Mary Monica remained loyal to Aideen, despite the actress's dark moods, obstinate opinions and sometimes airs of grandeur. She always thought of Aideen as a girl with a strong Catholic faith and a kind heart. O'Connor had fans in America and friends in the Abbey, but there's a searing honesty in Mary Monica's letter to the infant Christine Shields in which she says, 'I loved her very much.'[74]

When she found herself stuck in Cobh, O'Connor had much to tell her cloistered friend and much she may have found impossible to reveal. There's no way of knowing if the nun knew about O'Connor's love for a married man, and if she supported or advised the actress. As the leader of a sodality group of 170 young women, the nun did know the possible future that lay in store for women who fell pregnant out of wedlock.[75] Kay Swift counselled love and passion; Sister Mary Monica stood for Catholic faith and prayer. In the serene grounds of the Sisters of Mercy Convent and the hushed cathedral, the nun continued to pray for O'Connor's peace and happiness.

Choate had left her to make the decision about the UK production, but she would not give up an opportunity to be with Shields. Hunt's offer of a part in the UK production of *Kindred* was politely declined and money somehow found to buy a ticket to New York. In O'Connor's suitcase the morning she embarked, like a talisman, was the final draft of Paul Vincent Carroll's play *Kindred*. On the dark green cover of the manuscript, the playwright had written, 'To Aideen, Bon Voyage, Paul.'[76]

Shields was filming in Hollywood when O'Connor arrived in New York, and he thought it better she stay where she had 'more companionship'.[77] She was familiar with the Whitby apartments on West 45th Street, where they'd be living. Only a few blocks from the Hotel Edison, the Whitby lacked the glamour of the hotel but was very comfortable. It was a community of people working on Broadway, quietest before noon and humming with parties until late. It had been built as a residential hotel, complete with bellhops and barbershop, maid service, a shoe repair stand and even Christmas parties in the lobby. During the depression that began in 1929, it was converted into small studio units.[78] There, Choate and his actress wife Iris Whitney kept an apartment always full of fresh flowers where they entertained O'Connor. Despite their close friendship, from the start of her stay, she and Shields constantly felt that they were a burden to Choate and his wife.[79]

When Choate arranged a reading of the new play *Kindred* in New York for potential investors, in the audience of invited guests was the then composer for Radio City Music Hall and the Director of Light Music for the World Fair, Kay Swift. O'Connor had high hopes she might invest, declaring her a 'grand person' and insisting, 'I know she will [help] if she can'.[80] Swift was impressed and excited by the play, eager to give her ideas to Choate although she admitted she had no available 'monya'.[81] Despite her elegant wardrobe and busy social life, Swift was struggling to support herself financially. There was little chance she could invest in *Kindred*, although her jovial mood may have given the producers a different impression.

Swift was still 'the old carthorse. Always feeling so well it's hardly decent.'[82] Her positivity and worldly wisdom could always provide O'Connor with a chuckle and a distraction from the pressing concerns of theatre life. The Beekman Place apartment where Swift lived and entertained was decorated in zebra-print rugs; her bedroom and dressing room were painted (walls and ceiling) in shrimp pink.[83] Framed studio portraits of Gershwin, some signed in an ebony ink that echoed his own dark handsome profile, hung on the walls of her lounge. Along with various other ornaments and treasures she had taken from the Warburg townhouse, there was a baby grand piano.[84] Here, Swift composed and played incessantly. She kept jottings of compositions wherever paper fell, and coffee cups marked with lipstick surrounded her. Each time she sat there, Swift removed her gold bangles (a gift from Gershwin) and set them on the piano top. They sparkled and trembled as she played.[85]

On the first Sunday morning of September 1939, O'Connor was listening to the wireless in the Choates' apartment when Neville Chamberlain's speech was broadcast on BBC radio. The sentence 'His Majesty's government has declared war on Germany' chilled her, casting a lifelong memory.[86] Going back to her life in Ireland was now not only difficult but potentially dangerous.

There was a reunion with Shields in time to celebrate her 26th birthday, but soon both couples (Choate and wife Iris Whitney; O'Connor and Shields) were working on *Kindred*, 'going over the script word for word, indicating possible cuts and adjustments which we will later go over with Dick [Madden] for his approval.'[87] Up until August, O'Connor was cast in the main role of Agnes. Then a decision was made, putting her out of the part.

It's unclear whether the original casting was just an arrangement by Choate and Shields to secure her visa, or if it was a dreadful surprise when she was replaced by well-known Broadway performer Haila Stoddard. In any event, her sense of indebtedness to Choate overrode any anger about her re-casting in a minor role, Alice. Around the same time, Swift left O'Connor's life as dramatically as she'd entered, eloping with a cowboy to a farm in Oregon. To fill her days until rehearsals began, and to combat her sense of uselessness, O'Connor began volunteering with the Red Cross, working from nine to four every day.[88]

After months of idle days for O'Connor, trying to contribute to the war effort or reading and window-shopping, the long-awaited rehearsals for *Kindred* began at the end of November. Shields had a starring role and Barry Fitzgerald was also in the cast. Reunited with her Irish companions and hard at work, even if her part was minor, the actress saw the days fly by; her theatrical life was back on track. A week into rehearsals, distressing news from home reached her. Frolie Mulhern had died on 17 November at her home on Ailesbury Road. Stunned by grief, O'Connor wrote in her journal that she simply couldn't believe it was true.[89] Deprived of the opportunity to say goodbye and pay her respects to the Mulhern family at the funeral, O'Connor buried pain and upset to carry on with dignity among a group of people who had never met her friend.

Mulhern's relatives told me that family stories report that Frolie died suddenly and quietly on a Friday evening, her heart giving out as she sat at the fire with her mother. Her young nephew woke on Saturday morning to a quiet house; his beloved aunt had gone and Belvedere, the house, was in mourning.[90] The fortune teller in San Francsico had been right about an untimely death, although it wasn't Ria Mooney's. In the death notice published in the newspaper the next day, the list of mourners is exceptionally long. The large collection of clerics in the grieving extended family confirms Aideen's comments about the Mulherns' religious background. She was buried with her father in Enniskillen. In the obituary, the *Irish Independent* said of her career: 'Her high ideals, courage and good humour adorned all she undertook, and the company will be the poorer for her death.'[91] The *Fermanagh Herald* chose to emphasise her religious faith: 'She was a splendid type of sterling Catholic young lady, exemplifying in high degree the highest qualities of a member of the Catholic Church.'[92] For this newspaper, her embodiment of a religious lady, adhering to the teachings of the Catholic Church, was more important than her career.

Frolie and Aideen parted when Aideen took the train to Cobh in the summer of 1939. Frolie was then considering joining her friend in New York. She may have held onto dreams of reuniting with Wickes and appearing on Broadway again. Nobody knows what Frolie ultimately wanted; she may have died before making a decision about travelling to New York.

Hunt's official history of the theatre, *The Abbey: Ireland's National Theatre 1904–78*, omits any reference to Frolie Mulhern's death, or indeed to her acting. Holloway remarked on her passing in his diary three days after her death. He described her as, 'full of the joy of life and she carried that joy into her parts on stage' and said, 'Both the company and the audience loved her.'[93] Holloway's assessment of Mulhern after her death included the following comment: 'I liked both herself and her playing very much indeed and often thought on her fame in the days to come, for she had it in her to excel as an actress of rare gifts.'[94] There is faint damnation in Holloway's assessment that she 'had it in her' to prove a gifted actress. Already she was a gifted actress. But it is true that since her return from the Abbey company's American tour in 1938, Frolie was growing in stature and in dramatic range. She was poised on the edge of a very successful career, rich with possibilities. Her loss would be felt by O'Connor and other close friends, but the impact she might have made at the Abbey Theatre was a loss to Irish theatre audiences that cannot be measured.

Kindred

After a few weeks of rehearsals for *Kindred*, the actors left together for Princeton, a town 80 kilometres outside of New York. It opened in the McCarter Theatre, at the edge of the Princeton University campus, on 23 December 1939. They immediately travelled back by train to the New

York opening. It was a tense Christmas day, for the next morning Arthur Shields had to pay an urgent visit to a doctor. *Kindred* would premiere that evening at the Maxine Elliott Theatre, but he was suffering from chest pain.

A pencilled note in Shields' diary for the following day, a Wednesday, records: 'Kindred a failure.'[95] Sixteen performances after opening night, it closed. The spectacular flop left Shields with a 20 per cent share in bankruptcy. Rehearsals of the old reliable, O'Casey's *Juno and the Paycock*, began even before *Kindred* closed, on 4 January. Under the stress, Shields was admitted to Lenox Hill Hospital on the Upper East Side and diagnosed with tuberculosis. O'Connor continued to perform in *Juno and the Paycock*, playing a part now so familiar to the actress it was like reciting a prayer. O'Casey's description for Mary Boyle reads:

> Two forces are working in her mind—one, through the circumstances of her life, pulling her back; the other, through the influence of books she has read, pushing her forward. The opposing forces are in her speech and her manners.[96]

Similar forces were working on O'Connor, but it was no longer the simple 'backwards or forward' decision she had contemplated as a younger Mary.

It's a long, hard trek from the Whitby Building up to Lenox Hill Hospital, particularly if the weather is bad and there is no money for taxis. The walk leads away from the dazzling white lights of Broadway, past the large department stores up the length of Park Avenue and right up to the east side of Central Park. O'Connor had to make this trek, while ensuring that she was back in the theatre each evening in time to perform. On her way, she passed the Warburg townhouse where Kay Swift's ex-husband still lived with her three daughters. It was a stark reminder of the luxury that Swift had given up for love and her career.

The year of 1939 had been bookended with the deaths of W. B. Yeats and of Frolie Mulhern and had contained little but worry and relentless struggle for O'Connor and Shields. At least they had been a support to each other; now Shields' serious illness left the actress isolated. As she trudged up and down to the hospital, sometimes with Iris Whitney or Barry Fitzgerald, the weight of worry about the future became heavier. Only in her private journals did she admit that she now longed for one thing only: to go home.[97] War, or love, or shame, or a combination of all three, kept her where she was.

Equity contracts reveal that O'Connor earned $150 a week to appear in *Kindred* in 1939. After it closed, her salary decreased to $100 a week for her part of Mary in *Juno and The Paycock* (1940) and then to $50 a week for appearing with actor Hale Norcross in *Tanyard Street* (1941).[98] It was increasingly difficult for her to manage on her own; her reliance on Shields was not just emotional but financial.

Shields was still seriously ill, but his condition was improving. After *Juno and the Paycock*, he took the doctors' advice to travel to California to recuperate in sunshine and dry air. Barry Fitzgerald travelled with him. Both men had hopes of finding film work to improve their financial situation. Once again, Shields left O'Connor behind. She had been cast in a small part in a Terence Rattigan play and was hoping it would improve her situation with Equity.

A few weeks into rehearsal for the production at the Hudson Theatre, O'Connor arrived back to the Whitby apartment bereft and Shields received a distressed call. The connection was bad; O'Connor was crying.[99] Shields had to wait for an explanation. Choate wrote:

> By the time you receive this letter Aideen will be arriving and will give you all the details

of how Cooper railroaded her out of his show. Unfortunately, she couldn't reach me at the time all the damage was done. [...] The new director wanted a different type in the part and when Cooper refused to pay Aideen off, the new director and Homolka simply decided that they would make it so uncomfortable for her that she would leave of her own accord.[100]

O'Connor was the third actress to leave the production; the *New York Times* announced that English actress Maria Temple would assume the role.[101] O'Connor's experiences in Dublin had made her tough; yet given the traumatic events of the previous few months, a hasty and emotional flight to the West Coast is easy to understand. Cooper was insisting that the actress had broken her contract and owed him $200–a sum of money she simply didn't have.[102]

O'Connor said farewell to Choate and Iris Whitney, before heading for Grand Central Station. A round trip ticket from New York to Hollywood that year would have cost $90, the equivalent of just over $1,000 in today's money.[103] It was a huge investment for an actress that had been deprived of two week's salary for walking out of a show. O'Connor walked under the widespread wings of the American eagle, through the wooden swing door and into the Vanderbilt Hall waiting room. The green marble Tiffanys' clock high on the wall counted down the minutes before she could board. Returning to Dublin wasn't possible; onwards to Hollywood was O'Connor's only option.

Hollywood and housework

A few years after their parting in New York, Kay Swift found herself tiptoeing across the landing to the bathroom from the guest room of the Shields' Hollywood apartment. She was intimidated by the hush and found the quiet the couple lived in utterly discomfiting.[104] Having avoided using the bathroom as much as possible, Swift was 'near death' close to midnight and braved the expedition in bare feet. To her horror, when she pulled the plug, she broke the mechanism and the plumbing 'roared like a wolf for three days'.[105] Despite the spacious surroundings, it was not a pleasant place to stay. Shields was still weak, and O'Connor's unhappiness was rumbling under the floorboards.

1843 North Cherokee Avenue was a good address, on a steep hill, one block away from the bookshops, cinemas and restaurants of Hollywood Boulevard. The four-storey apartment block was built in 1926, with an entrance discreetly hidden by a fountain and shaded by palm trees. The darkness in the white marble lobby was dispelled by a chandelier; the mahogany front doors of the apartments ran down narrow corridors that all led to sash windows with cast-iron fire escapes. Climbing the stairs to the third floor, the low hum of people in their homes was audible. O'Connor was weary and melancholy. She abhorred the heat and boredom of her empty days in Hollywood:

> I read about two books a day – nothing else to do in this god awful town. We have moved into another apt in this building. It is lovely. Big airy rooms and nice furniture and decorations. [...] My cooking has become most proficient![106]

Six months after her arrival, O'Connor was feeling unwell. Shields wasn't strong enough to nurse her, and the stomach pains became so intense that she visited the doctor and was admitted to hospital with acute appendicitis.[107] During the early tours with the Abbey, O'Connor had used heavy painkillers provided by Bazie Magee to help with menstrual pains. Later, doctors had prescribed liver extract.[108] These pains were different. The casual, social drinking of the theatre crowd had intensified during her sojourn in New York and her journals shortly after she arrived in Hollywood suggest that it was getting out of control. This time, she stayed in hospital for ten days.

Symptoms of appendicitis include a lack of appetite, a painful bloated abdomen and general fatigue. These symptoms could also indicate cirrhosis of the liver brought on by excessive alcohol intake. If the patient refused to acknowledge the extent of her problem or to be truthful about her consumption of alcohol, there was little a doctor could do to help. The doctors removed her appendix and O'Connor went home to recuperate. Now both she and her partner were weak and struggling to find work. But Shields had a plan: he was in discussions with producer Jack Kirkland to direct *Tanyard Street*, on Broadway.[109]

This play about an Irish soldier in the Spanish Civil War seeking a miracle, written by Irish playwright Louis D'Alton, had been produced on the Abbey stage in January 1940 as *The Spanish Soldier*. There, the rich comedy and social satire had delighted audiences and critics. Kirkland agreed to sponsor the production on condition Barry Fitzgerald was included in the cast, and so in December (later than planned) all three Irish actors went back briefly to New York. After the premiere had been postponed twice, the play opened in February 1941.

D'Alton had written *The Spanish Soldier* to stake a claim as a serious dramatist, but Broadway audiences came mainly to laugh at the famous comedian Barry Fitzgerald in the role of Mossy Furlong.[110] Shields directed and played the soldier Kevin McMorna. In the final act, Kevin tells his lover Hessy that he has decided to join the priesthood. Hessy was played by the singularly titled 'Margo'. According to the *New York Sun*, Margo was Mexican, born as Maria Margarita Guadalupe Bolado Castilla.[111] O'Connor, as the only Irish woman in the cast, played the minor role of Nanno Deasy. (In Dublin, this part was played by Phyllis Ryan: her young rival continued to haunt her.) The play ran for only 22 performances. Critics hated it; Atkinson of the *New York Times* was amazed Fitzgerald had agreed to appear in it.[112] Soon, all three actors were back in Hollywood. O'Connor's performance in *Tanyard Street* would be her last appearance on the stage.

Staying in Hollywood, Kay Swift said she 'loved being with' Shields and O'Connor. She declared they were 'kindness itself.'[113] Yet, her discomfort in a home devoid of life is clear from her letters. Shields was 'delicate', recuperating slowly from his TB and O'Connor, Swift observed, was 'wearied from the extra work entailed by my visit'.[114] Barry Fitzgerald came most evenings for the dinner O'Connor prepared, providing light relief for Swift, but the silence during the day and O'Connor's moods left the vivacious Swift uncomfortable.

Doing her best to cater for her friend, O'Connor put a hot water bottle in Swift's guest bed while she was out, only for the composer to discover on her return that it was leaking. A horrified O'Connor roused Shields from his bed to take some of his bedding to refresh the guest bed. A very awkward Swift had to sit 'in state' while her hostess remade the bed for her; the accident was another shameful episode for a struggling O'Connor.[115] Shields and Kay Swift were in their beds by nine each evening, to make the early mornings in the studio. During the cool nights, O'Connor had time to read, write letters, to imagine how different her life might be if the war ended or she found acting work of her own, and to drink. Swift tried to get a hotel room; none were to be found in the vicinity.

The sexy, hard-drinking and rarely-eating Kay Swift, with her leopard-skin coat, silk gowns and red lipstick had been replaced in Oregon by a calmer, plain-living woman who would not contemplate a dalliance with an unsuitable man. Swift had embodied the frank sexuality and liberated femininity of 1920's New York, a femininity that both thrilled and intimidated the

Abbey actresses. Now, Swift had written a wholesome tale of the devoted wife and housekeeper, *Who Could Ask for Anything More?*, which fitted with the ideals of 1940s California. Aideen tried to take on these ideas of womanhood, but it was not a role she relished. While Shields was at the studio, she was meant to be the diligent housewife. In the evenings, she entertained their guests with her 'most proficient' cooking and cocktails.[116]

There was a temporary reprieve when O'Connor paid a visit to Selznick's studio and after reading for them, began rehearsing a part in a film with the Irish actress Geraldine Fitzgerald. They 'worked like fury—till 2am most mornings' until Equity questioned her status and there was a disagreement over money.[117] Shields also had misgivings about her working in movies. O'Connor told Choate that she'd reluctantly left it because, 'although I wanted to do it, Boss was terribly against it'.[118] Despite his previous support for her career, Shields disliked the idea of O'Connor being exploited in the film industry. He was happy that she was 'housekeeping and reading and keeping as cheerful as the news of the war will permit any of us.'[119] He felt: 'She misses New York but is good at settling down anywhere.'[120] In her eagerness to please, to convince Shields that she could settle anywhere with good humour, caring for him and for his brother, O'Connor hid the extent of her loneliness and unhappiness.

To celebrate her 28th birthday, Shields took O'Connor to Musso Franks' restaurant on Hollywood Boulevard.[121] It was a rare social occasion for her, now that she often stayed at home if he was working or socialising at the studios. A waiter in a scarlet waistcoat escorted them to their table. The red leather booths were often full of movie stars eating the trademark steaks and drinking some of the best cocktails in Hollywood. It was one of her favourite spots, but it had been almost a year since she'd worked and there seemed little to celebrate. Nobody could help how old she felt, or how drab she believed she looked.[122] After dinner and drinks, the couple could walk the short distance back to the apartment.

December came and the couple muddled through the holiday as best as they could without family and Irish tea. Kay Swift was also far from her family. She called it the 'nostalgic old Nina Twaddle of a day' and lamented, 'all those choice regrets we have on Dec[ember] 25th.'[123] But Swift found solace in the fact she was 'so damned necessary' to her new husband. Being needed by those around you, she decided, was the real 'payola'.[124] O'Connor felt nothing but a burden to Shields and Fitzgerald. Her choice regrets of 25 December were not so easily allayed.

That Christmas, there remained the prospect that O'Connor's career could be salvaged, and her life could turn around. On St Stephen's Day, as the Irish couple still called it, in 1941, Shields walked down the hill to the Post Office to send a wire to Choate. It read:

> Aideen goes to Vancouver January 6th. A letter as you suggest would be very helpful writing. Boss.[125]

There was little Shields could do to support his lover, but he used his contacts to help her American visa application. O'Connor had to take a tram and then a train, carrying with her clothes for a few days as well as all the papers connected with her emigration status. Included in those carefully guarded papers was a letter from Kay Swift (now Mrs Faye Hubbard) addressed to the American Counsel General in Vancouver. The letter certified that Swift 'enjoys an annual income from a trust fund in excess of $10,000.'[126] Swift had not simply filled in some paperwork to help an old work contact. Swift had offered as security for Aideen's visa the trust fund set up by her first husband's parents as a dowry. Swift now had no financial security except the Warburg Trust Fund; yet she didn't hesitate to offer it to O'Connor to help her stay in the country.

Both Shields and O'Connor had previously visited the Canadian city with the Abbey company. He particularly enjoyed how it contained 'interesting looking oriental people' and offered 'something queer around every corner.'[127] But this trip was different, and not simply because she was alone. The actress later said:

> I had a real taste of a country at war in Vancouver. There the people were alert 24 hours a day. There were restrictions and partial blackouts and army life got the first place with civilians second. I guess that this will gradually happen here.[128]

O'Connor returned to North Cherokee with the right to residency for five years under the quota system, but also with 'rare fevers and miseries together with shaky legs, high temperature, dizzy head and a swollen and festered leg'.[129] The vaccinations she had before leaving for Canada left her feeling thoroughly unwell and she took to bed for a number of weeks, her hands wavering aimlessly over the keys each time she tried to compose a letter.[130] Shields nursed her, but he was depressed about work and considering switching agents to improve his career chances. Eventually, her symptoms passed and Shields began a new round of the studios led by a new agent. Alone again during the day, she applied to the Red Cross for volunteer work and was disgusted when they declined her offer on the basis that she didn't know braille. She told Eddie Choate in January 1942:

> Well, I ask you! Braille! They are the snuttiest [sic] crowd and seem to be trying to keep the Red Cross for the social and movie crowd when everyone in the country is needed.[131]

Frequently, O'Connor wrote about World War II. There is a sense of political naïvety in her commentary though she is characteristically practical and frank. She wrote to Choate about it as early as 1939 from Dublin and in January 1942 she shared a real pride in the British forces: 'And boy, wasn't Churchill wonderful in his speeches here and in Canada. Whatta man!'[132]

Some months after O'Connor arrived in Hollywood, huge anti-war rallies were held in Los Angeles. Thirty-five thousand people crowded the Hollywood Bowl and surrounding hillsides to voice their resistance to the fighting. But the industrial and economic boom emanating from the European conflict generated huge wealth. In October 1939, the US had signed a Neutrality Act to say that they were not getting involved in World War II, but on 4 November they passed an amendment to allow them to sell arms to European countries. By May 1940, Roosevelt was talking about the US as an 'Arsenal of Democracy'.

Later that year, O'Connor grew concerned about Ireland's place in the conflict: 'Eire is now so insular, so cut off by her own will from contact from the rest of the world.' She was reading William Shirer's *Berlin Diary*.[133] The actress swung between ferocious homesickness, dying to escape the cloying heat and lethargy of Hollywood, and delight to be free of Abbey politics, conservative Irish society and family conflicts. She often felt guilty about her distance from the war, telling Choate:

> We feel so useless and SAFE over here – with plenty of food and clothes and amusement when we ought to be sharing the rationing and the anxiety and the work and the hardships that the people in Eire are having – or we should be doing something in England.[134]

The letters sent to Choate are neatly typed, dated and with corrections and necessary punctuation inserted by hand. They are the work of an organised and engaged lady. It is in transcribing the letters she wrote during this time that one can sense the erratic rhythm of her thoughts and her repetitive tales. It's then one feels the mood swings of someone inebriated. O'Connor's flurries of affection, fiery outbursts and frank analyses of events are the only clues to her private struggle; there are no other signs of her drinking habits or any evidence of possible attempts by herself, Barry or Arthur to address the issue.

'I STILL LOATHE HOLLYWOOD,' O'Connor wrote in 1942.[135] Tellingly, this wasn't a letter home, but a confession she made to Choate. While Shields was often away on location, or shooting at the studios, she was at home. The local second-hand bookshops helped pass time, and her bedroom became a retreat for the slightest hurt or injury, but two other places started to figure largely in her days. The rooftop of North Cherokee was open to residents, a quiet retreat where one could watch the neighbourhood unseen. Photographs of her here (from the private collection of Christine Shields) show a reflective woman, sitting among potted plants in the early evening light. The other refuge she found was the cinemas of Hollywood Boulevard. Alone in the darkness, O'Connor could immerse herself in another world, or simply drink unnoticed, although family members were aware of this habit.[136] Her journals show that she would attend two or three screenings on her own during the week, and then bring Shields with her to watch her favourites over again on his free days.[137]

War rationing was increasingly impinging on the Hollywood diet, but in December O'Connor and Shields arrived at Barry Fitzgerald's new house on Gardner Street to share an enormous turkey and British plum pudding. Outside, the sun was blazing but Fitzgerald managed to get some logs and created a proper fire inside to remind them of home.[138] Despite the luxuries, O'Connor was not feeling well and was capable of doing little. On doctor's advice, Shields booked a week in the Biltmore Hotel in downtown Los Angeles, and they left for a holiday.

The couple returned home to the wet season in Hollywood. The rain rarely abated, pushing houses into the sea on the coast at Malibu and keeping many awake at night. Temperatures were also below their normal level. Despite the damp, O'Connor was refreshed and full of good intentions. Reflecting that she was now three and a half years in America, she was cheered by the recent 'grand' war news and believed 'things are really looking up for the allies'.[139] She hoped things were looking up for herself, telling Choate: 'I really am thoroughly ashamed of myself' for her lack of letters, and urging him to help her keep her promises. She signs off the letter 'God bless you', as if she is now relying on faith to help her.[140]

News of the sudden death of Bazie Magee in October 1943 reached Hollywood faster than one would expect given war conditions. The couple wasted no time; five days later Shields attended his doctor for pre-marital blood tests.[141] There was a quiet wedding ceremony on 10 November. If O'Connor did organise a Catholic ceremony in the church she attended, where Father Coughlan was parish priest, I could find no record of it despite weeks of searching. After years of union, the marriage was a brief moment, no more than a passing reference in a letter to Choate: '[H]e and I were married last week. We are very happy about it.'[142] The official arrangement was a precursor to other matters: Shields was preoccupied with the fate of his son Adam, who was moving around between family members in Dublin. His priority was to bring Adam to Hollywood.

Barry Fitzgerald had been a constant presence in her life since O'Connor's love affair with Shields had stabilised. Fitzgerald's comic talent not only brought humour into her home; his film success gave him an income that allowed him to support O'Connor and Shields when needed. Particularly when his brother was ill, Fitzgerald ensured the couple never went without. Chance events in March 1944 might have tested O'Connor's loyalty to her brother-in-law, although her actions do not show any doubt.

One Wednesday evening, O'Connor cooked dinner and prepared drinks for Shields and his brother as usual, before they waved Fitzgerald off in his car. Around midnight, she received a call to say that her brother-in-law had been in an accident and had been arrested. The *Los Angeles Times* reported that Fitzgerald was driving along Hollywood Boulevard when he failed to stop at the junction of Sycamore Street. He didn't see two women crossing the street; Mary Farrer was killed and her daughter Edna Torrance seriously injured.[143]

Shields and O'Connor went straight to the local jail after the call. Fitzgerald was now a rising star and the studio producers quickly stepped in to solve the problem. Jerry Geisler, an expensive and well-known lawyer to the stars, was hired to defend Fitzgerald and details on the case still prove difficult to find. There were suggestions that bad lighting was the issue; others believe he had been drinking but this was reported as unproven.[144] For weeks after the accident, the couple lived with the much-shaken Fitzgerald at his home. O'Connor reveals little about what she said or how she felt about the incident although it is mentioned in later letters.[145]

The accident shook all three members of the Shields family to their core. If anything could force O'Connor to reconsider her drinking, it was the events of that night. Her journals and medical records suggest that her health problems were now an endless cycle of urgent illness; good intentions and fresh starts; followed by a gradual return to drinking in secret. After the war ended, she had a new house, a step-son and, soon, a pregnancy. She continued to drink.

Two years after the war ended, O'Connor was seven months pregnant when her 18-year-old stepson Adam arrived from Ireland. He was enrolled at Hollywood High School to finish his education. Kay Swift, who had relocated to Beverly Hills, thought Adam 'very nice, & his reactions to America are anything but dull'.[146] Swift had visited their home on Sierra Bonita Avenue and heard of Shields' career developments. It caused her to reflect, as cheerful as always: 'Peoples' ships do come in, sometimes late. Everything's clicking for Boss, after so much hell.'[147] If everything was clicking for Shields, Swift had little idea how desperately O'Connor was struggling.

Five weeks after Swift's letter, O'Connor gave birth prematurely to a daughter, Christine Frances. She was named for Shields' most important role, as Christy Mahon in *The Playboy of the Western World*, and for Frolie (Frances) Mulhern. The dark-haired, blue-eyed baby arrived in a 'great rush'.[148] Christine was brought home by Arthur Shields and Mae Clarke, a nanny; O'Connor was kept in hospital for ten days for further treatment. The house was now full. As well as Adam and Mae Clarke, Bid Shields Mortishead (Arthur's sister) and her daughter Una arrived from Ireland in November to visit and help the new mother. On the day of her christening, Irish actress Sara Allgood stood as her godmother.[149] Later photographs, in Christine Shield's private collection, show Allgood watching from a distance, smiling, as Christine toddles away from O'Connor's arms in their new back garden.

The house on Sierra Bonita Avenue was a split-level clapboard house, not far from their first home on North Cherokee Avenue. It had a bright, open-plan kitchen, a room where Shields could keep his stamp collection and two bedrooms upstairs under the eaves. Downstairs, there was a cool, dark room in the centre of the house, which the couple set up as a 'green room'. The walls were lined with books and there was a desk for a typewriter and an easy chair for reading. On the shelves, first editions of Yeats' poetry and Synge's plays sat alongside fiction.[150]

Shields was away working more and more, as his film career progressed. Despite the company of his family and a new baby, O'Connor was generally melancholy and pining for him. It isn't clear how well O'Connor hid her drinking at home, but she was attending a physician who had diagnosed the cause of her stomach pains as cirrhosis of the liver (degeneration of liver tissue generally caused by long-term alcoholism).[151]

In a moving letter written in January 1947, O'Connor wrote to her husband in New York to tell him, 'All I want is to be with you, even if it's in Timbuctoo'.[152] The letter takes her through day and night, keeping him up to date on life at home. Monday afternoon's entry reads: 'I wanted to fly to NY last night to be with you – I kept very busy – made formula like mad and did a wash so that I wouldn't cry into the bathroom towels'.[153] By 6am on Tuesday:

> Not much sleep as Christine talked most of the night! A cold dreary dawn. Longing for my cup of tea. I have the kettle on. Wish you were here. I always feel terribly alone and lonely in the cold early mornings.[154]

There was frustration that Shields was working and travelling so much: 'Boss – look if you would prefer me not to join you at all please tell me'.[155] The truth of a marriage may be impossible to know for anyone outside the union. Even in O'Connor's most frustrated, angry and emotional moments, she loved her husband deeply. She respected his opinion on everything from the latest film to her own career development, and she supported and encouraged his endless round of meetings and auditions in Dublin, New York and Hollywood. Shields' early notes show his growing affection for O'Connor, but later there are hints of his practical commitment. Throughout their marriage, Shields ensured that while he was not around, others were looking out for her. Choate assisted her in New York and various members of the Shields family came to Hollywood to help with baby Christine while he was away working.

Shooting for the Renoir film *The River* took place in India in 1950. While Shields was in Calcutta, his agent Vernon Jacobson had instructions to supervise O'Connor's finances. Vernon (known as Jake) accompanied the actress to the bank and ensured she had sufficient cash before arranging his own commission and sending money on to his client. Once, he overlooked his own debts rather than leave O'Connor short. In his letter to Calcutta he said, 'Arthur, I didn't take any of the $2,869.33 [...] I'll wait until I get the other money'.[156] He reported that, 'The family are fine and Christine is really growing and seems in great form'.[157]

A pencilled note in Arthur's diary for a Sunday in May 1950 reads, 'Learned of Aideen's illness'.[158] He had returned to Hollywood after shooting finished in late April, to learn his wife's illness was now fatal. According to family members, he knew of her drinking but perhaps hoped all her visitors would help moderate it. Choate served as his confidante. Shields wrote to him: 'It is all hopeless, and the sooner God takes the poor thing, the easier it will be for her'.[159]

On the other side of the Atlantic, Vincent De Paul O'Connor and his daughters were also dealing with this shocking news. As late as June 1949, their neighbour, Maire Judge, daughter of Abbey actors Eileen Crowe and F. J. McCormick, had been exchanging letters with the actress. Judge sent gossip from the Gate Theatre (where she worked) and family news. O'Connor sent *Hollywood Reporter* magazine and shared tit-bits of her 'glamorous' life in Los Angeles.[160] Her sisters had no idea that O'Connor was an alcoholic. Until the very end, she presented to certain people as a vivacious woman living an idyllic life in the city of dreams.

O'Connor had spent much time in the 'green room' at Sierra Bonita and now her bed was set up there. Christine has an early memory of being brought into the dark room, crying with fear and an instinct that something was deeply wrong. Her mother was admitted to hospital shortly after that painful moment.[161] There was no possibility of O'Connor seeing her father or sisters again. For years, the actress had abhorred the fuss of American holidays. In 1950, as Independence Day dawned on the 4 July, she slipped away. She was 36 years old, the same age at which her own mother had passed away. And like the final insult of a harsh Hollywood system, on her death certificate she was deemed a 'housewife'.[162]

There was 'general sorrow' in the Abbey Theatre when news of her passing reached Dublin.[163] Eileen Crowe was asked to speak to the press, and mass was offered at St Mary's Pro-Cathedral on Marlborough Street. In their home at Sierra Bonita Avenue, Shields was bereft. His sister Bid wrote of her sadness and advised he 'must just battle it out and think of Christine'.[164]

In September 2011, Christine Shields and I together paced the hills of Holy Cross Cemetery in Culver City in the noonday sun to find her mother's grave. The 200 acres of parched grass are dotted here and there by low, gnarly trees and criss-crossed by lines of small, neat plaques. Christine Shields didn't visit much growing up and the O'Connor family never saw Aideen's grave. Arthur chose to be buried with his brother in Dean's Grange Cemetery in Dublin; Aideen rests in Culver City alone. When we found it, we used tissue and water to scrub from the surface moss that blurred the stencilled letters. The standard plaque barely fits a name and date, but here there are two names. She is buried as 'Una Mary Shields (1913–1950)' and then, in brackets, is the name 'Aideen O'Connor'. The two names symbolise the facets of her life she never managed to merge successfully: the desire to perform professionally as Aideen and to find personal fulfilment as Una.

No hagiography

I believe that the process of constructing a narrative such as this allows for a celebration of O'Connor's human features: her determination, focus and potential, as well as the love for Arthur Shields that defined much of her life. In tandem with a study of the life of another women in the company, it also allows for the exposure of fundamental truths about Irish theatre, society and attitudes to women in the 1930s. O'Connor was repeatedly punished for behaviour deemed outside of standards at the National Theatre. She was a real woman: complex and flawed, challenged and challenging. This is not a hagiography, but the presentation of a vital Irish lady and actress in all her facets, and of how the parts she played impacted her off-stage reality. It also demonstrates how her ultimate performance as a fulfilled housewife running a home and caring for her husband wore her down.

W. B. Yeats once feared it was 'almost impossible for us to find a passionate woman actress in Catholic Ireland'.[165] Women from outside of Ireland, Yeats insisted:

> have far more sensitive instruments, are far more teachable in all that belongs to expression but they lack simplicity of feeling, their minds are too full of trivial ideas, and they seldom seem capable of really noble feelings.[166]

Aideen O'Connor was a Catholic woman who repeatedly displayed her passionate nature and noble feelings. Throughout her working life, she engaged with scripts, writers and directors in a way that proved her intelligence and her capacity to absorb and debate ideas. In her training at the Abbey School, and later in her work on the UK and American stage, her physicality developed, and she mastered the use of her sexuality to expand her acting range. Yet, it was this passion and exposure of a more liberated sexuality that led to her exclusion from the Abbey company and thus to her emigration. She was punished in her career, her ambitions thwarted, for her off-stage behaviour. For all of Yeats' despair, his theatre could not escape the repressive atmosphere in Irish society. In the 1930s, and for decades afterwards, it refused to countenance such expressions of femininity, ostracising such women, or making it clear there was no future for them.

O'Connor could not, and would not, countenance a career or a life for herself that did not include performing in the theatre. She was part of the first wave of Irish women to risk a professional career as a performer by demanding her personal life be kept separate from her work. She sought to be accepted in America as an actress, not just an 'Abbey player' with a familiar repertoire of national stereotypes. She set a path that has often been travelled since by Irish actresses seeking success and fame in Hollywood. In this light, that Aideen O'Connor ultimately failed to have a long-lasting or what is conceived as a 'successful' performance career becomes less important than the fact she followed through on her decision to 'stick to the stage for good or evil now'.[167]

Conclusion

In November 1959, Arthur Shields paid a visit to Dublin from his home in Los Angeles and he reported back to his third wife, Laurie, that he'd had dinner with old female colleagues from the Abbey company: Eileen Crowe, May Craig and Maureen Delany. He shared with Laurie his enjoyment of their 'two-hour talk about old times'.[1] Many of the old times discussed featured three actresses not there that night: Frolie Mulhern (died 1939), Aideen O'Connor (died 1950), and Ria Mooney.

The cosy scene from 1959, with the older generation of Abbey actors united and sharing memories with an old friend raises the question: can such longevity of career be deemed success? On the surface, May Craig, Eileen Crowe and Maureen Delany would appear to have managed their careers and balanced their personal lives (and religious faith) with their dramatic art in a form that brought them fulfillment, stability and comfort. All three continued to perform long after they reached the age of retirement. Privately, we do not know. None of these women left a record of their thoughts. One could go further and suggest that this management of their career and personal lives was connected to the conditions and constraints imposed on their generation of women: to their theatre and social training. They were successful, but they had inherited and internalised personal and professional limits; everything they achieved and all they chose to forego was placed within these invisible parameters for women set by Irish society during the Free State period.

If one accepts that this is the case, then the later generation of women struggled because they didn't follow their predecessors closely. Or, perhaps, we could say, they chose to struggle rather than follow the old model. We may view them as victims of changing times, or casualties of bad decisions. But I choose to focus on the agency of these women. All were part of the first wave of professional Irish actresses at the National Theatre that sought to be recognised for their theatrical work and not for their lifestyle. They developed artistic integrity and technique that demanded a full separation of their theatrical performances from their personal lives when such separation was not granted to them in Ireland.

O'Connor made a bid for a life that was as yet out of the reach of Irish women: a theatre actress, living in Hollywood with a man already married to someone else. It may have been bound to end in disappointment, but there is much to admire in her determination to live her life on her own terms. Mooney experienced both the exoticism and the discipline of performing with Le Gallienne and the Civic Repertory Theatre Company, as well as working as a lead actress at the Gate Theatre and teaching many generations of actors in New York and in Dublin. She earned her living as an implicitly feminist director with the Gaiety Theatre, the Experimental Theatre Group in the Peacock Theatre and, in the latter years of her career, at the Abbey Theatre. Despite opportunities elsewhere, she persisted in returning to use her talents in the Irish National

Theatre where she was invariably mistreated. Her contribution to the work of the institution and to theatre in general has not been recognised for its complexity and variety.

In a letter to a student, Lilian Foley, in 1936, Ria Mooney spoke of her own challenges and complexes as a young performer and said:

> Most people like to think it's love — or lack of it that keeps women from being good actresses. It may sometimes be so — but nine times out of ten it is something much more prosaic...[2]

She was speaking specifically about money, but that connects the challenges to the wider issues of economy, families, society. These biographies demonstrate how their gender, class and material circumstances shaped their artistic careers.[3]

As lower-middle-class girls, O'Connor and Mooney most readily fit the category of working actors developing a craft. They retained their position through tireless work, on and off the stage, to maintain themselves financially. Both biographies show evidence of constant reading and an ongoing interest in theories developing around acting, performance, teaching and in theatre outside of Ireland. At the same time, the breadth of Mooney's career and her commitment to theatre marks her as a radical modernist artist rather than a performer honing a 'craft'.

Mooney and O'Connor were successful in forging professional and personal lives with forays into independence and liberation, very different from the women that came before them. They were exposed to the role models of certain American women that had a lasting impact on their own sense of self and potential. Overseas, in their work and lives, they sought to be recognised as professional performers and theatre artists, not merely 'Abbey actresses'. They set the path for generations of actresses that would come after them, providing the model for Irish women that seek to impress on the world their talent and spirit, and to assert themselves as performers worthy of international honours.

The porous distinctions between 'public' and 'private' and between 'professional' and 'amateur', the overlaps and exceptions, make the careers and lives of the Abbey Theatre actresses of the 1930s a particularly complex group to study in depth. This exploration of an actress's precarious position within Irish society comes from an in-depth study of individual lives. In seeking out the individual, the particular circumstances of these women, patterns emerge. The induction of these patterns allows a new understanding of the lives and work of female performers in the Free State.

I hope that this composite biography, which incorporates elements of theatre history and of performance theory, serves as a form of feminist historiography. Joan Wallach Scott has set out the ideal form for feminist history. Scott states this history should be:

> not the recounting of great deeds performed by women but the exposure of the silent and hidden operations of gender. [...] With such an approach, the history of women critically confronts the politics of existing histories and inevitably begins the rewriting of history.[4]

This book seeks to contribute to such a re-writing of Irish theatre history. It does so to produce a re-constituted archive of Irish theatre, an archive that I hope may allow us to think differently about the future.

I completed this manuscript thousands of kilometres from where it began, seated in Yale University's Beinecke Library. Far from being strange, it was fitting that I could only garner a proper sense of perspective on these Irish women when I was in America. It was a glorious, golden Connecticut autumn, in the weeks before Trump was elected president of the US. There was a sense of momentum about everything, as if the world was intent on speeding up and hurtling into a future nobody could control. The only thing I could control was to turn up in the library every morning and finish my manuscript.

My relationship with these women was so intimate that I had no idea how it would ever come to a satisfactory conclusion. To say it was intimate is not to say it was always easy or pleasant. It was often tedious, tense, frequently infuriating and sometimes bordering on toxic. Staying in Hollywood, I had the most terrifying dreams about Aideen visiting me.

I was in Yale, on a generous fellowship, with the express purpose of doing nothing but researching Eva Le Gallienne and finishing my manuscript. In the event, there was another task I had to complete while I was there. In November 2015, Ireland's National Theatre announced its theatre programme for the centenary year of 2016 entitled 'Waking the Nation.' Following the announcement, there was a massive public outcry at the representation of (or lack of) women in the programme. The furore led to the formation of a movement called #WakingTheFeminists, which set out to redress the consistent underrepresentation of female writers, directors and other professionals in all aspects of Irish theatre. I found myself working on the Research Committee for the movement, producing the first quantitative analysis of the position of women in Irish theatre over a ten-year period. The report was being launched at a public meeting at the end of November 2016. Hence, I found myself in Connecticut having Skype meetings; checking Excel spreadsheets and reviewing tables of figures and drafts of speeches at odd hours of the day, often in the tiny, spartan room where I was staying, as others in the boarding house slept. Generally, I detest such administrative work when I'm researching and writing. But now, there seemed no conflict in these tasks. In fact, it felt like the work I'd been doing to get to know these women, revealing their stories, their strength and their suffering, had added to the energy that precipitated #WakingTheFeminists. Aideen and Ria wouldn't just approve of it; they'd be at the front lines. And so that was where I was, on their behalf. It was a transition from the chauvinism and feminist struggles of the 1930s, to the endemic gender issues in Irish theatre today. A biographer separating from a subject (or subjects, in this case) is as complex and painful as any relationship breakdown. My work with #WakingTheFeminists helped that process; I started to feel that when some kind of equality was restored in the theatre, that their ghosts would rest a little easier.

It's now over a decade since I discovered Aideen's letters in the archive and began this work. I've fought incessantly along the way, for funding, access to archives, recognition for their stories. I've fought for the importance of remembering and honouring these women in ways I might never have had the strength to fight for myself. With care and attention, I've built up an alternative archive of Irish theatre, which places these women, their work and their contribution, at the centre of it, letting the men drift into secondary roles and bit parts. I've done that to show that it can be done, and that it garners a complex and rich version of Irish theatre history for any researcher. As with any archive, its use, its meaning and significance, is in how it can be mined and shaped and used. But I know that this book is simply that: another archive and another way of telling a story.

Róisín McBrinn – Artistic Director of the Gate Theatre

In Dublin today, both the Gate Theatre and the Abbey Theatre have female artistic directors: Caitríona McLaughlin and myself. We are not the first, and we will not be the last, but this book has made me consider anew all of the wonderful women, including Ria, Aideen and Frolie who paved the way for our achievements and the continuing growth and evolution of Irish theatre. Their work and travels connected them and Irish theatre with international influences whose impact can still be felt today.

When Micheál MacLiammóir wrote the foreword to Ria Mooney's 1978 memoir, he revealed how much he esteemed her – despite her discretion and avoidance of theatre gossip! He spoke of the 'reality and understanding' she brought to her roles, as well as her studious intensity and her focus on craft. To learn that Ria Mooney provided both the Gate and the Abbey with a direct link to Stanislavski – She trained and assisted with Eva Le Gallienne – was such an exciting revelation. Ria's sense of excellent theatre never wavered, despite the pressures consistently heaped on her. Her adaptation of *Wuthering Heights* was such a success it was brought back by the Gate to support the box office (a familiar challenge!) and she would go on to nurture some of Ireland's greatest acting talent as well as bringing to the stage for the first time the work of Brian Friel. What a legacy!

Every artistic director knows about risk; it is the consistent thread in everything we do. We explore, we nurture and we strive consistently to connect audiences with the best of theatre. The evolution of our form is also a vital ambition and bold investment in the future is a big part of what I'm charged with at The Gate. Ria did all this without ever having the title of Artistic Director. And so well!

I have been inspired to read about the risks these women took with their personal reputations, their financial stability, and their own wellbeing, all in devotion to Irish theatre. To hear their stories is to be heartened, and to recognise we are part of a wonderful legacy that should be celebrated. Congratulations to Ciara O'Dowd for highlighting these wonderful women and for illuminating and reinstating their place in Irish theatre history.

Notes

CHAPTER 1: AIDEEN O'CONNOR (1913–50)

1. Shields Family Archive, James Hardiman Library, University of Galway, Green room photo, T13/B/13.
2. Abbey Theatre: Scrapbooks: Vol. 27: American Tour 1935: National Library of Ireland, Dublin, NLI Mss 25,511-23.
3. Shields Family Archive, Visa papers, T13/A/469.
4. Brinsley MacNamara, *Margaret Gillan: A Play in Three Acts*, (London: Allen & Unwin, 1934), p. 12.
5. Census of Ireland, Dublin County, District Electoral Division (DED) Rathmines and Rathgar East, unpaginated, household no. 53 Hollybank Avenue, Vincent De Paul O'Connor, digital image, National Archives of Ireland, *Census of Ireland 1901/1911* (http://www.census.nationalarchives.ie: accessed 5 Feb. 2023); original manuscript not cited.
6. Ibid.
7. Padraig Yeates, *Lockout Dublin: 1913* (Dublin: Gill & Macmillan, 2000), p. 1.
8. Ibid., p. 131.
9. Padraig Yeates, 'The Dublin 1913 Lockout' in *History Ireland*, vol. 9, no. 2. (2001), pp 31–6.
10. Yeates, *Lockout Dublin: 1913*, pp 134–6.
11. Shields Family Archive, Visa application, T13/A/465.
12. Yeates, 'The Dublin 1913 Lockout', pp 31–6.
13. 'Death Certificate of Clara O'Connor, Dublin South Register 2149079', Irish Genealogy, accessed 31 Jan. 2023.
14. Lilian Roberts Finlay, *Always in my Mind*, (Kerry: Brandon Press, 1999), p. 97.
15. Shields Family Archive, Letter to Vincent O'Connor, T13/A/436.
16. M. J. Dolan Papers, National Library of Ireland, Dublin, Adjudications sheet, NLI Mss 22,556.
17. Shields Family Archive, Acting Certificate 1933, T13/A/445.
18. Ibid., Postcard, T13/A/446.
19. Ibid., Letter to Eddie Choate, T13/A/155(15).
20. Marianne Cosgrave, Mercy Congregational Archivist, Email to the author, 10 Dec. 2013.
21. Shields Family Archive, Shields T13/A/518 (1).
22. Seán O'Casey, *Three Plays: Juno and the Paycock, Shadow of a Gunman and The Plough and the Stars*, Introduced by J. C. Trewin, (New York, NY: St Martin's Press, 1957), p. 179.
23. Michael J. O'Neill, *Lennox Robinson*, (New York: Twayne Publishers Inc, 1964), p. 149.
24. Teresa Deevy Papers, Manuscripts and Archives, Trinity College Dublin, Letter to Florence Hackett, 1935, TCD MS 10722/5.
25. Lennox Robinson, *Selected Plays of Lennox Robinson*, ed. Christopher Murray, (Gerrards Cross, Buckinghamshire: Colin Smythe, 1982), p. 202.
26. May Craig's scrapbook is in the UCD Archives with her papers; O'Connor's is in the Shields Family Papers at the University of Galway. It is my understanding that the Mulhern family donated her scrapbook to the Abbey Theatre after her death and it subsequently transferred to the National Library of Ireland, where it can be viewed on microfiche.
27. Abbey Theatre: Scrapbooks: Vol. 27: American Tour 1935, National Library of Ireland, Dublin, NLI Mss 25,511-23.
28. Ibid.

29. Census of Ireland, Fermanagh County, District Electoral Division (DED) Enniskillen East, unpaginated, household no. 10 Belmore Street, Bridget Mulhern, digital image, National Archives of Ireland, *Census of Ireland 1901/1911* (http://www.census.nationalarchives.ie: accessed 5 Feb. 2023); original manuscript not cited.

30. Shields Family Archive, Letter to Eileen and Maeve, Mar. 1935, T13/A/437.

31. Helen De Geus, Personal Interview, Dublin, 10 Sept. 2016.

32. George Shiels, *Selected Plays of George Shiels 1886–1949*, ed. Christopher Murray; Leonard L. Milberg Irish Theater Collection (Gerrards Cross, Buckinghamshire: Colin Smythe, 2008), p. 133.

33. Ibid.

34. Ibid.

35. Abbey Theatre: Scrapbooks: Vol. 22: American Tour 1932–3, National Library of Ireland, Dublin, NLI Mss 25,511-23.

36. Robinson, *Selected Plays of Lennox Robinson*, ed. Christopher Murray, p. 69.

37. Helen De Geus, Personal Interview, Dublin, 10 Sept. 2016.

38. Ibid.

39. Shields Family Archive, Letter addressed to Arthur Shields from the Abbey Theatre, T13/A/117.

40. Ibid., Letter to Vincent O'Connor, 1935, T13/A/436.

41. Ibid., Memorandum of Agreement with Elbert Wickes, 1934, T13/A/106 (1).

42. Ibid., Statement made by Lennox Robinson, 1934, T13/A/108 (1).

43. Ibid.

44. 'Scythia arrives here a day late', in *Daily Boston Globe (1928–1960)*, 9 Oct. 1934, p. 13.

45. Ibid.

46. Abbey Theatre: Scrapbooks: Vol. 23: American Tour 1934–5, National Library of Ireland, Dublin, NLI Mss 25,511-23.

47. Ibid.

48. Ibid.

49. Shields Family Archive, Letter to Eileen O'Connor, T13/A/437.

50. Abbey Theatre: Scrapbooks: Vol. 23: American Tour 1934–5, National Library of Ireland, Dublin, NLI Mss 25,511-23.

51. Ibid.

52. Ibid.

53. Shields Family Archive, Letter to Eileen O'Connor, T13/A/437.

54. Ibid.

55. Abbey Theatre: Scrapbooks: Vol. 23: American Tour 1934–5: National Library of Ireland, Dublin, NLI Mss 25,511-23.

56. Ibid.

57. Robinson, *Selected Plays of Lennox Robinson*, , p. 211.

58. Ibid., p. 203.

59. Abbey Theatre: Scrapbooks: Vol. 23: American Tour 1934–5: National Library of Ireland, Dublin, NLI Mss 25,511-23.

60. Ibid.

61. Ibid.

62. Ibid.

63. Lennox Robinson, *The Far-Off Hills: A comedy in three acts.* (London: Chatto & Windus, 1959), p. 33.

64. May Craig Papers, UCD Archives Collection, UCD, Dubin, Newspaper cutting, LA28/116.

65. Robinson, *The Far-Off Hills*, p. 33.

66. Ibid., p. 34.

67. Ibid., p. 35.

68. Shields Family Archive, Letter to Vincent O'Connor, T13/A/436.

69. Ibid.

70. Ibid., Letter to Eileen and Maeve O'Connor, T13/A/437.

71. Ibid.

72. Ibid.

73. Ibid.

74. Ibid.

75. Ibid.

76. Ibid.
77. Ibid.
78. Ibid.
79. F. R. Higgins Papers, National Library of Ireland, Dublin, Correspondence, NLI Mss 27,897(2).
80. Shields Family Archive, Scrapbook of newspaper cuttings, T13/A/560.
81. There are various versions of events at this time. This reflects the account by Christopher Murray in his biography, *Seán O'Casey: Writer at Work – A Biography*, (Dublin: Gill & Macmillan, 2004), p. 242.
82. Shields Family Archive, Scrapbook, T13/A/560.
83. Ibid.
84. Seán O Casey, *Three More Plays: The Silver Tassie, Purple Dust and Red Roses for Me*, Introduced by J. C. Trewin, (London: Macmillan, 1983), pp 38–9.
85. Seán O'Casey Papers, The Henry W. and Albert A. Berg Collection of English and American Literature, The New York Public Library, New York, Folio Notebook 6, V6 p. 39.
86. Ibid.
87. O Casey, *Three More Plays*, p. 95.
88. Ibid., p. 38.
89. Shields Family Archive, Scrapbook, T13/A/560.
90. Seán O'Casey, *Rose and Crown*, (London: Macmillan, 1952), p. 51.
91. Shields Family Archive, Scrapbook, T13/A/560.
92. Diaries of Joseph Holloway, Recording Theatrical Performances in Dublin and His Views Thereon, Including Newscuttings and Programmes Relating Thereto, 1930–9, National Library of Ireland, Dublin, NLI Mss 1971, p. 347.
93. Abbey Theatre Minute Book 1936–1937, University of Galway, Asset Id 3604, 3558.
94. Ibid.
95. Ibid.
96. Shields Family Archive, Notes by Laurie Shields, T13/A/512.
97. Diaries of Joseph Holloway, p. 342.
98. Ibid., p. 347.
99. James Matthews, *Voices: A Life of Frank O'Connor*, (New York: Atheneum Press, 1983), p. 145.
100. Shields Family Archive, Scrapbook, T13/A/560.
101. Ibid.
102. Ibid.
103. Shields Family Archive, Notes by Laurie Shields, T13/A/512.
104. Ibid., Scrapbook, T13/A/560.
105. Ibid.
106. Ibid.
107. Ibid., Production photograph, T13/B/202.
108. Paul A. Doyle, *Paul Vincent Carroll*, (Lewisburg, PA.: Bucknell UP, 1971), p. 30.
109. Paul Vincent Carroll, *Shadow and Substance: A Play in Four Acts*. (London: Macmillan, 1938), pp 9–10.
110. Lennox Robinson, *The Irish Theatre: lectures delivered during the Abbey Theatre festival, held in Dublin in August 1938*, (New York, NY: Haskell House, 1971), p. 209.
111. Phyllis Ryan, *The Company I Kept: Revelations from the Life of Ireland's Most Distinguished and Independent Theatrical Manager*, (Dublin: Townhouse Press, 1996), p. 74.
112. Ibid.
113. Shields Family Archive, Scrapbook, T13/A/560.
114. May Craig Papers, UCD Archives Collection, UCD, Dublin, Newspaper cutting, UCD Mss LA28/219.
115. Ibid.
116. Ryan, *The Company I Kept*, p. 74.
117. Shields Family Archive, Notes, T13/A/512.
118. Papers of William Denis Johnston, Manuscripts and Archives, Trinity College Dublin Library, Dublin, TCD Mss 10066/165.
119. Ibid.
120. Ann Saddlemyer, ed., *W. B. Yeats and George Yeats: The Letters*, (London: Oxford UP, 2011), Letter from W. B. Yeats to George Yeats, 16 Mar. 1937, p. 459.
121. Ibid., p. 460.
122. Ibid.

123. Ann Treanor, 'Behind the Abbey Scenes', in *Irish Press*, July 28 1938.

124. Ibid.

125. Ibid.

126. Saddlemyer, ed., *W. B. Yeats and George Yeats: The Letters*, Letter from George to W. B. Yeats, 16 Mar. 1937, p. 460.

127. Ibid.

128. Christine Shields, Personal Interviews, California, Sept. 2011.

129. Saddlemyer, ed. *W. B. Yeats and George Yeats: The Letters*, Letter from George to W. B. Yeats, 16 Mar. 1937, p. 461.

130. Shields Family Archive, Pocket diaries, T13/A/372 (1).

CHAPTER 2: RIA MOONEY (1903–73)

1. Viv Gardner, 'By herself: the actress and autobiography, 1755–1939', in *The Cambridge Companion to the Actress*, eds, Maggie Gale and John Stokes, (Cambridge: Cambridge UP, 2007), p. 178.

2. Mary J. Corbett, 'Performing identities: Actresses and autobiography', in *Biography*, vol. 24, no. 1. (Winter 2001), p. 15.

3. Val Mulkerns, ed., 'Players and the painted stage: Autobiography of Ria Mooney: Part 1', in *George Spelvin's Theatre Book* (Spring/Summer 1978), p. 29.

4. Ibid., p. 57.

5. Ibid., p. 131.

6. Robert A. Schanke, *The Shattered Applause: The Lives of Eva Le Gallienne*, (Carbondale and Edwardsville, IL: Southern Illinois UP, 1992), p. xvi.

7. Corbett, 'Performing identities: Actresses and autobiography', p. 15.

8. Mulkerns, ed., 'Players and the painted stage: Autobiography of Ria Mooney: Part 1', p. 83.

9. Ibid., p. 9.

10. Ibid., p. 27.

11. Ibid., p. 12.

12. Ibid., p. 29.

13. Krause, ed., *The Letters of Seán O'Casey 1910–1941*, p. 142.

14. Ibid.

15. Ibid.

16. Ibid., p. 139.

17. Ibid.

18. Ibid., p. 144.

19. Ibid.

20. Ibid., pp 146–7.

21. Adrian Frazier, *Hollywood Irish: John Ford, Abbey Actors and the Irish Revival in Hollywood*, (Dublin: Lilliput Press, 2010), p. 72.

22. In fact, while on tour with the play in January 1928, Richards was signing off letters to her husband from 'your little red-nosed Norah', directly referencing the script and suggesting that she had her own way of softening the term if decorum required. (Johnston TCD Mss 10066/287/2632)

23. Krause, ed., *The Letters of Seán O'Casey 1910–1941*, p. 165.

24. Mulkerns, ed., 'Players and the painted stage: Autobiography of Ria Mooney: Part 1', p. 43.

25. Ibid.

26. Ibid.

27. Krause, ed., *The Letters of Seán O'Casey 1910–1941*, p. 147.

28. Mulkerns, ed., 'Players and the painted stage: Autobiography of Ria Mooney: Part 1', p. 46.

29. Bernard Adams, *Denis Johnston: A Life.* (Dublin: Lilliput Press, 2002), p. 80.

30. Seán O'Casey, *Three Plays: Juno and the Paycock, Shadow of a Gunman and The Plough and the Stars*, Introduced by J. C. Trewin, (New York: St Martin's Press, 1957), p. 175.

31. Ibid.

32. Mulkerns, ed., 'Players and the painted stage: Autobiography of Ria Mooney: Part 1', p. 45.

33. Papers of William Denis Johnston, Trinity College Dublin, Letter from Shelah Richards, TCD MSS 10066/287/2638.

34. Mulkerns, ed., 'Players and the painted stage: Autobiography of Ria Mooney: Part 1', p. 62.

35. Ibid.

36. Ibid.

37. Papers of William Denis Johnston, Trinity College Dublin, Letter from Shelah Richards, TCD MSS 10066/287/2633.

38. Ibid.

39. Ibid.

40. Helen Sheehy, *Eva Le Gallienne: A Biography*, (New York, NY: Alfred Knopf, 1996), p. 152.

41. Ibid.

42. Sheehy, *Eva Le Gallienne: A Biography*, p. 179.

43. Ibid., pp 144–58.

44. Ibid., p. 57.

45. Eva Le Gallienne, *At 33*, (London: John Lane, Bodley Head Ltd, 1934), p. 164.

46. Ibid., p. 147.

47. Ibid.

48. Eva Le Gallienne, *With a Quiet Heart*, (New York, NY: Viking, 1953), p. 15.

49. Le Gallienne, *At 33*, p. 198.

50. Ibid., p. 201.

51. Sheehy, *Eva Le Gallienne: A Biography*, p. 76.

52. The manner in which Hapgood's translation differs from Stanislavski's writing and its inconsistencies, deletions and erroneous substitutions is clearly set out in Carnicke's chapter 'The US Publication Maze' in *Stanislavsky in Focus*. (pp 76–93) Carnicke also explains how 'dual consciousness' ensured the mental health of actors was protected, in a manner never observed by the American Method.

53. Le Gallienne, *At 33*, p. 168.

54. Patrick Laffan letter, Private collection, shared with the author in 2013.

55. Sheehy, *Eva Le Gallienne: A Biography*, p. 84.

56. Le Gallienne, *At 33*, p. 181.

57. Sheehy, *Eva Le Gallienne: A Biography*, p. 134.

58. Ibid.

59. Ibid., p. 198.

60. Ibid., p. 194.

61. Ibid., p. 118.

62. Ibid.

63. Papers of William Denis Johnston, Trinity College Dublin, Letter to Shelah Richards, Mar. 1927, TCD MSS 10066/165.

64. James McGlone, *Ria Mooney: The Life and Times of the Artistic Director of the Abbey Theatre 1948–1963* (North Carolina: McFarland & Co., 2002), p. 28.

65. Micheál MacLiammóir, *All For Hecuba*, (Dublin: Progress House, 1961), p. 167.

66. Ibid.

67. Shields Family Archive, James Hardiman Library, University of Galway, Letter from P. V. Carroll, T13/A/150(44).

68. Le Gallienne, *At 33*, p. 147.

69. George Jean Nathan, 'The Theatre' *American Mercury*, vol. 13, no 5, (Mar. 1928), p. 377.

70. Ibid.

71. Sheehy, *Eva Le Gallienne: A Biography*, p. 164.

72. Ibid., p. 274.

73. Helen Dore Boylston, *Carol Goes Backstage*, (Boston, MA: Little, Brown and Co., 1947), p. 97.

74. Ibid., p. 98.

75. Ibid.

76. Ibid.

77. The relationship of manipulation and control between a male director and female actor (a relationship which Malague examines in relation to the 'American Method') is here abandoned.

78. Sharon Marie Carnicke, *Stanislavsky in Focus: An Acting Master for the Twenty-First Century*, Edn 2, (New York, NY: Routledge, 2009), p. 3.

79. May Sarton, *I Knew a Phoenix*, (UK: The Women's Press Ltd, 1995), p. 152.

80. Ibid., p. 156.

81. Ibid.
82. Carnicke, *Stanislavsky in Focus: An Acting Master for the Twenty-First Century*, p. 29.
83. Boylston, *Carol Goes Backstage*, p. 155.
84. Carnicke, *Stanislavsky in Focus: An Acting Master for the Twenty-First Century*, p. 214.
85. Boylston, *Carol Goes Backstage*, p. 105.
86. Mulkerns, ed., 'Players and the painted stage: Autobiography of Ria Mooney: Part 1', p. 90.
87. Civic Repertory Theatre Records, Yale Collection of American Literature, Beinecke Rare Book and Manuscript Library, Production Files, *La Locandiera*, YCAL Mss 343.
88. Carnicke, *Stanislavsky in Focus: An Acting Master for the Twenty-First Century*, p. 30.
89. Mulkerns, ed., 'Players and the painted stage: Autobiography of Ria Mooney: Part 1 '), p. 91.
90. Ibid., p. 45.
91. Vincent Dowling, *Astride the Moon: A Theatrical Life*, (Dublin: Wolfhound Press, 2000), p. 174.
92. Roz Dixon, '"All of Ireland is our orchard": Maria Knebel's production of *The Cherry Orchard* at the Abbey in 1968', in *Ibsen and Chekhov on the Irish Stage*, eds, Roz Dixon and Irina Ruppo Malone, (Dublin: Carysfort Press, 2012), p. 158.
93. Mulkerns, ed., 'Players and the painted stage: Autobiography of Ria Mooney: Part 1', p. 71.
94. Ibid.
95. Sheehy, *Eva Le Gallienne: A Biography*, p. 176.
96. Ibid., p. 179.
97. Jean-Jacques Bernard, *The Sulky Fire: Five Plays*, trans. J. L. Firth, (London: Jonathan Cape, 1939), p. 195.
98. Sheehy, *Eva Le Gallienne: A Biography*, p. 179.
99. Bernard, *The Sulky Fire: Five Plays*, trans. J. L. Firth, p. 195.
100. Ibid., p. 10.
101. Ibid., p. 232.
102. Ibid.
103. McGlone, *Ria Mooney: The Life and Times of the Artistic Director of the Abbey Theatre 1948–1963*, p. 32.
104. Brooks Atkinson, 'The Play: The Abbey Theatre players open an engagement', *New York Times*, 4 Oct. 1937, p. 17.
105. Sarton, *I knew a Phoenix*, p. 158.
106. Civic Repertory Theatre Records, Yale Collection of American Literature, Beinecke Rare Book and Manuscript Library, CRTC Cashbook, YCAL Mss 343.
107. McGlone, *Ria Mooney: The Life and Times of the Artistic Director of the Abbey Theatre 1948–1963*, p. 35.
108. Sheehy, *Eva Le Gallienne: A Biography*, p. 181.
109. Ibid., p. 189.
110. Mulkerns, ed., 'Players and the painted stage: Autobiography of Ria Mooney: Part 1', p. 91.
111. Ibid., p. 92.
112. Civic Repertory Theatre Records, Yale Collection of American Literature, Beinecke Rare Book and Manuscript Library, Production files, Box 23, YCAL Mss 343.
113. Le Gallienne, *At 33*, p. 255.
114. Sheehy, *Eva Le Gallienne: A Biography*, p. 168.
115. This strain in her work will be considered in detail at a later point in this chapter.
116. Boylston, *Carol Goes Backstage*, p. 144.
117. Ibid., pp 116–17.
118. Ibid., p. 119.
119. McGlone, *Ria Mooney: The Life and Times of the Artistic Director of the Abbey Theatre 1948–1963*, p. 32.
120. Papers of William Denis Johnston, Trinity College Dublin, Letter from Shelah Richards, 25 Jan. 1928, TCD MSS 10066/287/2632.
121. Papers of William Denis Johnston, Trinity College Dublin, Letter from Shelah Richards, 2 Feb. 1928, TCD MSS 10066/287/2633.
122. 'Rita Romilly Benson dead at 79; Actress taught at Arts Academy', *New York Times*, 7 Apr. 1980, D11.
123. Mulkerns, ed., 'Players and the painted stage: Autobiography of Ria Mooney: Part 1 ', p. 62.
124. McGlone, *Ria Mooney: The Life and Times of the Artistic Director of the Abbey Theatre 1948–1963*, p. 43.
125. Mulkerns, ed., 'Players and the painted stage: Autobiography of Ria Mooney: Part 1', p. 62.
126. Ibid., p. 98.
127. McGlone, *Ria Mooney: The Life and Times of the Artistic Director of the Abbey Theatre 1948–1963*, p. 32.
128. Sheehy, *Eva Le Gallienne: A Biography*, p. 164.

129. McGlone, *Ria Mooney: The Life and Times of the Artistic Director of the Abbey Theatre 1948–1963*, p. 43.
130. Mulkerns, ed., 'Players and the painted stage: Autobiography of Ria Mooney: Part 1', p. 97.
131. McGlone, *Ria Mooney: The Life and Times of the Artistic Director of the Abbey Theatre 1948–1963*, p. 44.
132. Sheehy, *Eva Le Gallienne: A Biography*, p. 198.
133. Ibid.
134. Mulkerns, ed., 'Players and the painted stage: Autobiography of Ria Mooney: Part 1', p. 96.
135. Ibid., pp 69–70.
136. Ibid.
137. Ibid., p. 30.
138. Ibid., p. 74.
139. Val Mulkerns, Personal Interview, Dublin, 13 July 2012.
140. Mulkerns, ed., 'Players and the painted stage: Autobiography of Ria Mooney: Part 1', p. 88.
141. Sheehy, *Eva Le Gallienne: A Biography*, p. 201.
142. Ibid.
143. Dore Boylston, *Carol Goes Backstage*, p. 127.
144. Mulkerns, ed., 'Players and the painted stage: Autobiography of Ria Mooney: Part 1', p. 93.
145. Brooks Atkinson, 'Plays and players of the mid-February stage', *New York Times*, 15 Feb. 1931, p. 105.
146. Ibid.
147. Sheehy, *Eva Le Gallienne: A Biography*, p. 214.
148. Papers of William Denis Johnston, Trinity College Dublin, Letter from Shelah Richards, Sept. 1931, TCD MSS 10066/287/2651.
149. McGlone, *Ria Mooney: The Life and Times of the Artistic Director of the Abbey Theatre 1948–1963*, p. 47.
150. Val Mulkerns, ed., 'Players and the painted stage: Autobiography of Ria Mooney, Part 2', *George Spelvin's Theatre Book* (Autumn/Winter 1978), p. 88.
151. Henry W. and Albert A. Berg Collection of English and American Literature, The New York Public Library. 'Seán and Me' (Rosie Redmond played by Ria Mooney) *The Plough and the Stars* Abbey Theatre, *The New York Public Library Digital Collections*, 1926, Mss 7OB5715. https://digitalcollections.nypl.org/items/4c3ae020-3481-0137-cf17-47b92197baeb
152. Mulkerns, ed., 'Players and the painted stage: Autobiography of Ria Mooney: Part 1', p. 101.
153. May Craig Papers (1889–1972), UCD Archives, Dublin, Scrapbook undated, IE UCDA LA28/116.
154. Mulkerns, ed., 'Players and the painted stage: Autobiography of Ria Mooney, Part 2', p. 104.
155. McGlone, *Ria Mooney: The Life and Times of the Artistic Director of the Abbey Theatre 1948–1963*, p. 60.
156. MacLiammóir, *All For Hecuba*, p. 167.
157. Ibid.
158. Mulkerns, ed., 'Players and the painted stage: Autobiography of Ria Mooney: Part 1', p. 105.
159. 'Wuthering Heights Revived', in *Irish Independent*, 13 Feb. 1935, p. 6.
160. 'The Gate Theatre: Wuthering Heights Revived', in *Irish Times*, 13 Feb. 1935, p. 8.
161. Mulkerns, ed., 'Players and the painted stage: Autobiography of Ria Mooney: Part 1', p. 106.
162. This jibe is recorded by Lauren Arrington, referring to a letter to Fred Higgins from Ethel Mannin (9 Feb. 1939) in Ria Mooney Papers, NLI Acc 6548.
163. Ibid., p. 108.
164. Mulkerns, ed., 'Players and the painted stage: Autobiography of Ria Mooney: Part 1', p. 108.
165. Ibid.
166. Ibid.
167. 'New play at the Abbey: *Parnell of Avondale*', in *Irish Times*, 2 Oct. 1934, p. 6.
168. Lilian Roberts Finlay, *Always in my Mind*, (Kerry: Brandon Press, 1999), p. 177.
169. This second production was directed by Hugh Hunt in October 1935.
170. Mulkerns, ed., 'Players and the painted stage: Autobiography of Ria Mooney: Part 1', p. 109.
171. Teresa Deevy Papers, Trinity College Manuscript Collections, Trinity College, Dublin, Letter to F Hackett, 8 May 1935, IE TCD Mss 10722/8.
172. Ibid., Letter to F Hackett, 24 Apr. 1935, IE TCD Mss 10722/6.
173. Ibid., Letter to F Hackett, 8 May 1935, IE TCD Mss 10722/8.
174. Ibid.
175. Ibid.
176. Teresa Deevy, *Three Plays: Katie Roche; The King of Spain's Daughter and The Wild Goose*, (London: Macmillan, 1939), p. 23.

177. Teresa Deevy Papers, Trinity College Manuscript Collections, Trinity College, Dublin, Unpublished lecture, IE TCD Mss 10722/81.
178. Ibid., Letter to F Hackett, 1934, IE TCD Mss 10722/1.
179. Ibid.
180. Ibid., Letter to F Hackett, 8 May 1935, IE TCD Mss 10722/8.
181. Diaries of Joseph Holloway, 1930–9, National Library of Ireland, Dublin, Aug. 1936, NLI Mss 1971.
182. Ibid.
183. Deevy, *Three Plays: Katie Roche; The King of Spain's Daughter and The Wild Goose*, p. 28.
184. Ibid., p. 25.
185. Ibid., p. 40.
186. Ibid., p. 108.
187. Ibid., p. 113.
188. Ibid.
189. Ibid., p. 114.
190. Ibid., p. 113.
191. Teresa Deevy Papers, Trinity College Manuscript Collections, Trinity College, Dublin, Letter to F Hackett, 5 Apr. 1936, IE TCD Mss 10722/15.
192. Ibid., Letter to F Hackett, 1949, IE TCD Mss 10722/49.
193. Mulkerns, ed., 'Players and the painted stage: Autobiography of Ria Mooney. Part 2', p. 90.
194. Before the release of his collection, *Intercessions*, he removed this poem from the manuscript, along with others. It was subsequently published in 1946, in a collection entitled *Lough Derg and Other Poems*. The title of the poem had also changed: from 'Actress Attracting' to 'Poet and Comic Muse'. Denis Devlin, *Lough Derg and Other Poems*, (New York, NY: Reynal & Hitchcock, 1946).
195. Sarah Bennett, ed., *The Letters of Denis Devlin*, (Cork: Cork UP 2020), p. 114.
196. Ibid.
197. Ibid., p. 131.

INTERLUDE: THE AMERICAN TOUR OF 1937/38

1. Elbert Wickes Theater Arts Collection, Special Collections, The Claremont Colleges Library, Claremont, California, Office Inventory, Box 4,2.
2. Elbert Wickes Theater Arts Collection, Special Collections, The Claremont Colleges Library, Claremont, California, Letter to F. R. Higgins, Box 4,2.
3. Elbert Wickes Theater Arts Collection, Special Collections, The Claremont Colleges Library, Claremont, California, Press statement, Box 4,2.
4. Elbert Wickes Theater Arts Collection, Special Collections, The Claremont Colleges Library, Claremont, California, Letter to F. R. Higgins, Box 4,2.
5. Ibid.
6. Ibid.
7. Ibid.
8. Elbert Wickes Theater Arts Collection, Special Collections, The Claremont Colleges Library, Claremont, California, Telegram to F. R. Higgins, Box 4,2.
9. Shields Family Archive, Press articles, T13/A/561(17).
10. Anne Saddlemyer, ed., *W. B. Yeats and George Yeats: The Letters*, (London: Oxford UP, 2011), p. 491.
11. F. R. Higgins Papers, National Library of Ireland, Dublin, Letter from F. R. Higgins to May Higgins, NLI Mss 27,883(7).
12. Frank O'Connor, *My Father's Son*, (Belfast: Blackstaff Press, 1994), p. 314.
13. F. R. Higgins Papers, National Library of Ireland, Dublin, Letter from F. R. Higgins to May Higgins, NLI Mss 27,883(8).
14. F. R. Higgins Papers, National Library of Ireland, Dublin, Letter from F. R. Higgins to May Higgins, NLI Mss 27,883(7).
15. Ibid.
16. Ibid.
17. Ibid.

18. Her physical attributes are evident in photographs of Delany in the Abbey Theatre Digital Archive and Shields Papers, both accessible at Hardiman Library, University of Galway.

19. D. Dayton, 'Maureen Delany: Off Stage', in *New York Sun*, 6 Dec. 1934.

20. Abbey Theatre: Scrapbooks: Vol. 23: American Tour 1934–5: National Library of Ireland, Dublin, NLI Mss 25,511-23.

21. F. R. Higgins Papers, National Library of Ireland, Dublin, Letter from F. R. Higgins to May Higgins, NLI Mss 27,883(7).

22. Ibid.

23. Val Mulkerns, ed., 'Players and the painted atage: Autobiography of Ria Mooney: Part 1', *George Spelvin's Theatre Book* (Spring/Summer 1978), p. 85.

24. F. R. Higgins Papers, National Library of Ireland, Dublin, Letter from F. R. Higgins to May Higgins, NLI Mss 27,883(7).

25. Ibid.

26. Ibid.

27. Teresa Deevy Papers, Trinity College Manuscript Collections, Trinity College, Dublin, Letter to F Hackett, 8 May 1935, IE TCD Mss 10722/12.

28. May Craig Papers, UCD Archives, University College Dublin, Newspaper cuttings, Mss IE UCDA LA28/231.

29. Sarah Bennett, ed., *The Letters of Denis Devlin*, (Cork: Cork UP, 2020), Letter to Ria Mooney, 8 Nov. 1937, p. 124.

30. Sarah Bennett, ed., *The Letters of Denis Devlin*, (Cork: Cork UP, 2020), Letter to Ria Mooney, 4 Aug. 1938, p. 138.

31. F. R. Higgins Papers, National Library of Ireland, Dublin, Letter from F. R. Higgins, NLI Mss 27,883(7).

32. Theatre Guild Archive, Yale Collection of American Literature, Beinecke Rare Book & Manuscript Library, Connecticut, Letter to Theresa Helburn, YCAL Mss 436.

33. Shields Family Archive, Letter to Eileen O'Connor, T13/A/428.

34. Ibid.

35. Ibid., Letter to Eileen O'Connor, T13/A/439.

36. Saddlemyer, ed., *W. B. Yeats and George Yeats: The Letters*, p. 511.

37. Shields Family Archive, Letter to Eileen O'Connor, T13/A/439.

38. F. R. Higgins Papers, National Library of Ireland, Dublin, Letter from F. R. Higgins to May Higgins, NLI Mss 27,883(7).

39. Shields Family Archive, Letter to Eileen O'Connor, T13/A/440.

40. Abbey Theatre Scrapbooks: Vol. 27: American Tour 1935, National Library of Ireland, Dublin, Mss 25,511-23.

41. Elbert Wickes Theater Arts Collection, Special Collections, The Claremont Colleges Library, Claremont, California, Press cuttings, Box 4,2.

42. O'Connor, *My Father's Son*, p. 326.

43. Ibid.

44. Elbert Wickes Theater Arts Collection, Special Collections, The Claremont Colleges Library, Claremont, California, Letter to F. R. Higgins, Box 4,2.

45. Saddlemyer, ed., *W. B. Yeats and George Yeats: The Letters*, p. 544.

46. Abbey Theatre Scrapbooks: Vol. 27: American Tour 1937, National Library of Ireland, Dublin, Mss 25,511-23.

47. Nicolas Grene and Christopher Morash, eds, *Irish Theatre on Tour*, (Dublin: Carysfort Press, 2005), p. 44.

48. Ibid.

49. Barry Monahan, *Ireland's Theatre on Film: Style, Stories and the National Stage on Screen*, (Dublin: Irish Academic Press, 2009), p. 100.

50. Ibid.

51. Shields Family Archive, Letter to Eileen O'Connor, T13/A/441.

52. Ibid., Letter to Eileen O'Connor, T13/A/440.

53. Ibid., Letter to Eileen O'Connor, T13/A/441.

54. Ibid.

55. Ibid., Photos of train platforms, T13/B/326-7.

56. Ibid., Letter to Eileen O'Connor, T13/A/441.

57. Abbey Theatre Scrapbooks: Vol. 27: American Tour 1937, National Library of Ireland, Dublin, Mss 25,511-23.
58. Ibid.
59. Frank O'Connor, *My Father's Son*, (Belfast: Blackstaff Press, 1994) p. 311.
60. Elbert Wickes Theater Arts Collection, Special Collections, The Claremont Colleges Library, Claremont, California, Press cuttings, Box 6,4.
61. Ibid.
62. Elbert Wickes Theater Arts Collection, Special Collections, The Claremont Colleges Library, Claremont, California, Letter from Arthur Shields, Box 4,11.
63. Ibid.
64. Ibid.
65. Charles Frances Peters, 'A Historical Survey of the Biltmore Theatre', Unpublished Dissertation, California: University of Long Beach, 1969.
66. Ibid.
67. Elbert Wickes Theater Arts Collection, Special Collections, The Claremont Colleges Library, Claremont, California, Letter to F. R. Higgins, Box 4,2.
68. Ibid.
69. Ibid.
70. Elbert Wickes Theater Arts Collection, Special Collections, The Claremont Colleges Library, Claremont, California, Stories: Agents' File, Box 5,6.
71. Elbert Wickes Theater Arts Collection, Special Collections, The Claremont Colleges Library, Claremont, California, Letter from Arthur Shields, Box 4,2.
72. Elbert Wickes Theater Arts Collection, Special Collections, The Claremont Colleges Library, Claremont, California, Letter to F. R. Higgins, Box 4,2.
73. Hugh Hunt, *The Abbey: Ireland's National Theatre 1904–78*, (Dublin: Gill & Macmillan, 1979), p. 162.
74. Elbert Wickes Theater Arts Collection, Special Collections, The Claremont Colleges Library, Claremont, California, Letter from F. R. Higgins, Box 4,2.
75. Elbert Wickes Theater Arts Collection, Special Collections, The Claremont Colleges Library, Claremont, California, Letter from Arthur Shields, Box 4,2.
76. Elbert Wickes Theater Arts Collection, Special Collections, The Claremont Colleges Library, Claremont, California, Letter from Gertrude Lamothe, Box 5.
77. Ibid.
78. Ibid.
79. Ibid.

CHAPTER 3: RIA AGAIN: AFTER THE 1937/38 TOUR

1. Val Mulkerns, ed., 'Players and the painted stage: Autobiography of Ria Mooney: Part 1', *George Spelvin's Theatre Book* (Spring/Summer 1978), p. 113.
2. Ibid., p. 120.
3. Sarah Bennett, ed., *The Letters of Denis Devlin*, Letter to Ria Mooney, 4 Aug. 1938, (Cork: Cork UP, 2020) p. 138.
4. Ria Mooney Papers, NLI Acc 6548, National Library of Ireland, Dublin.
5. James McGlone, *Ria Mooney: The Life and Times of the Artistic Director of the Abbey Theatre 1948–1963*, (North Carolina: McFarland & Co., 2002), p. 71.
6. Una Troy Papers, National Library of Ireland, Dublin, Letter from Ria Mooney, Mss 35,687(9).
7. Ibid., Newspaper cuttings, Mss 35,687(9).
8. Ibid., Letter from Lennox Robinson, Mss 35,687(9).
9. Ibid., Newspaper cuttings, Mss 35,687(9).
10. Ibid., Una Troy Papers, National Library of Ireland, Dublin, Newspaper cuttings, Mss 35,687(9).
11. Ibid., Letter from Robinson, Mss 35,687(9).
12. Ibid., NLI Acc 5526, *Mount Prospect*, Act 1 Scene 1, p. 8, Mss 35,687(9).
13. Ibid., NLI Acc 5526, *Mount Prospect*, the novel, p. 544, Mss 36,685(2).
14. Hugh Hunt, *The Abbey: Ireland's National Theatre 1904–78*, (Dublin: Gill & Macmillan, 1979), p. 157.
15. Una Troy Papers, National Library of Ireland, Dublin, *Mount Prospect*, Act 1 Scene 1, p. 10, Mss 35,687(9).

16. Ibid., *Mount Prospect*, the novel, p. 468, Mss 36,685(2).

17. Ibid., *Mount Prospect*, the novel, p. 469, Mss 36,685(2).

18. Ibid., *Mount Prospect*, Act 1 Scene 2, Mss 35,687(9).

19. Ibid., *Mount Prospect*, Act 1 Scene 2, Mss 35,687(9).

20. Ibid., *Mount Prospect*, the novel, p. 558, Mss 36,685(2).

21. Ibid., *Mount Prospect*, the novel, p. 563, Mss 36,685(2).

22. 'Abbey Theatre: Mount Prospect', in *Irish Times*, 23 Apr. 1940, p. 4.

23. Una Troy Papers, National Library of Ireland, Dublin, Newspaper cuttings, Mss 35,687 (9).

24. Abbey Theatre Minute Books, ADM–00003559_1932-1936, 2 Aug. 1935, p. 135.

25. Abbey Theatre Minute Book, ADM–00003559_1936-1937, 14 Feb. 1936, p. 19.

26. Ibid.

27. Val Mulkerns, ed., 'Players and the painted stage: Autobiography of Ria Mooney. Part 2', *George Spelvin's Theatre Book* (Spring/Summer 1978), p. 69.

28. Ibid., p. 68.

29. Anne Saddlemyer, ed., *W. B. Yeats and George Yeats: The Letters*, (London: Oxford UP, 2011), p. 467.

30. Lennox Robinson, *Ireland's Abbey Theatre: A History: 1899–1951*, (Port Washington, NY: Kennikat Press, 1968), pp 154–5.

31. Saddlemyer, ed., *W. B. Yeats and George Yeats: The Letters*, p. 467.

32. Ian R Walsh, *Experimental Irish Theatre After W. B. Yeats*, (London: Palgrave Macmillan, 2012), p. 41.

33. The Henry W. and Albert A. Berg Collection of English and American Literature, The New York Public Library, New York, Jack Yeats Correspondence, Berg Mss 170B6454.

34. Hilary Pyle, *Jack B. Yeats: A Biography*, Second Edition, (London: Andre Deutsch Ltd, 1989), p. 154.

35. Mulkerns, ed., 'Players and the painted stage: Autobiography of Ria Mooney. Part 2', p. 111.

36. Ibid.

37. Pyle, *Jack B. Yeats: A Biography*, p. 154.

38. 'The Peacock Theatre', in *Irish Times*, 6 June 1939, p. 6.

39. Ibid.

40. McGlone, *Ria Mooney: The Life and Times of the Artistic Director of the Abbey Theatre 1948–1963*, p. 71.

41. 'Mr F. R. Higgins' in *Irish Times*, 11 Jan. 1941; ProQuest Historical Newspapers: *The Irish Times* and *The Weekly Irish Times*, p. 8.

42. Jack B. Yeats, *La La Noo*, (Shannon: Irish UP, 1971), p. 1.

43. Ibid.

44. Marilyn Gaddis Rose, *Jack B. Yeats. Painter and Poet*, (Berne : Herbert Lang, 1972), p. 35.

45. Yeats, *La La Noo*, p. 10.

46. Ibid., p. 23.

47. Ibid., p. 10.

48. The Henry W. and Albert A. Berg Collection of English and American Literature, The New York Public Library, New York, Jack Yeats Correspondence, Berg Mss 170B6454.

49. Ibid.

50. Ibid.

51. Vincent Dowling, *Astride the Moon: A Theatrical Life*, (Dublin: Wolfhound Press, 2000), p. 163.

52. Mulkerns, ed., 'Players and the painted stage: Autobiography of Ria Mooney, Part 2', p. 69.

53. Ibid., .p. 84.

54. Ibid.

55. Dowling, *Astride the Moon: A Theatrical Life*, p. 161.

56. Ibid.

57. Theatre Guild Archive, Yale Collection of American Literature, Beinecke Rare Book & Manuscript Library, Connecticut, Letter to Theresa Helburn, YCAL Mss 436.

58. Mulkerns, ed., 'Players and the painted stage: Autobiography of Ria Mooney. Part 2', p. 85.

59. Ibid., p. 102.

60. Ibid., p. 104.

61. Theatre Guild Archive, Yale Collection of American Literature, Beinecke Rare Book & Manuscript Library, Connecticut, Letter to Theresa Helburn, YCAL Mss 436.

62. Mulkerns, ed., 'Players and the painted stage: Autobiography of Ria Mooney. Part 2', p. 113.

63. Theatre Guild Archive, Yale Collection of American Literature, Beinecke Rare Book & Manuscript Library, Connecticut, Letter to Theresa Helburn, YCAL Mss 436.

64. Ibid.
65. Ibid.
66. Dowling, *Astride the Moon: A Theatrical Life*, pp 203–4.
67. Eugene O'Neill, *Long Day's Journey Into Night*, ed., Harold Bloom, 2nd edn, (New Haven, CT and London: Yale Nota Bene Books, 1989), p. 12.
68. Ibid., p. 13.
69. Ibid., p. 12.
70. Dowling, *Astride the Moon: A Theatrical Life*, p. 206.
71. McGlone, *Ria Mooney: The Life and Times of the Artistic Director of the Abbey Theatre 1948–1963*, p. 184.
72. 'Excellent acting by Abbey players' in *Irish Independent*, 29 Apr. 1959, p. 10.
73. Ibid.
74. Patrick Laffan, Personal Interview, Dublin, 3 July 2013.
75. McGlone, *Ria Mooney: The Life and Times of the Artistic Director of the Abbey Theatre 1948–1963*, p. 185.
76. Dowling, *Astride the Moon: A Theatrical Life*, p. 164.
77. Patrick Laffan, Personal Interview, Dublin, 3 July 2013.
78. Ibid.
79. 'Fine study of Saint in new play at Abbey', in *Irish Press*, 7 Aug. 1962, p. 6.
80. Hugh Hunt, *The Abbey: Ireland's National Theatre 1904–78*, (Dublin: Gill & Macmillan, 1979), p. 185.
81. Mulkerns, ed., 'Players and the painted stage: Autobiography of Ria Mooney, Part 2', p. 116.
82. Patrick Laffan, Personal Interview, Dublin, 3 July 2013.
83. Mulkerns, ed., 'Players and the painted stage: Autobiography of Ria Mooney, Part 2', p. 116.
84. Ibid.
85. Lyric Theatre Archive, James Hardiman Library, University of Galway, Letter from Ria Mooney, T4/851.
86. Ibid.
87. Mulkerns, ed., 'Players and the painted stage: Autobiography of Ria Mooney. Part 2', p. 119.
88. Theatre Guild Archive, Yale Collection of American Literature, Beinecke Rare Book & Manuscript Library, Connecticut, Letter to Theresa Helburn, YCAL Mss 436.
89. Letter to Lilian Robert Finlay, 1936, Family Private Collection.
90. Ibid.
91. Ibid.
92. Letter to Patrick Laffan, June 1962, copy shared with the author.
93. Mulkerns, ed., 'Players and the painted stage: Autobiography of Ria Mooney. Part 2', p. 119.
94. Sharon Marie Carnicke, *Stanislavsky in Focus: An Acting Master for the Twenty-First Century*, 2nd edn, (New York, NY: Routledge, 2009), p. 3.

CHAPTER 4: AIDEEN AGAIN: AFTER THE 1937/38 TOUR

1. Shields Family Archive, James Hardiman Library, University of Galway, Letter to Eileen O'Connor, T13/A/441.
2. Ibid., Letter to Maeve O'Connor, T13/A/442.
3. Ibid.
4. Ibid., Letter to Eileen O'Connor, T13/A/441.
5. Ibid., Letter to Maeve O'Connor, T13/A/442.
6. Val Mulkerns, ed., 'Players and the painted stage: Autobiography of Ria Mooney: Part 1', in *George Spelvin's Theatre Book* (Spring/Summer 1978), p. 116.
7. Ibid.
8. Ibid.
9. Shields Family Archive, Letter to Eileen O'Connor, T13/A/440.
10. Ibid.
11. Ibid., Letter to Eileen O'Connor, T13/A/439.
12. Ibid.
13. Helen de Geus and Mary McCullough, Personal interviews, Dublin, 10 Sept. 2016 and 9 Apr. 2010.
14. 'Popular Abbey Actress Dead', *Fermanagh Herald*, 24 Nov. 1939, p. 8.
15. Shields Family Archive, Letter to Eddie Choate, T13/A/150 (41).
16. Ibid., Letter from Arthur Shields to Eddie Choate, T13/A/150 (30).

17. Mary Rynne Papers, James Hardiman Library Special Collections, University of Galway, *Pilgrims* Mss, Act 1.

18. Ibid., Act 3.

19. 'Ennis Woman's First Play', *Irish Independent*, 11th Oct. 1938, 12.

20. Shields Family Archive, Letter to Eddie Choate, T13/A/150 (27).

21. Abbey Theatre: Scrapbooks: Vol. 27: American Tour 1937–8: National Library of Ireland, Dublin, Unknown paper, N.d., Mss 25,511-23.

22. Ibid.

23. Ibid.

24. Shields Family Archive, Letter to Eileen O'Connor, T13/A/444.

25. Tricia O'Beirne, '"In a position to be treated roughly": F. R. Higgins in the Abbey Theatre Minute Books', in *New Hibernia Review*, vol. 22, no. 1, 2018, pp 120–34.

26. Abbey Theatre Minute Books, ADM–00003559_1937-1939, p. 215.

27. Ibid., p. 222.

28. A. Dent, 'Abbey Theatre Drama Festival' in UK *Spectator*, 18 Aug. 1938, p. 15.

29. Ibid.

30. 'What does it mean?' in *Evening Herald*, 11 Aug. 1938, N.p.

31. Tricia O'Beirne, '"In a position to be treated roughly": F. R. Higgins in the Abbey Theatre Minute Books', in *New Hibernia Review*, vol. 22, no. 1, 2018, pp 120–34.

32. Papers of William Denis Johnston, Trinity College Dublin Library, Dublin, Letter from Shelah Richards, TCD MSS 10066/287/2649.

33. Abbey Theatre Minute Books, ADM–00003559_1939-1940, p. 17.

34. Shields Family Archive, Letter to Eddie Choate, T13/A/150 (20).

35. Ibid.

36. Anne Saddlemyer, ed., *W. B. Yeats and George Yeats: The Letters*, (London: Oxford UP, 2011), Letter from George to W. B. Yeats, 24 Mar. 1937, p. 544.

37. Tricia O'Beirne, '"In a position to be treated roughly": F. R. Higgins in the Abbey Theatre Minute Books', in *New Hibernia Review*, vol. 22, no. 1, 2018, pp 120–34.

38. K. Clive, 'Echoes of the Town', in *Irish Times*, 26 Aug. 1938, p. 4.

39. Ibid.

40. Adrian Frazier, *Hollywood Irish: John Ford, Abbey Actor and the Irish Revival in Hollywood*, (Dublin: Lilliput Press, 2010), p. 128.

41. Ibid.

42. 'From the drama mailbag', in *New York Times*, 29 Jan. 1939, X3.

43. Ibid.

44. Christine Shields, Personal interview, California, 18 Sept. 2011.

45. Shelah Richards Papers, Irish Theatre Archive, Dublin City Library and Archive, Pearse Street, Dublin, *Spring Meeting* playbill, ITA/128/1/1.

46. Ibid.

47. M. J. Farrell and John Perry, *Spring Meeting: A Comedy in Three Acts*, (London: Samuel French Ltd, 1938), p. 7.

48. Ibid., p. 9.

49. Ibid., p. 11.

50. Ibid., p. 43.

51. Ibid., p. 37.

52. Teresa Deevy, *Three Plays: Katie Roche; The King of Spain's Daughter and The Wild Goose*, (London: Macmillan, 1939), p. 113.

53. Mary Lasker Papers, Columbia University Library, Rare Book and Manuscript Library, New York, Folder 259.

54. May Craig Papers, UCD Archives Collection, UCD, Dubin, 'Reminiscence' , LA28/240.

55. Mary Lasker Papers, Columbia University Library, Rare Book and Manuscript Library, New York, Folder 259.

56. Ibid., Folder 544.

57. Vicki Ohl, *Fine and Dandy: The Life and Work of Kay Swift*, (New Haven, CT and London: Yale UP, 2004), p. 219.

58. Mary Lasker Papers, Columbia University Library, Rare Book and Manuscript Library, New York, Folder 259.

59. Shields Family Archive, James Hardiman Library, University of Galway, Letter to Eddie Choate, T13/A/150(21).

60. Ibid., Letter to Eddie Choate, T13/A/150(28).

61. Ibid., Letter to Eddie Choate, T13/A/150(27).

62. Ibid., Letter to Eddie Choate, T13/A/150(28).

63. Ibid., Letter to Eddie Choate, T13/A/150(20).

64. Ibid., Letter from P. V. Carroll, T13/A/150(44).

65. Ibid., Letter to Eddie Choate, T13/A/150(41).

66. Ibid., Letter to Eddie Choate, T13/A/150(30).

67. Ibid., Letter to Eddie Choate, T13/A/150(28).

68. Ibid., Telegram to Eddie Choate, T13/A/150(43).

69. Ibid., Note from Eddie Choate, T13/A/150(43).

70. Ibid., Letter to Eddie Choate, T13/A/150(41).

71. Ibid., Letter to Eddie Choate, T13/A/150(46).

72. Shields Family Archive, James Hardiman Library, University of Galway, Letter from P. V. Carroll, T13/A/150(44).

73. Ibid.

74. Shields Family Archive, Letter to Arthur Shields, T13/A/518(1).

75. Marianne Cosgrave, Mercy Congregational Archivist, message to the author, 10 Dec. 2013, Email.

76. Shields Family Archive, Manuscript, T13/A/124.

77. Shields Family Archive, Letter to Eddie Choate, T13/A/151(27).

78. E Neuffer, 'In 45th street apartments, time of change for actors', in *New York Times*, 4 Jan. 1988.

79. Shields Family Archive, , Letter from Arthur Shields, T13/A/45(1)-(2).

80. Shields Family Archive, Letter to Eddie Choate, T13/A/150(21).

81. Shields Family Archive, Letter to Eddie Chaote, T13/A/150(4).

82. Mary Lasker Papers, Columbia University Library, Rare Book and Manuscript Library, New York, Folder 544.

83. Mary Lasker Papers, Columbia University Library, Rare Book and Manuscript Library, New York, Folder 259.

84. Katharine Weber, *The Memory of All That: George Gershwin, Kay Swift and my Family's Legacy of Infidelities*, (New York, NY: Broadway Paperbacks, 2011), p. 133.

85. Ibid.

86. Shields Family Archive, Letter to Eddie Choate, T13/A/155(15).

87. Ibid., Letter from Eddie Choate, T13/A/151(32).

88. Ibid., Letter to Eddie Choate, T13/A/155(3).

89. Christine Shields, Personal interviews, California, Sept. 2011.

90. Helen De Geus, Personal Interview, Dublin, 10 Sept. 2016.

91. 'Death of Abbey actress', in *The Irish Independent*, 18 Nov. 1939, p. 11.

92. 'Popular Abbey actress dead', in *Fermanagh Herald*, 24 Nov. 1939, p. 8.

93. Robert Hogan and Micheal J. O'Neill, eds, *Joseph Holloway's Abbey Theatre: A Selection from His Unpublished Journal 'Impressions of a Dublin playgoer'*, (Carbondale, IL: Southern Illinois UP, 1967), vol. 3, p. 38.

94. Ibid., p. 38.

95. Shields Family Archive, Pocket diaries of Ar, T13/A/372 (3).

96. Seán O'Casey, *Three Plays: Juno and the Paycock, Shadow of a Gunman and The Plough and the Stars*, Introduced by J. C. Trewin, (New York, NY: St Martin's Press 1957), p. 5.

97. Christine Shields, Personal Interviews, California, Sept. 2011.

98. Shields Family Archive, Contracts, T13/A/454.

99. Ibid., Letter to Eddie Choate, T13/A/151(27).

100. Ibid., Letter from Eddie Choate, T13/A/153(57).

101. 'News of the Stage: "Heavenly Express"', *New York Times*, 18 Apr. 1940, p. 32.

102. Shields Family Archive, Letter to Eddie Choate, T13/A/153(57).

103. David Kipen, *Los Angeles in the 1930s: The WPA Guide to the City of Angels*, (Berkeley, CA: University of California Press, 2011), p. xxxiii.

104. Mary Lasker Papers, Columbia University Library, Rare Book and Manuscript Library, New York, Folder 544.
105. Ibid.
106. Shields Family Archive, Letter to Eddie Choate, T13/A/154(6).
107. Ibid., Medical records, T13/A/471.
108. Ibid., Letter to Eileen O'Connor, T13/A/441.
109. Ibid., Letter to Eddie Choate, T13/A/153.
110. Ciara O'Farrell, *Louis D'Alton and the Abbey Theatre*, (Dublin: Four Courts Press, 2004), p. 111.
111. W. Morehouse, 'Amusements: Broadway After Dark', in *New York Sun*, 21 Feb. 1941, p. 6.
112. 'The Play: Barry Fitzgerald appears in *Tanyard Street*', in *New York Times*, 5 Feb. 1941, p. 16.
113. Mary Lasker Papers, Columbia University Library, Rare Book and Manuscript Library, New York, Folder 544.
114. Ibid.
115. Ibid.
116. Shields Family Archive, Letter to Eddie Choate, T13/A/154(6).
117. Ibid.
118. Ibid.
119. Ibid., Letter to Eddie Choate, T13/A/154(3).
120. Ibid.
121. Christine Shields, Personal interview, California, Sept. 2011.
122. Ibid.
123. Mary Lasker Papers, Columbia University Library, Rare Book and Manuscript Library, New York, Folder 259.
124. Ibid.
125. Shields Family Archive, Telegram to Eddie Choate, T13/A/154(44).
126. Ibid., Visa papers, T13/A/467.
127. Adrian Frazier, *Hollywood Irish: John Ford, Abbey Actor and the Irish Revival in Hollywood*, (Dublin: Lilliput Press, 2010), p. 116.
128. Shields Family Archive, Letter to Eddie Choate, T13/A/155(3).
129. Ibid.
130. Ibid.
131. Ibid.
132. Ibid.
133. Ibid., Letter to Eddie Choate, T13/A/155(9).
134. Ibid., Letter to Eddie Choate, T13/A/154(6).
135. Ibid., Letter to Eddie Choate, T13/A/155(12).
136. Christine Shields, Personal Interviews, California, Sept. 2011.
137. Ibid.
138. Shields Family Archive, Letter to Eddie Choate, T13/A/155(15).
139. Ibid.
140. Ibid.
141. Ibid., Medical records, T13/A/366.
142. Ibid., Letter to Eddie Choate, T13/A/155(19).
143. 'Barry Fitzgerald faces court in traffic death', in *Los Angeles Times*, 9 Jan. 1945, A1.
144. Ibid.
145. Shields Family Archive, Letter to Eddie Choate, T13/A/155(23).
146. Mary Lasker Papers, Columbia University Library, Rare Book and Manuscript Library, New York, Folder 544.
147. Ibid.
148. Shields Family Archive, T13/A/155(28).
149. Ibid.
150. Christine Shields, Personal Interviews, California, Sept. 2011.
151. Shields Family Archive, Medical records, T13/A/472.
152. Ibid., Letter to Arthur Shields, T13/A/241.
153. Ibid.
154. Ibid.

155. Ibid.
156. Ibid., Letter to Arthur Shields, T13/A/211(7).
157. Ibid.
158. Ibid., Pocket diaries, T13/A/372(10).
159. Ibid., Letter to Eddie Choate, T13/A/156.
160. Ibid., Letter from Maire Judge, T13/A/450.
161. Christine Shields, Personal Interviews, California, Sept. 2011.
162. Shields Family Archive, Death certificate, T13/A/472.
163. Ibid., Letter from Bid Shields, T13/A/252(1).
164. Ibid.
165. Frazier, *Behind the Scenes: Yeats, Horniman and the struggle for the Abbey Theatre*, p. 188.
166. Ibid.
167. Shields Family Archive, Letter to Eileen O'Connor, T13/A/437.

Conclusion

1. Shields Family Archive, James Hardiman Library, University of Galway, Letter to Laurie Shields, T13/A/519.
2. Ria Mooney Letter to Lilian Roberts, 1936, family collection, shared with the author.
3. Shields Family Archive, Letter to Eddie Choate, T13/A/150(41).
4. Joan Wallach Scott, *Gender and the Politics of History*, (New York, NY: Columbia UP, 1999 Revised edn), p. 27.

Appendices

1. 'An End a Beginning', *The Irish Times* (1921–), Dec. 06, 1922, p. 4. ProQuest, https://ucd.idm.oclc.org/login?url=https://www.proquest.com/historical-newspapers/end-beginning/docview/520478807/se-2.
2. Liam O'Dowd, 'Church, State and women: The aftermath of partition', *Gender in Irish Society*, eds, Curtin, Chris; Jackson, Pauline; O'Connor, Barbara, (Galway: Galway UP, 1987), p. 13.
3. Ibid.
4. Maria Luddy, 'Sex and the single girl in 1920s and 1930s Ireland', *The Irish Review (1986–)*, no. 35, Irish Feminisms, (Summer 2007), p. 80.
5. Tom Inglis, *Moral Monopoly: The Rise and Fall of the Catholic Church in Modern Ireland*, (Dublin: UCD Press, 1998), p. 68.
6. Ibid., p. 33.
7. Myrtle Hill, *Women In Ireland: A Century of Change*, (Belfast: Blackstaff Press, 2003), pp 99–100.
8. *Catholic Bulletin and book review*, Oct. 1936, vol. XXVI, no 10, p. 795
9. James Smyth, 'Dancing, depravity & all that jazz', in *History Ireland*, vol. 1, no. 2 (Summer 1993), pp 51–4.
10. *Catholic Bulletin and book review*, Dec. 1934, vol. XXIV, no 12, p. 999.
11. *Catholic Bulletin and book review*, Oct. 1936, vol. XXVI, no 10, p. 795.
12. Smyth, 'Dancing, depravity & all that jazz', pp 51–4.
13. 'Survey by Dublin Senior Justice – Edward J. Little', in *Irish Times*, 7 Feb. 1938, p. 4.
14. Caitriona Clear, *Women of the House: Women's Household Work in Ireland 1922–61: Discourses, Experiences, Memories*, (Dublin: Irish Academic Press, 2000), p. 187.
15. Clear, *Women of the House: Women's Household Work in Ireland 1922–61: Discourses, Experiences, Memories*, p. 274.
16. Adrian Frazier, *Hollywood Irish: John Ford, Abbey Actor and the Irish Revival in Hollywood*, (Dublin: Lilliput Press, 2010), p. 59.
17. By the early 1930s, the mode had deteriorated as more actors transferred from the populist drama at the Queen's Theatre to the Abbey. The audience knew what to expect from each performer and anticipated the 'turn' of their favourite, eager to see improvisation.
18. Elizabeth Brewer Redwine, *Gender, Performance, and Authorship at the Abbey Theatre*, (Oxford: Oxford UP, 2021), p. 181.
19. Alan Cole, 'Acting at the Abbey', *University Review*, vol. 2, no. 13, 1962, pp 37–52. JSTOR, http://www.jstor.org/stable/45241847.

20. Sharon Marie Carnicke, *Stanislavsky in Focus: An Acting Master for the Twenty-First Century*, 2nd edn (New York, NY: Routledge, 2009, Kindle edn), LOC 2865.

21. Ibid., 2883.

22. Ibid., 2924.

23. Ibid., 2873.

24. Christopher Morash and Shaun Richards, *Mapping Irish Theatre: Theories of Space and Place*, (Cambridge and New York, NY: Cambridge UP, 2013), p. 7.

Appendix 1

Gender in the Irish Free State period (1922–37)

Details of Ireland's class structure and an analysis of the operations of gender during the 1930s are interweaved with the biographical details of these women in such a way that to extract and present them in some sort of objective light is potentially fatal to the narrative. However, here follows a brief legal and sociological framework to the period under focus for those in need of wider historical context.

The Irish Free State (Saorstát Éireann) was established in December 1922, when legal acts passed through the British parliament establishing the new dominion state. There was an increasingly bitter civil war continuing in Ireland, being fought between those who insisted the Free State was not the Republic they had fought for, and those who supported the Anglo-Irish Treaty as a necessary step to independence from Britain. Saorstát Éireann was described in the *Irish Times* editorial as an 'almost bewildering moment of transition' with the Irish left to shape their own future.[1] That moment would continue until December 1937, when president Éamon de Valera (supported by leaders from the Catholic Church) authored a new Constitution stripped of any reference to the British Crown. On 29 December 1937, when Bunreacht na hÉireann (Ireland's Constitution) came into operation, the Irish Free State was succeeded by Éire (Ireland), a sovereign, independent, democratic state.

Historian Mary E. Daly has highlighted that the history of women in Ireland in the twentieth century is unique, while bearing similarities to that of other European countries. All across Europe after World War I, dominant ideologies confined the role of women to the family. With mass unemployment and economic stagnation, most labour movements were ambivalent on the question of females in the workplace while falling birth rates concerned all national governments, for various reasons. Between the establishment of the Irish Free State and World War II, the partition of Ireland and the restoration of public order were key political issues for the government. The social ideologies that emanated from the religious and political spheres during this period had long-standing implications for women.

In an essay entitled 'Church, state and women: The aftermath of partition', Liam O'Dowd draws out the reciprocal relationship between the Protestant churches in the North and the Catholic Church in the Free State and demonstrates the 'substantial theological differences' between the churches on women's role in society.[2] O'Dowd argues that the prominence of Marian cults in Irish Catholicism from the nineteenth century onwards separated sex from sexuality, thus contributing to the Catholic idealisation of motherhood.[3] Such theological differences created practical differences, whereby Protestant clergy emphasised the spiritual contract of marriage and the individual conscience, while the Catholic clergy sought to police the family.

Many commentators, such as Maria Luddy and Mary Daly, have written of how the Free State and the Catholic Church shaped the function and place of women through issues relating to sexuality. As Luddy points out, 'the politicization of sexual behaviour had been a feature of Irish nationalism from the late nineteenth century,' but from the 1920s, it was believed that the bodies of women threatened the morality of the State.[4] Moral regulation lay in the imposition of standards of idealised conduct for women.

The conservatism of the states (both nationalist and unionist), the ideology of the Catholic Church and the laissez-faire political ideology of the time all militated against the participation of women in public life. Sociologist Tom Inglis has explored the social grounding of loyalty to the Catholic Church and demonstrated the close link between religious capital and social acceptance and respect.[5] He insightfully suggests that it is an error to interpret the position of women as victims, as hopeless or powerless; but their gender made their power radically different. In fact, women could gain and hold power only by virtue of their display of sexual morality. The fact remains that the ideological separation of public and private (familial) spheres, which was enforced by the material and class conditions of the time, has obscured women's subordination, in terms of class and gender, as well as the full dimensions of their social role.[6]

The Free State Act of 1935 gave the Minister for Industry and Commerce powers to prohibit women from working in some industries, and to prevent employers taking on more women than men. The Employment Act, in the same year, extended the marriage bar to all civil service posts, requiring women holding state employment to resign upon marriage. While paid work was considered appropriate, and even healthy, for single women, it did not reflect well on a husband to have a wife in the workplace. The rate of married Irish women in paid employment remained at around 6 per cent until the 1960s.[7] A small number of married women of the Abbey company were in that minority.

By the 1930s, the number of Irish women emigrating was at its greatest for decades; female emigrants far outnumbered the male. Ireland's practical and social problems (lack of marriage opportunities, lack of employment opportunities, poverty) were matched by a threat the Catholic Church viewed as treacherous. In the editorial of the *Catholic Bulletin* in October 1936, one commentator wrote of: 'the general wave of immorality [...] which seems already to have quenched in so many souls every sense of modesty and dignity, conscience and responsibility [...]'[8] The chief sources of such immorality were the darkness, motor cars and dancing. Not all dancing, but particular forms of dancing. In a Lenten Pastoral in 1924, Cardinal Logue made a speech saying: 'Irish dances do not make degenerates.'[9] Traditional Irish ceilí dances had strict, rigid postures, which maintained decorum and kept the genders far apart. Unlike the barbarous, sultry movements brought on by jazz music. In the *Catholic Bulletin* McGlinchy explained:

> Many of the modern kinds of dance are such as would offend the moral sense of a decent pagan. They deliberately pander to the lower instincts, and are proximate occasions of sins of the flesh.[10]

He goes further:

> If the circumstances mean [...] the form of dance is likely to arouse passion and lead to sin, it is wrong .... Oh, for a general revival of our grand old Irish dances! Dances and dancing as carried on at the present time are, generally speaking, a dangerous occasion of sin for the young.[11]

The Gaelic League, championing the Irish language and music, were at the forefront of the campaign to outlaw 'pagan' music. At the main anti-jazz rally in Co. Leitrim, a letter was read out from Cardinal MacRory, where he did his best to distance himself from the evil activity: 'I know nothing about jazz dancing.' Although he did know enough to state they were 'suggestive and demoralizing.'[12]

In 1935 The Public Dance Halls Act made it impossible for a dance to be held in Ireland without the sanction of the clergy, the police and the judiciary. In a survey of this particular legislation in 1938, a Dublin Senior Justice spoke of how a 'nervous and overwrought generation' born during the Great War had an insatiable craving 'to multiply means of excitement.'[13] Such 'craving' led to the popularity of betting houses, picture houses and public dancing. In response to the pressure from the Church and from the public, legislation was enacted to ensure the licensing, supervision and control of dance halls.

With the proposed introduction by the Irish government of the Children's Allowance in 1943 came a robust debate about paying this money (for each third and subsequent child) directly to mothers. But an awareness of the responsibilities borne by women didn't translate into a political acknowledgment of their role. Fears that such payments would isolate fathers and lead to the nationalisation of mothers and children won out. The father's place as head of the Irish family unit was underlined when the payments were awarded to him. This decision is significant precisely because, as Caitriona Clear deduced from her widespread investigations, 'it is notable that in a variety of locations and household economies [...] the woman was seen as the person who controlled vital resources.'[14]

In this, as in many other aspects of life, there was a clear contradiction between the national ideal and the social reality. It is imperative to bear this contradiction in mind when considering the lives of individual women during this time. The Abbey Theatre actresses of this study were in a unique position in this regard, at a remove from the social barriers and pressures, although never exempt from them. As actresses in the National Theatre, supported by the government and ostensibly championing the national ideal, their work was more respectable than women in music halls or other entertainments. They were single women, earning their own money and managing their own affairs. While they struggled to fully separate their public performances (with the necessary displays of sexuality) from their private lives, they were some of the few women in the Irish Free State moving between the two spheres.

The index of Caitriona Clear's extensive study *Women of the House: Women's Household Work in Ireland 1922–61* skips directly from 'Abortion' to 'Advice to women: beauty and appearance'.[15] Actresses don't figure in Clear's study and there is a notable lack of information on this particular form of labour during that period. This means the role in society of an Abbey Theatre actress during the Free State period is a particularly complex case study of the operations of gender and class in Irish society during this time.

Appendix 2

Performance styles in Ireland's National Theatre

With no recorded demonstrations of the performance style of these actresses, one might forever grope in the imagination to envision their performances, to understand how their craft appeared in action. Even in the depths of our imaginings, we are liable to draw on examples of contemporary acting, either in theatre or film. Other readers may bring to this an international perspective: the work of European and international performers in history, and now, often varies greatly from that on the Irish stage. Therefore, I'd like to draw your imaginative speculations towards specific images of Irish acting at the turn of the century that are useful to shape our understanding of these performances. I also set out a theory around acting in the 1930s that may assist understanding of how the artistic and social melded in the Abbey Theatre.

Many of the women involved in the foundation of the Abbey Theatre began their theatrical experience as members of Inghinidhe na hÉireann, as political campaigners and organisers. As such, they wrote and performed speeches on a speaker's platform, or gave impassioned lectures on a street corner: they used the bold gestures, rousing words and volume levels such rebellious work demanded. But soon those serious about acting started to work with W. G. Fay, performing 'Tableaux Vivant'. These were stage images, or living pictures. The performers were costumed, posed and suitably lit in postures emblematic of important moments in national history. Crucially, they were silent: nobody spoke. Such static images continued to be used by the nationalist movement as displays of rebellion and protest, long after the actors and actresses began searching for other modes of performance.

Into (and out of) this tradition of silent images arrived a one-act play by Yeats and Lady Gregory. The premiere of *Cathleen ni Houlihan*, on 2 April 1902, set in play the most potent metaphor of Irish womanhood to this day. Set in Mayo in 1798 (the year of a major republican rebellion), the drama of the play unfolds in a traditional peasant cottage. Into the home of Mrs Gillane comes a poor old woman (Cathleen ni Houlihan) who has no worldly goods but retains her dignity and belief in a united Ireland free of English rule. Cathleen appeals to her children to offer their lives to Ireland.

At the inauspicious theatrical venue of St Teresa's Church Hall on Clarendon Street, the eponymous role was played by Maud Gonne, then President of Inghinidhe na hÉireann and the Vice-President of the Irish National Theatre Society (INTS). At this point, Gonne was at the height of her fame in Ireland as a political campaigner. She was known as an ardent nationalist and was a strikingly beautiful woman, who brought to every public appearance an erotic charge.

Accounts of the first night of this production often focus on the shock and awe caused by Gonne's appearance; arriving in costume and late to the cramped hall, she dramatically swept through the audience and alighted on the tiny stage to take her cue. Gonne was over six foot tall, taller than any of the other actors, and she had a thick, grey wig perched on her head. In her booming, melodious voice she urged the men of Ireland to come to her aid. Many audience members may have been unsure if they were attending a political rally or a play. For some members of Inghinidhe na hÉireann, it was both. *Cathleen ni Houlihan* had a propagandist function. Once understood as a parable and nationalist call to arms, the play became both popular and controversial. That vision of an Irish woman, performing simultaneously as a political symbol and a dramatic character, reflects a particular type of performance that overshadowed Irish actresses on the national stage for years to come.

In the early decades of the INTS and then the Abbey company, the Fay brothers (William and Frank) trained all members of the company in 'restraint' and 'teamwork'.[16] Derived from the French Conservatoire and André Antoine's company, the Théâtre Libre, this style kept the focus on the language of the text, the essence of a playwright's theatre.[17] W. G. Fay trained extensively in elocution. Thus, when they began to work with the actresses on traditional theatrical performances the emphasis was on clear enunciation and proper projection. Speeches were recited like poetry; dialogue like lyrical verse delivered facing the audience. The animated business of the British melodrama was anathema to Frank Fay, while a light tempo of the voice was crucial. He believed there should be no physical action while an actor was speaking and the eyes of the entire cast rested always on the speaker, much like a spotlight moving from 'star' to 'star'. The actresses, then, were most often still. In their acting style, many learnt never to draw attention to themselves, particularly their physicality, but to put all emotion into pitch and tone of voice. Remaining silent and elegant in deportment was now a requirement, rather than a display of protest.

In very recent times, Elizabeth Brewer-Redwine has interrogated the role of female performers in canonical Irish texts first performed in the Abbey Theatre. Her book, *Gender, Performance and Authorship at the Abbey Theatre,* insightfully reassesses how actresses contributed to the writing of the plays without receiving any credit for their work. But their contributions were private, generally covert and carefully negotiated. She explains that Abbey 'creators', Yeats, Lady Gregory and even Sara Allgood herself, returned again and again to 'an insistence on a familiar, nearly motionless female body performing memory.'[18] Alan Cole, tracing the Abbey acting style from the 1900s, notes that many erred in thinking there to be no style in Irish acting, but simply actors 'being themselves'. In fact, the actors under the Fay brothers had to play:

> knowing that their purpose was to reproduce men and women like themselves—naturally, since the characters in the plays were ordinary Irish men and women like themselves— but in circumstances, not ordinary but unique, and furthermore, dramatized.[19]

The emphasis, then, is on the reproduction of the types in the dramatic circumstances.

In his writings on the theory of acting, Constantin Stanislavsky also used Fay's example of the great Coquelin the Elder. Stanislavsky adopted the term Coquelin himself used for his art: 'representation'.[20] The theatre of 'representation' occupies the penultimate rung in Stanislavsky's hierarchy of acting styles. Such theatre places the actor at the creative nexus of theatrical production, and thus values the actor as much as Stanislavsky does, although there are particular issues.[21] In this mode of performing, the actor strives to reveal the inner life of the character and to communicate genuine emotion, by selecting specific details. Stanislavsky says of the characters created by representational actors: 'The spectator immediately sees that these are not just ordinary people whom we meet in life, but personages, whom we see in paintings and about whom we read in books.'[22] Thus, they are 'types'; the actors' performances are reproducible works of art. Such work can give rise to great heights of virtuosity. However, this mode also creates the risk that the personality and charisma of the actor may detract from the performance. In extreme cases, the level of emphasis on the person of the actor (or 'star') may entirely obscure the character.

In representation, Carnicke explains, 'the actor juggles both a "first self" (the artist) and a "second self" (the canvas); in acting, the first self shapes the second.'[23] In the Irish context of the 1930s, this representation of types while retaining the presence of the performer's own personality on stage was crucial to maintaining respectability in the eyes of society. With 'representation', the distinction between actor and character is maintained by the performer and acknowledged by the audience throughout. This acceptance by the audience of the two 'selves' was key to the theatrical experience of visiting the Abbey in the 1930s. It was fostered by the familiarity between the audiences and the performers, much like they were watching people they knew personally perform privately in their own home. Such a mode of working allowed women in particular an opportunity to present certain behaviour deemed unacceptable off stage, without any besmirching of their personal reputation. Thus, the acting style of 'representation' gained particular importance for women performing on stage in the repressive atmosphere of the Free State. When younger actresses, notably Ria Mooney as Rosie Redmond, experimented with more psychological modes of working and immersion into character, this had consequences for their reputation and their place in the company, as these biographies explore.

Morash and Richards, in *Mapping Irish Theatre*, explore the French Marxist Henri Lefebvre's notion of 'representational space', in the context of Irish theatre.[24] Completing the triad of space, Lefebvre posits alongside perceived (spatial practice) and conceived space (space of representation), this representational space. Coded, often heavy with symbolism and metonymy, representational space can realise the social imaginary within a separate sphere. It has a force that is only unleashed when the perceived space of the spectators and the represented space of the writer and performers come together. It can be passively experienced by an audience and does not directly, or overtly impact on perceived space or social reality. In such a liminal space on the stage, a space that mirrored but was entirely separate from 'reality', women could gain and yield power that was not 'truthful' in the Irish context. It offered a theatrical 'representational' space for women to emote fully, to 'play' with ideas of choice and experiment with liberation, without ever fully embracing it or posing a threat to the social order established. Thus, actresses of the time were privileged, dancing around the edges of the 1937 Constitution's requirement that their place be in the home, caring for husbands and children, without agency, financial or otherwise.

Manuscript Collections

Abbey Archives Database, Abbey Theatre—Amharclann na Mainistreach. Web. http://www.abbeytheatre. ie/archives/person_detail.

Abbey Theatre Digital Archive, University of Galway, James Hardiman Library Special Collections, Galway.

Abbey Theatre Minute Books, University of Galway, Digital Collections, Galway.

Abbey Theatre Scrapbooks, National Library of Ireland, Dublin.

The Henry W. and Albert A. Berg Collection of English and American Literature, The New York Public Library, New York.

Civic Repertory Theatre Records, Yale Collection of American Literature, Beinecke Rare Book and Manuscript Library, Yale University, New Haven, Connecticut.

May Craig Papers (1889–1972), IE UCDA LA28, UCD Archives, Dublin.

Teresa Deevy Papers, Trinity College Manuscript Collections, IE TCD Mss 10722, Trinity College, Dublin.

M. J. Dolan Papers, National Library of Ireland, Dublin.

F. R. Higgins Papers, Acc No 4113, National Library of Ireland, Dublin.

Diaries of Joseph Holloway, 1930-39, National Library of Ireland, Dublin.

Papers of (William) Denis Johnston (1889–1984), Trinity College Manuscript Collections, IE TCD Mss 10066, Trinity College, Dublin.

Mary Lasker Papers, Columbia University Library, Rare Book and Manuscript Library, New York.

Ria Mooney Papers, NLI Acc 6548, National Library of Ireland, Dublin.

Shelah Richards Papers, ITA/128, Irish Theatre Archive, Dublin City Library and Archive, Pearse Street, Dublin.

Mary Rynne Papers, University of Galway, James Hardiman Library Special Collections, Galway.

Shields Family Papers, University of Galway, James Hardiman Library Special Collections, Galway.

Theatre Guild Archive, Yale Collection of American Literature, Beinecke Rare Book and Manuscript Library, Yale University, New Haven, Connecticut.

Una Troy Papers (1910–1993), NLI Acc 5526, National Library of Ireland, Dublin.

Elbert A. Wickes Papers: Theatre Impressario (1884–1974), Claremont Colleges, Honnold/Mudd Special Collections, California.

Works Cited

'Abbey Theatre', *Irish Times*, 23 March 1923: 4. Web.
'Abbey Theatre, Dublin-Mr Brinsley MacNamara's new play', *Irish Times*, 20 July 1933: 10. Web.
'Abbey players in Belfast', *Irish Independent*, 1 May 1934: 10. Web.
'Abbey Theatre: *Mount Prospect*', *Irish Times*, 23 April 1940: 4. Web.
Abbey Theatre Digital Archive, University of Galway, James Hardiman Library Special Collections, Galway.
Abbey Theatre Minute Books, University of Galway, Digital Collections, https://www.universityofgalway.ie/abbeytheatreminutebooks/collection/.
'Acting with a breaking heart.' *Leitrim Observer*, 8 July 1933: 6. Web.
Adams, Bernard, *Denis Johnston: A Life*, (Dublin: Lilliput Press, 2002). Print.
Adjudications' Sheet for the School of Acting, *c.*1925, M. J. Dolan Papers, NLI Mss. 22,556, National Library of Ireland, Dublin.
Arrington, Lauren, *W.B. Yeats, the Abbey Theatre, Censorship, and the Irish State: Adding the Half-Pence to the Pence* (Oxford: Oxford UP, 2010). Print.
Atkinson, Brooks, 'The play: In pastel shades', *New York Times*, 5 October 1928: 17. Web.
— 'Plays and players of the mid-February stage', *New York Times*, 15 February 1931: 105. Web.
— 'The play: The Abbey Theatre Players open an engagement', *New York Times*, 4 October 1937: 17. Web.
— 'The play: Barry Fitzgerald appears in *Tanyard Street*', *New York Times*, 5 February 1941: 16. Web.
'Auditor laid to rest', *Irish Independent*, 1 July 1933, n.p., *Papers of May Craig*, IE UCD LA28/219-4, UCD Archives, Dublin.
Backscheider, P., *Reflections on Biography* (London: Oxford UP, 1999). Print.
Barreca, Regina, *Last Laughs: Perspectives on Women and Comedy* (New York, NY and London: Gordon & Breach, 1988). Print.
'Barry Fitzgerald faces court in traffic death', *Los Angeles Times*, 9 January 1945: A1.
Benedetti, Jean, *Stanislavski: An Introduction* (New York, NY: Routledge, 2004). Print.
Bennett, Susan, 'Theatre history and women's dramatic writing', *Women, Theatre and Performance: New Histories, New Historiographies*, eds, Maggie Gale and Viv Gardner (Manchester: Manchester UP, 2000), pp 46–60. Print.
Bernard, Jean-Jacques, *The Sulky Fire: Five Plays*, trans., J. L. Firth (London: Jonathan Cape, 1939). Print.
Bernstein, Robin, 'Dances with things: Material culture and the performance of race', *Social Text*, vol. 27, no. 101 (2009), pp 67–94. Print.
Bound Volume recording salaries paid to actors of the Abbey 1923–7, Abbey Theatre Digital Archive at NUI, Galway, ADM_00004384, p. 4.
Boston Globe, January 1938, *Papers of May Craig*, IE UCD LA28/219, UCD Archives, Dublin.
Boylston, Helen Dore, *Carol Goes Backstage* (Boston, MA: Little, Brown and Co., 1947). Print.
Bradley, Anthony and Maryann Gialanella Valiulis, eds, *Gender and Sexuality in Modern Ireland* (Amherst, MA: University of Massachusetts Press, 1997). Print.
Bratton, Jacky, 'Working in the margin: Women in theatre history,', *New Theatre Quarterly*, vol. 10, no. 38 (1994), pp 122–31. Print.
Brewer Redwine, Elizabeth, *Gender, Performance, and Authorship at the Abbey Theatre* (London: Oxford UP, 2021). Print.
Brown, Terence, *Ireland: A Social and Cultural History: 1922–2002* (London: Harper Perennial, 2004). Print.

Bulliet, C. J., *Unknown Newspaper*, February 1938, Abbey Theatre Scrapbooks: Volume 26 American Tour 1935, Mss 25,511-23, National Library of Ireland, Dublin.

Calvino, Italo, *Six Memos for the Next Millennium* (Cambridge, MA: Harvard UP, 1988). Print.

Carnicke, Sharon Marie, *Stanislavsky in Focus: An Acting Master for the Twenty-First Century*, 2nd edn (New York, NY: Routledge, 2009, Kindle edn).

Carroll, Paul Vincent, *Shadow and Substance: A Play in Four Acts* (London: Macmillan, 1938). Print.

Catholic Bulletin and Book Review, October 1936, vol. XXVI, no, 10.

Caulfield, Mary P., 'Inseparable and no longer subsequent: The relocation and representation of women in Irish theatre practices', *Theatre Research International*, no. 36, 2011, pp 276–7. Print.

Census of Ireland 1911, The National Archives of Ireland, n.d. www.census.nationalarchives.ie , Web. Accessed 22 March 2010.

Chicago Herald, 22 January 1935, Abbey Theatre Scrapbooks: Volume 26 American Tour 1935, Mss 25,511-23, National Library of Ireland, Dublin.

Clarke, Norma, 'From plaything to professional: The English actress, 1660–1990', *Gender & History*, vol. 5, no. 1 (Spring 1993), pp 120–4. Print.

Clear, Caitriona, 'The minimum rights of every woman? Women's changing appearance in Ireland, 1940–1966', *Irish Economic and Social History*, vol. 35 (2008) pp 68–80. Print.

Clear, Caitriona, *Women of the House: Women's Household Work in Ireland 1922–61: Discourses, Experiences, Memories* (Dublin: Irish Academic Press, 2000). Print.

Clive, K., 'Echoes of the town', *Irish Times*, 26 August 1938: 4. Web.

Cole, Alan, 'Acting at the Abbey', *University Review*, vol. 2, no. 13 (1962), pp.37–52, JSTOR, http://www.jstor.org/stable/45241847.

Conroy, Colette, *Theatre & The Body* (London: Palgrave Macmillan, 2010). Print.

Corbett, Mary J., 'Performing identities: Actresses and autobiography', *Biography*, vol. 24, no. 1, (Honolulu: Winter 2001) pp 15–24. Print.

Cork Examiner, 22 October 1935, *Papers of May Craig*, IE UCD LA28/116, UCD Archives, Dublin.

Cosgrave, M., Mercy Congregational Archivist, Message to the Author, 10 December 2013. Email.

Daly, Mary E., 'O Kathleen Ni Houlihan, your way's a thorny way: The condition of women in twentieth-century Ireland', *Gender and Sexuality in Modern Ireland*, eds, Anthony Bradley and Maryann Gialanella Valiulis (Amherst, MA: University of Massachusetts Press, 1997), pp 102–26. Print.

Davis, Tracy C., *Actresses as Working Women: Their Social Identity in Victorian Culture*, (London: Routledge, 1991). Print.

— 'The context problem', *Theatre Survey*, vol. 45, no. 2 (November 2004), pp 203–9. Print.

— 'A feminist methodology in theatre history', *Interpreting the Theatrical Past*, eds, T. Postlewait and B. McConachie (Iowa City, IA: University of Iowa Press, 1989), pp 59–76. Print.

— 'Private women and the public realm', *Theatre Survey*, vol. 35, no. 1 (May 1994), pp 65–71. Print.

Dayton, D., 'Maureen Delany: Off Stage', *New York Sun*, 6 December 1934, *Papers of May Craig*, UCD: LA28/116, UCD Archives, Dublin.

'Death of Abbey actress', *Irish Independent*, 18 November 1939: 11. Web.

De Búrca, Seán, 'F. J. McCormick and Eileen Crowe: Abbey stars', *Dublin Historical Record*, vol. 42, no. 3 (June 1989),pp 114–15. Print.

Deevy, Teresa, *Three Plays: Katie Roche; The King of Spain's Daughter and The Wild Goose*, (London: Macmillan, 1939). Print.

Dent, A., 'Abbey Theatre Drama Festival', UK *Spectator*, 18 August 1938: 15. Web.

Derrida, Jacques, 'Archive fever: A Freudian impression', trans., Eric Prenowitz, *Diacritics*, vol. 25, no. 2 (Summer 1995), pp 9–63. Print.

Detroit Evening Times, 23 January 1935, Abbey Theatre Scrapbooks: Volume 26 American Tour 1935, NLI Mss 25,511-23, National Library of Ireland, Dublin.

Detroit News, 24 January 1935, Abbey Theatre Scrapbooks: Volume 26 American Tour 1935, Mss 25,511-23, National Library of Ireland, Dublin.

Detroit Times, 22 January 1935, Abbey Theatre Scrapbooks: Volume 26 American Tour 1935, NLI Mss 25,511-23, National Library of Ireland, Dublin.

Diamond, Elin, *Unmaking Mimesis: Essays on Feminism and Theater* (London: Routledge, 1997).

Dixon, Roz, '"All of Ireland is our Orchard": Maria Knebel's production of *The Cherry Orchard* at the Abbey in 1968', *Ibsen and Chekhov on the Irish Stage*, eds, Roz Dixon and Irina Ruppo Malone (Dublin: Carysfort Press, 2012), pp 149–60. Print.

Dixon, Roz and Irina Ruppo Malone, eds, *Ibsen and Chekhov on the Irish Stage* (Dublin: Carysfort Press, 2012). Print.

D'Monté, Rebecca, 'Review of *Actresses as Working Women: their social identity in Victorian Culture*', *Feminist Review*, no. 46, Sexualities: Challenge & Change (Spring 1994), pp 94–7. Print.

Dolan, Jill, *Theatre and Sexuality* (London: Palgrave Macmillan, 2010). Print.

— *The Feminist Spectator as Critic* (Ann Arbor, MI: University of Michigan Press, 1988). Print.

Dowling, Vincent, *Astride the Moon: A Theatrical Life* (Dublin: Wolfhound Press, 2000). Print.

Doyle, Paul A., *Paul Vincent Carroll* (Lewisburg, PA: Bucknell UP, 1971). Print.

Drama in Los Angeles 1938, Scrapbook of unknown origin, Los Angeles Public Library.

Dublin Evening Mail, 28 February 1934, *Papers of May Craig*, IE UCD LA 28/219-1, UCD Archives, Dublin.

'Eileen Crowe Interview', *Boston Evening* Transcript, 29 April 1933, Abbey Theatre Scrapbooks, NLI Mss 25,489-25,523, National Library of Ireland, Dublin.

'Ennis woman's first play', *Irish Independent*, 11th October 1938: 12. Mary Rynne Collection, NUI Galway, James Hardiman Library Special Collections, Galway.

'Excellent acting by Abbey Players', *Irish Independent*, 29 April 1959: 10. Web.

Fallon, Gabriel, *Seán O'Casey: The Man I Knew* (London: Routledge & Kegan Paul, 1965). Print.

Farrell, M. J. and John Perry, *Spring Meeting: A Comedy in Three Acts* (London: Samuel French Ltd, 1938). Print.

Ferris, Louise, 'Review of *Actresses as Working Women: their social identity in Victorian Culture*', *Signs*, vol. 18, no. 1 (1992), pp 162–72. Print.

'Fine study of Saint in new play at Abbey', *Irish Press*, 7 August 1962: 6. Web.

Finlay, Lilian Roberts, *Always in my Mind* (Kerry: Brandon Press, 1999). Print.

Fitzpatrick Dean, Joan, *Riot and Great Anger: Stage Censorship in Twentieth-Century Ireland* (Madison, WI: Winsconsin UP, 1968). Print.

Fitzpatrick, Lisa, ed., *Performing Feminisms in Contemporary Ireland* (Dublin: Carysfort Press, 2013). Print.

Fitz-simon, Christopher, *The Irish Theatre* (London: Thames & Hudson, 1983). Print.

Foley, Timothy P., Lionel Pilkington, Sean Ryder and Elizabeth Tilley, eds, *Gender and Colonialism* (Galway: Galway UP, 1995). Print.

Foster, R. F., *Vivid Faces: The Revolutionary Generation in Ireland. 1890–1923* (London: Allen Lane, 2014). Print.

Franko, Mark and Annette Richards, eds, *Acting on the Past: Historical Performance Across the Disciplines* (Hanover, NH and London: Wesleyan UP, 2000). Print.

Frazier, Adrian, *Hollywood Irish: John Ford, Abbey Actor and the Irish Revival in Hollywood* (Dublin: Lilliput Press, 2010). Print.

— *Behind the Scenes: Yeats, Horniman and the struggle for the Abbey Theatre* (Berkeley, CA: University of California Press, 1990). Print.

Friel, Brian, *The Enemy Within* (Loughcrew: Gallery Books, 1992). Print.

Friel, Judy, 'Rehearsing Katie Roche', *Irish University Review*, vol. 25, no. 1, Silver Jubilee Issue: Teresa Deevy and Irish Women Playwrights (Spring/Summer 1995), pp 117–25. Print.

'From the drama mailbag', *New York Times*, 29 January 1939. X3. Web.

Gaddis Rose, Marilyn, *Jack B. Yeats. Painter and Poet* (Berne: Herbert Lang, 1972). Print.

Gale, Maggie B., *West End Women: Women and the London Stage, 1918–1962* (London and New York, NY: Routledge, 1996). Print.

Gale, Maggie and Anne Featherstone, 'The imperative of the archive: Creative archive research', *Research Methods in Theatre & Performance*, eds, Baz Kershaw and Helen Nicholson (New York, NY: Columbia UP, 2011). pp 17–40. Print.

Gale, Maggie B. and Viv Gardner, eds, *Women, Theatre & Performance: New Histories, New Historiographies* (New York, NY: Manchester UP, 2000). Print.

Gale, Maggie B. and John Stokes, eds, *The Cambridge Companion to the Actress*, (London: Cambridge UP, 2007). Print.

Gardner, Viv, 'By herself: the actress and autobiography, 1755 – 1939', *The Cambridge Companion to the Actress*, eds, Maggie Gale and John Stokes, pp 173–92. Print.

Ginzburg, Carlo, 'Checking the evidence: The judge and the historian', *Critical Inquiry*, vol. 18, no. 1 (Autumn 1991), pp 79–92. Print.

Gonzalez, Alexander G., *Modern Irish Writers: A Bio-Critical Sourcebook* (London: Aldwych Press, 1997). Print.

Gough, Kathleen, *Haptic Allegories: Kinship and Performance in the Black and Green Atlantic* (London: Routledge, 2014). Print.

Grene, Nicolas and Christopher Morash, eds, *Irish Theatre on Tour* (Dublin: Carysfort Press, 2005). Print.

Hill, Judith, *Lady Gregory: An Irish Life* (Cork: Collins Press, 2011). Print.

Hill, Myrtle, *Women In Ireland: A Century of Change* (Belfast: Blackstaff Press, 2003). Print.

Hogan, Robert, *After the Irish Renaissance: A Critical History of Irish Drama Since The Plough and the Stars* (London: Macmillan, 1968). Print.

Hogan, Robert and M. J. O'Neill, eds, *Joseph Holloway's Irish Theatre* (Dixon, CA: Proscenium Press, 1969). Print.

Hogan, Robert and Micheal J. O'Neill, eds, *Joseph Holloway's Abbey Theatre: A Selection from his Unpublished Journal 'Impressions of a Dublin playgoer'* (Carbondale, IL: Southern Illinois UP 1967). Print.

Hogan, Robert and Richard Burnham, *The Years of O'Casey, 1921–1926: A Documentary History* (Newark, DE: University of Delaware Press; Gerrards Cross, Buckinghamshire: Colin Smythe, 1992). Print.

Holloway, Joseph, Diaries, July – September 1936, NLI Mss 1971: 342, National Library of Ireland, Dublin.

Hunt, Hugh, *The Abbey: Ireland's National Theatre 1904–78* (Dublin: Gill & Macmillan, 1979). Print.

'Ibsen play at the Abbey', *Irish Independent*, 23 March 1923: 4. Web.

Ibsen, Henrik, *A Doll's House*, trans., Michael Meyer (London: Bloomsbury Publishing, 2008). Web. 12 September 2015.

Iles, Theresa, ed., *All Sides of the Subject: Women and Biography* (New York, NY: Teachers College Press, 1992). Print.

Inglis, Tom, *Moral Monopoly: The Rise and Fall of the Catholic Church in Modern Ireland* (Dublin: UCD Press, 1998). Print.

'Interview with May Craig', *Boston Globe*, July 1938, *Papers of May Craig*, IE UCD LA28, UCD Archives, Dublin.

Jackson, Shannon, *Professing Performance: Theatre in the Academy from Philology to Performativity* (New York, NY: Cambridge UP, 2004). Print.

'Katie Roche Review', *Daily Mirror*, 13 October 1937, *Papers of May Craig*, IE UCD LA 28/231, UCD Archives, Dublin.

Keaton, Maria, 'The mother's tale: Maternal agency in *Juno and the Paycock*', *New Hibernia Review*, vol. 3, no. 4 (1999), pp 85–97. Print.

Kershaw, Baz and Helen Nicholson, eds, *Research Methods in Theatre & Performance* (New York, NY: Columbia UP, 2011). Print.

Kipen, David, *Los Angeles in the 1930s: The WPA Guide to the City of Angels* (Berkeley, CA: University of California Press, 2011). Print.

Krause, David, ed., *The Letters of Seán O'Casey 1910–1941* (New York, NY: Macmillan, 1975). Print.

— *Seán O'Casey, the Man and his Work* (London: Macgibbon & Kee, 1960).

'Late Miss Mulhern', *Irish Independent*, 20 November 1939: 8. Web.

Lee, Joe, 'Women and the Church since the Famine', *Women in Irish Society: The Historical Dimension*, eds, M. MacCurtain and D. O Corrain (Westport: Greenwood Press, 1979).

Leeney, Cathy, *Irish Women Playwrights 1930–1939: Gender and Violence on Stage* (New York, NY: Peter Lang, 2010). Print.

Le Gallienne, Eva, *The Mystic in the Theatre: Eleonora Duse* (London: Bodley Head Ltd, 1966). Print.

Le Gallienne, Eva, *At 33* (London: John Lane, Bodley Head Ltd, 1934). Print.

Le Gallienne, Eva, *With a Quiet Heart* (New York, NY: Viking, 1953). Print.

Lepore, Jill, 'Historians who love too much: Reflections on microhistory and biography', *The Journal of American History*, vol. 88, no. 1 (June 2001), pp 129–44. Print.

Luddy, Maria, 'Sex and the single girl in 1920s and 1930s Ireland', *The Irish Review (1986–)*, no. 35, Irish Feminisms, (Summer 2007), pp 79–91.

MacLiammóir, Micheál, *All For Hecuba* (Dublin: Progress House, 1961). Print.

MacNamara, Brinsley, *Margaret Gillan: A Play in Three Acts* (London: Allen & Unwin, 1934). Print.

Malague, Rosemary, *An Actress Prepares: Women and 'The Method'* (New York, NY: Routledge, 2012). Print.

Mannion, Elizabeth, *The Urban Plays of the Early Abbey Theatre* (Syracuse, NY: Syracuse UP 2014). Print.

Marshall, Gail, *Actresses on the Victorian Stage: Feminine Performance and the Galatea Myth* (London: Cambridge UP, 1998). Print.

Matthews, James, *Voices: A Life of Frank O'Connor* (New York, NY: Atheneum Press, 1983). Print.

McGlinchy, J. PP VF, 'Maxims & counsels for the Christian family', *Catholic Bulletin*, December 1934, vol. XXIV, no. 12, p. 999.

McGlone, James, *Ria Mooney: The Life and Times of the Artistic Director of the Abbey Theatre 1948 – 1963* (North Carolina: McFarland & Co., 2002). Print.

Mikhail, Edward K., ed., *The Abbey Theatre: Interviews and Recollections* (London: Macmillan, 1988). Print.

Monahan, Barry, *Ireland's Theatre on Film: Style, Stories and the National Stage on Screen* (Dublin: Irish Academic Press, 2009). Print.

Monks, Aoife, *The Actor in Costume* (London: Palgrave Macmillan, 2009).

Moody, Jane, 'The state of the abyss: Nineteenth century performance and theatre historiography in 1999', *Journal of Victorian Culture* (Edinburgh UP), vol. 5, no. 1 (Spring 2000), pp 112–28. Print.

Morash, Christopher, *A History of the Irish Theatre: 1600 – 2000* (Cambridge and New York, NY: Cambridge UP 2002). Print.

Morash, Christopher and Shaun Richards, *Mapping Irish Theatre: Theories of Space and Place* (Cambridge and New York, NY: Cambridge UP, 2013). Print.

Morehouse, W., 'Amusements: Broadway after dark', *New York Sun*, 21 February 1941: 6. Web.

Mulkerns, Val, ed., 'Players and the painted stage: Autobiography of Ria Mooney: Part 1', *George Spelvin's Theatre Book* (Spring/Summer 1978). Print.

Mulkerns, Val, ed., 'Players and the painted stage: Autobiography of Ria Mooney: Part 2', *George Spelvin's Theatre Book* (Autumn/Winter 1978). Print.

Murphy, Daniel J., ed., *Lady Gregory's Journals: Volume 2, Books 30 to 44 – 21 February 1925 – 9 May 1932*, (London: Oxford UP, 1988). Print.

Murphy, Paul, *Hegemony and Fantasy in Irish Drama 1899 – 1949* (New York, NY: Palgrave Macmillan, 2008). Print.

Murray, Christopher, 'Shaw's Ibsen and the idea of an Irish theatre', *Ibsen and Chekhov on the Irish Stage*, eds, Roz Dixon and Ruppo Malone Irina (Dublin: Carysfort Press, 2012), pp 23–36. Print.

— *Seán O'Casey: Writer at Work – A Biography* (Dublin: Gill & Macmillan, 2004). Print.

Nathan, George Jean, 'The Theatre', *American Mercury*, vol. 13, no 5 (March 1928) pp 373–8. Print.

Neuffer, E., 'In 45th street apartments, time of change for actors', *New York Times*, 4 January 1988. Web.

'New play at the Abbey: *Parnell of Avondale*', *Irish Times*, 2 October 1934: 6. Web.

'News of the stage: "Heavenly Express"', *New York Times*, 18 April 1940: 32. Web.

New York World Telegraph, 3 December 1934, Abbey Theatre Scrapbooks, NLI Mss 25,489-25,523, National Library of Ireland, Dublin.

Normington, Katie and Jacky Bratton, Gilli Bush-Bailey and Jim Davis, 'Researching theatre history and historiography', *Research Methods in Theatre & Performance*, eds, Baz Kershaw and Helen Nicholson (New York, NY: Columbia UP, 2011), pp 86–110. Print.

O'Casey, Seán, *Three Plays: Juno and the Paycock, Shadow of a Gunman and The Plough and the Stars*, Introduced by J. C. Trewin (New York, NY: St Martin's Press, 1957). Print.

— *Three More Plays: The Silver Tassie, Purple Dust and Red Roses for Me*, Introduced by J. C. Trewin (London: Macmillan, 1983). Print.

— *Rose and Crown* (London: Macmillan, 1952). Print.

O'Donnell, F. J., 'Kingdom of God', *Evening Herald*, 22 October 1923: 2. Web.

O'Dowd, L., 'Church, State and women: The aftermath of partition', *Gender in Irish Society*, eds, Chris Curtin, Pauline Jackson and Barbara O'Connor (Galway: Galway UP, 1987).

O'Farrell, Ciara, *Louis D'Alton and the Abbey Theatre* (Dublin: Four Courts Press, 2004). Print.

Ohl, Vicki, *Fine and Dandy: The Life and Work of Kay Swift* (New Haven, CT and London: Yale UP, 2004). Print.

O'Neill, Eugene, *Long Day's Journey Into Night*, ed., Harold Bloom, 2nd edn (New Haven, CT and London: Yale Nota Bene Books, 1989). Print.

Peters, Charles Frances, 'A historical survey of the Biltmore Theatre', Diss. University of Long Beach, California, 1969. Print.

Phelan, Peggy, *Unmarked: The Politics of Performance* (London: Routledge, 1993). Print.

Pilkington, Lionel, *Theatre and the State in Twentieth-Century Ireland: Cultivating the People* (London: Routledge, 2001). Print.

— *Theatre and Ireland* (London: Palgrave Macmillan, 2010). Print.

— 'Staging the body in post-independence Ireland', *Ireland, Memory and Performing the Historical Imagination*, eds, Christopher Collins and Mary P. Caulfield (London: Palgrave Macmillan, 2014).

'Popular Abbey actress dead', *Fermanagh Herald*, 24 November 1939: 8. Web.

Postlewait, Thomas and Bruce McConachie, eds, *Interpreting the Theatrical Past: Essays in the Historiography of Performance*, American University Studies, series 7 (Iowa City, IA: University of Iowa Press, 1989), 1st edn. Print.

Pullen, Kirsten, *Actresses and Whores: On Stage and in Society* (New York, NY: Cambridge UP, 2004). Print.

Pyle, Hilary, *Jack B. Yeats: A Biography*, 2nd edn (London: Andre Deutsch Ltd, 1989). Print.

Quinn, Antoinette, 'Cathleen ni Houlihan writes back: Maud Gonne and Irish National Theater', *Gender and Sexuality in Modern Ireland*, eds, Anthony Bradley and Maryann Gialanella Valiulis, (Amherst, MA: University of Massachusetts Press, 1997), pp 39–59. Print.

Rattigan, Terence, *French Without Tears*, Introduced by Dan Rebellato, (London: Nick Hern Books, 2006). Print.

'Reminiscences', *Papers of May Craig*, UCD LA28/238, UCD Archives, Dublin.

'Review of *Professor Tim*', *Irish Times*, 5 November 1930, *Papers of May Craig*, IE UCD LA28/116, UCD Archives, Dublin.

'Rita Romilly Benson dead at 79; Actress taught at Arts Academy', *New York Times*, 7 April 1980: D11. Web.

Ritschel, Nelson O'Ceallaigh, *Performative and Textual Imaging of Women on the Irish Stage 1820–1920* (New York, NY: Mellen Press, 2006). Print.

Robinson, Lennox, *Curtain Up: An Autobiography* (London: Michael Joseph Ltd, 1942). Print.

— *Ireland's Abbey Theatre: A History: 1899 – 1951* (Port Washington, NY: Kennikat Press, 1968). Print.

— *The Far-Off Hills: A Comedy in Three Acts* (London: Chatto & Windus, 1959).

— *Selected Plays of Lennox Robinson*, ed., Christopher Murray (Gerrards Cross, Buckinghamshire: Colin Smythe, 1982). Print.

Robinson, Lennox with Mícheál Ó hAodha, *Pictures at the Abbey* (Portlaoise: Dolmen Press with the Irish National Theatre Society, 1983). Print.

Ryan, Phyllis, *The Company I Kept: Revelations from the Life of Ireland's Most Distinguished and Independent Theatrical Manager* (Dublin: Townhouse Press, 1996). Print.

Ryder, Sean, 'Gender and the discourse of young Ireland nationalism', *Gender and Colonialism*, eds, T. P. Foley, L. Pilkington, S. Ryder and E. Tilley (Galway: Galway UP, 1995), pp 210–24. Print.

Saddlemyer, Anne, ed., *W.B. Yeats and George Yeats: The Letters*, (London: Oxford UP, 2011). Print.

— *Theatre Business: The Correspondence of the First Abbey Theatre Directors: William Butler Yeats, Lady Gregory, and J. M. Synge*, (Gerrards Cross, Buckinghamshire: Colin Smythe; University Park, PA: Pennsylvania State UP, 1982).

San Francisco News, 2 April 1935, *Papers of May Craig*, IE UCD LA28/116, UCD Archives, Dublin.

Sarton, May, *I Knew A Phoenix* (Great Britain: The Women's Press Ltd, 1995). Print.

Schanke, Robert A., *The Shattered Applause: The Lives of Eva Le Gallienne* (Carbondale and Edwardsville, IL: Southern Illinois UP, 1992). Print.

Schneider, Rebecca, *Performing Remains: Art and War in Times of Theatrical Reenactment* (Oxon: Routledge, 2011). Print.

Schrank, Bernice, 'Dialectical configurations in *Juno and the Paycock*', *Twentieth Century Literature*, vol. 21 (1975), pp 439–54. Print.

Schrank, Bernice and William Demastes, *Irish Playwrights, 1880–1995: A Research and Production Sourcebook* (London: Greenwood Press, 1997). Print.

Scott, Joan Wallach, *Gender and the Politics of History* (New York, NY: Columbia UP, 1999, rev. edn). Print.

— 'Gender: A useful category of historical analysis', *The American Historical Review*, vol. 91, no. 5 (1986), pp 1053–75. Print.

Scott, Joan Wallach and Louise Tilly, *Women, Work, and Family* (London: Routledge, 1989). Print.

'Script of Mrs Grogan and the Ferret', *Papers of May Craig*, IE UCD LA28/226, UCD Archives, Dublin.

'Scythia arrives here a day late', *Daily Boston Globe (1928–1960)*, 9 October 1934: 13. Web.

Sheehy, Helen, *Eva Le Gallienne: A Biography* (New York, NY: Alfred Knopf, 1996). Print.

Shiels, George, *Selected Plays of George Shiels 1886–1949*, ed., Christopher Murray, Leonard L. Milberg Irish Theater Collection (Gerrards Cross, Buckinghamshire: Colin Smythe, 2008). Print.

Sihra, Melissa, ed., *Women in Irish Drama: A Century of Authorship and Representation* (London: Palgrave Macmillan, 2007). Print.

Sitzmann, Marion, *Indomitable Irishery: P V Carroll*, (Salzburg: Institut für Englische Sprache und Literatur, Universität Salzburg, 1975). Print.

Smyth, James, 'Dancing, depravity & all that jazz', *History Ireland*, vol. 1, no. 2 (Summer 1993), pp 51–4. Print.

Stanislavski, Constantin, *An Actor's Work*, trans., Jean Benedetti (Oxon: Routledge, 2008). Print.

Stanislavski, Constantin *An Actor's Handbook*, trans., Elizabeth Hapgood (London: Metheun Press, 1990). Print.

Steedman, Carolyn, *Dust: The Archive and Cultural History (Encounters)* (Manchester: Manchester UP, 2001). Print.

— 'Something she called a fever: Michelet, Derrida & dust', *The American Historical Review*, vol. 106, no. 4 (October 2001), pp 1159–80. Print.

Stiegler, W. G., 'Irish player combines stage & home life', *No Title*, 23 December 1931, *Papers of May Craig*, IE UCD LA 28/219 – 1, UCD Archives, Dublin.

Stroppel, Elizabeth C., 'Reconciling the past and the present: Feminist perspectives on the method in the classroom and on the stage', *Method Acting Reconsidered*, ed., D. Krasner (New York, NY: St Martin's, 2000) pp 111–23. Print.

'Survey by Dublin Senior Justice – Edward J. Little', *Irish Times*, 7 February 1938: 4. Web.

Synge, John Millington, *In the Shadow of the Glen* (London: Bloomsbury Publishing, 1981). Web.

— *The Playboy of the Western World and Other Plays*, ed., Anne Saddlemyer (London: Oxford UP, 2008). Print.

Taylor, Diana, *The Archive and the Repertoire: Performing Cultural Memory in the Americas* (Durham, NC: Duke UP, 2003). Print.

The Cambridge Gownsman, 20 February 1937, *Papers of May Craig*, IE UCD LA28/219, UCD Archives, Dublin.

'"The Emperor Jones" at the Abbey: Mr. Mayne's conception of the negro', *Irish Times*, 26 July 1927: 6. Web.

'The Gate Theatre: *Wuthering Heights* revived', *Irish Times*, 13 February 1935: 8. Web.

'The Peacock Theatre', *Irish Times*, 6 June 1939: 6. Web.

'The Theaters', Abbey Theatre Scrapbooks: Volume 27 American Tour 1937 – 38, NLI Mss. 25,511-23, National Library of Ireland, Dublin.

'The Words Upon the Window Pane', *Irish Independent*, 18 November 1930: 12. Web.

Treanor, A., 'Behind the Abbey scenes', *Irish Press*, 28 July 1938. Web.

Trotter, Mary, *Ireland's National Theaters Political Performance & the Origins of the Irish Dramatic Movement* (Syracuse, NY: Syracuse UP, 2001). Print.

— *Modern Irish Theatre* (Cambridge: Polity Press, 2008).

Wagner-Martin, Linda, *Telling Women's Lives: The New Biography*, (New Brunswick, NJ: Rutgers UP, 1994). Print.

Walsh, Ian R., *Experimental Irish Theatre After W. B. Yeats* (London: Palgrave Macmillan, 2012). Print.

Walsh, Eibhear, ed., *Selected Plays of Irish Playwright Teresa Deevy, 1894–1963*, Studies in Irish literature, vol. 10 (Lewiston, NY: Edwin Mellen Press, 2003). Print.

Warfel, G., Interview, *Detroit News*, 23 February 1933, *Papers of May Craig*, IE UCD LA28/231, UCD Archives, Dublin.

Weber, Katharine, *The Memory of All That: George Gershwin, Kay Swift and my Family's Legacy of Infidelities* (New York, NY: Broadway Paperbacks, 2011). Print.

Welch, Robert, *The Abbey Theatre, 1899 to 1999 – Form and Pressure* (London: Oxford UP, 1999). Print.

'What Does It Mean?', *Evening Herald*, 11 August 1938: n.p. Print.

Woods, Leigh, 'Actors' biography and mythmaking: The example of Edmund Kean', *Interpreting the Theatrical Past: Essays in the Historiography of Performance*, eds, Thomas Postlewait and Bruce McConachie, pp 230–47. Print.

'Wuthering Heights revived', *Irish Independent*, 13 February 1935: 6. Web.

Yeats, Jack B., *La La Noo* (Shannon: Irish UP, 1971). Print.

Yeates, Padraig, 'The Dublin 1913 Lockout', *History Ireland*, vol. 9, no. 2 (2001), pp 31–6. Print.

— *Lockout Dublin: 1913* (Dublin: Gill & Macmillan, 2000). Print.

Yeats, William B., *The Words Upon the Window Pane: A Play in One Act* (Dublin: The Cuala Press, 1934). Print.

Zemon-Davis, Natalie, '"Women's history" in transition: The European case', *Feminist Studies*, vol. 3, no. 3/4 (Spring/Summer 1976) pp 83–103. Print.

Interviews Conducted

DeGeus, Helen, Personal Interview, Dublin, 10 September 2016.
Laffan, Patrick, Personal Interview, Dublin, 3 July 2013.
McCullough, Mary, Personal Interview, Dublin, 9 April 2010.
Mulkerns, Val, Personal Interview, Dublin, 13 July 2012.
Shields, Christine, Personal Interview, Hollywood, CA, 18th, 19th, 20th September 2011.
Slott, Susan, Personal Interview, Dublin, 1 October 2011.

Index